First World War
and Army of Occupation
War Diary
France, Belgium and Germany

40 DIVISION
120 Infantry Brigade
Princess Louise's (Argyll & Sutherland Highlanders)
14th Battalion
27 May 1916 - 31 March 1918

WO95/2611/1

The Naval & Military Press Ltd
www.nmarchive.com
Published in association with The National Archives

Published by

The Naval & Military Press Ltd

Unit 10 Ridgewood Industrial Park,

Uckfield, East Sussex,

TN22 5QE England

Tel: +44 (0) 1825 749494

www.naval-military-press.com

www.nmarchive.com

This diary has been reprinted in facsimile from the original. Any imperfections are inevitably reproduced and the quality may fall short of modern type and cartographic standards.

© **Crown Copyright**
Images reproduced by permission of The National Archives, London, England, 2015.

Contents

Document type	Place/Title	Date From	Date To
Heading	WO95/2611/1		
Heading	40th Division 120th Infy Bde 14th Bn Argyll & Suth'd Hdrs Jun 1916-Mar 1918 From UK to 14 Div 42 Bde		
War Diary	Blackdown	27/05/1916	04/06/1916
War Diary	Southampton Docks	04/06/1916	05/06/1916
War Diary	Le Havre	06/06/1916	06/06/1916
War Diary	Equedeques	07/06/1916	15/06/1916
War Diary	Annequin	16/06/1916	16/06/1916
War Diary	Hohenzollern Sector	16/06/1916	19/06/1916
War Diary	Annequin	20/06/1916	22/06/1916
War Diary	BHQ Coys in Trenchs	23/06/1916	23/06/1916
War Diary	Baqanneqvinn Camp Hoacnzollern Sector	24/06/1916	26/06/1916
War Diary	Bruay	27/06/1916	30/06/1916
Heading	War Diary 14th (S) Bn Aug & Suth'd Highrs Volume 2 (July 1916) Vol 2		
War Diary	Bruay	01/07/1916	04/07/1916
War Diary	Le Brebis in Reserve	05/07/1916	10/07/1916
War Diary	Maroc	11/07/1916	18/07/1916
War Diary	Les Brebis	19/07/1916	21/07/1916
War Diary	South Maroc	21/07/1916	30/07/1916
War Diary	Smaroc sapport near Chaech	31/07/1916	31/07/1916
War Diary	Bruay	01/07/1916	01/07/1916
War Diary	Les Brebis	04/07/1916	04/07/1916
War Diary	North Maroc in Support	11/07/1916	11/07/1916
War Diary	Left fire Line	15/07/1916	15/07/1916
War Diary	Les Brebis	18/07/1916	18/07/1916
War Diary	South Maroc nea left Calan Suder	21/07/1916	21/07/1916
War Diary	S Maroc in Bill et in Support	30/07/1916	30/07/1916
Heading	War Diary 14th (S) Bn Arg & Suth'd Highrs August 1916 Volume 3		
War Diary	S Maroc	01/08/1916	04/08/1916
War Diary	Loos	05/08/1916	07/08/1916
War Diary	Loas No 2 Sub Section	07/08/1916	07/08/1916
War Diary	Loos	08/08/1916	09/08/1916
War Diary	SE Maroc	10/08/1916	12/08/1916
War Diary	Les Berbis	13/08/1916	16/08/1916
War Diary	Bolly Grenay	17/08/1916	20/08/1916
War Diary	Calonne Left Sub Sector	20/08/1916	20/08/1916
War Diary	Calonne L Sub Sec	21/08/1916	24/08/1916
War Diary	Calonne Support C Bn	24/08/1916	31/08/1916
Miscellaneous	War Diary 14th (S) Bn Argyll & Sutherland Hdrs		
War Diary	Petit Sains	01/09/1916	04/09/1916
War Diary	Maroc	05/09/1916	05/09/1916
War Diary	Left Sefsuton	06/09/1916	07/09/1916
War Diary	Maroc Left S.S.	08/09/1916	11/09/1916
War Diary	Maroc l. Sar Sa	11/09/1916	11/09/1916
War Diary	NE maroc Support	12/09/1916	12/09/1916
War Diary	NE Maroc	13/09/1916	14/09/1916
War Diary	NE Maroc Support Bn	15/09/1916	19/09/1916
War Diary	Les Brebis	20/09/1916	22/09/1916

War Diary	14 Bis Les Bn	22/09/1916	22/09/1916
War Diary	14 Bis Left	23/09/1916	30/09/1916
Miscellaneous	War Diary Sept 1916 14 Bn Argyll & Sutherland Highlanders		
Heading	144 (S) Arg & Suth'd Highrs Volumes October		
War Diary	14 Bis Sector Left Bn Trncehs	01/10/1916	02/10/1916
War Diary	14 Bis Sector	03/10/1916	03/10/1916
War Diary	Morl to Auth mazingarbe	04/10/1916	07/10/1916
War Diary	Momed to 14 Bis Secton Leftr Battalion tro	08/10/1916	08/10/1916
War Diary	14 Bis Section	11/10/1916	11/10/1916
War Diary	Moved to Bn Support Bn Hulluln	12/10/1916	12/10/1916
War Diary	Support Bn Hulluch	13/10/1916	25/10/1916
War Diary	Les Brebis	26/10/1916	26/10/1916
War Diary	Moved to Bruay	27/10/1916	27/10/1916
War Diary	Moved to Monchy Breton	28/10/1916	29/10/1916
War Diary	Move to Ternas	29/10/1916	29/10/1916
War Diary	Ternas	30/10/1916	31/10/1916
Miscellaneous	Appendix A		
Miscellaneous	List A Casualties to 14 A to hrs Appendix A		
Operation(al) Order(s)	Operation Orders No. 28 by Major H. Buru-Murdoch, Commdg 14th (S) Bn Arg & Suth'd. Hrs	07/12/1916	07/12/1916
Miscellaneous	14th (S) Bn. Argyll & Sutherland Highlanders Appendix B		
Miscellaneous	14th (Service) Battalion Argyll & Sutherland Highlanders.		
Miscellaneous	14th (S) Battn. Argyll & Sutherland Highlanders.	29/10/1916	29/10/1916
Miscellaneous	Move Order by Capt JD Mackie Comdg 122nd (S) Bn Hrs	27/10/1916	27/10/1916
Miscellaneous	Move Orders Bb Capt JD Mackie Comdg 14 (S) Bn. Ars Hrs.	27/10/1916	27/10/1916
Operation(al) Order(s)	Operations Order No. 31 by Major Hrs Watson Comdg 14th (S) Bn A & S Hrs	25/10/1916	25/10/1916
Operation(al) Order(s)	Operation Order No. 30 by Capt JD Mackie Comdg 14th (S) Bn Arg & Suth'd Hrs	17/10/1916	17/10/1916
Operation(al) Order(s)	Operation Order No. 28 by Major Buru-Murdoch Commdg 14th (S) Bn A & S Highrs	11/10/1916	11/10/1916
Operation(al) Order(s)	Operation Order No. 27 by Major E.C. Hill Whitson Comdg 14th (S) Bn, Hrs	07/10/1916	07/10/1916
Operation(al) Order(s)	Operation Order No. 26 by Major E.C. Hill Whitson Commdg 114th Bn As Hrs	30/10/1916	30/10/1916
War Diary	Ternas	01/11/1916	01/11/1916
War Diary	Moved to Petit Bouret	02/11/1916	03/11/1916
War Diary	Moved to Wavans and Beauvoir Riviere	04/11/1916	04/11/1916
War Diary	Moved to Ribeaucourt	05/11/1916	09/11/1916
War Diary	Ribeaucourt	10/11/1916	10/11/1916
War Diary	Moved to Bonneville	11/11/1916	12/11/1916
War Diary	Doullens	13/11/1916	13/11/1916
War Diary	Moved to Thievres	14/11/1916	14/11/1916
War Diary	Thievres	15/11/1916	21/11/1916
War Diary	Moved to Huts at Amplier	22/11/1916	22/11/1916
War Diary	Moved to Montrelet	23/11/1916	23/11/1916
War Diary	Moved to Yaucourt	24/11/1916	27/11/1916
War Diary	Yaucourt	28/11/1916	30/11/1916
War Diary	Yaucourt	01/12/1916	13/12/1916
War Diary	Moved to Camp III	14/12/1916	15/12/1916
War Diary	Camp No III	16/12/1916	24/12/1916

War Diary	Moved to Trenhes	26/12/1916	26/12/1916
War Diary	North Bouchavesnes	28/12/1916	30/12/1916
War Diary	Trenches North Bouchavesnes	26/12/1916	30/12/1916
War Diary	Trenches North Bouchavesnes	31/12/1916	31/12/1916
War Diary	Moved to Camp 21		
War Diary	Camp 21 on the Suzanne Maricourt Road	01/01/1917	01/01/1917
War Diary	Camp 2	02/01/1917	03/01/1917
War Diary	Moved to Support to trenches Rancourt	04/01/1917	05/01/1917
War Diary	Support Bn Rancourt	06/01/1917	07/01/1917
War Diary	Right Bn Rancourt	08/01/1917	11/01/1917
War Diary	Moved to Rancourt to Camp 21	12/01/1917	12/01/1917
War Diary	Camp 21	13/01/1917	18/01/1917
War Diary	Reserve Bn Bouchavesnes North Section	19/01/1917	19/01/1917
War Diary	Asquith Flats	19/01/1917	21/01/1917
War Diary	Moved to Rt Bn. Bouchavesnes North	22/01/1917	24/01/1917
War Diary	Right Bn Bouchavesnes North Section	25/01/1917	25/01/1917
War Diary	Move Down the Line to Camp 24	26/01/1917	26/01/1917
War Diary	Moved to Camp 124 to Corbis	27/01/1917	27/01/1917
War Diary	Corbie	28/01/1917	31/01/1917
Miscellaneous	Appendix Casualties for Jan 1917		
War Diary	Corbie	01/02/1917	11/02/1917
War Diary	Bray	12/02/1917	24/02/1917
War Diary	Camp III	25/02/1917	28/02/1917
Miscellaneous	Appendix A D.R.O. No 925 is published		
Miscellaneous	Move Orders by Major A.D. Carmichael Commdg 14th (S) By Arg & Suths Hdrs	09/02/1917	09/02/1917
Miscellaneous	Move Orders No. 3 by Major A.D. Carmichael Commg 14th (S) Bn Arg & Suth'd Hrs	28/02/1917	28/02/1917
War Diary	Camp III on Bray Meaulte Road	01/03/1917	06/03/1917
War Diary	Moved to Camp 19	07/03/1917	07/03/1917
War Diary	Moved to Road Wood	08/03/1917	08/03/1917
War Diary	Road Wood	09/03/1917	09/03/1917
War Diary	Moved to Left Battalion to ant ye	10/03/1917	12/03/1917
War Diary	Moved to Howitz cr Wood	13/03/1917	15/03/1917
War Diary	Moved up again Left Section	16/03/1917	17/03/1917
War Diary	Moved to German Reserve trench		
War Diary	Advanced	19/03/1917	20/03/1917
War Diary	Advanced out post line at Driencourt Templeux la Fosse	20/03/1917	20/03/1917
War Diary	Moved down to Duy outs E. of Haut Allaines	21/03/1917	24/03/1917
War Diary	Moved to Linger Campneaon Curlu	25/03/1917	31/03/1917
Miscellaneous	Casualties during March 1917 Appendix A		
Heading	War Diary 14th A. &. S. Hdrs April 1917		
War Diary	Linngen Camp	01/04/1917	16/04/1917
War Diary	Etricourt	17/04/1917	18/04/1917
War Diary	Equancourt	19/04/1917	20/04/1917
War Diary	Dessart Wood	21/04/1917	23/04/1917
War Diary	S.W. and S & Beaucamp	24/04/1917	24/04/1917
War Diary	Beaucamp	24/04/1917	25/04/1917
War Diary	Goorerucourt Wood	25/04/1917	30/04/1917
Operation(al) Order(s)	Appendix "B" Extract from Battalion Order No. 59 Para 2 of 6th April 1917		
Operation(al) Order(s)	14th (S) Bn Arg & Suth Highlanders Order No. 13	15/04/1917	15/04/1917
Operation(al) Order(s)	120th Infantry Brigade Order No. 91	15/04/1917	15/04/1917
Miscellaneous	March Table to accompany 120th Infantry Brigade Order No. 91		
Miscellaneous	C Form. Messages And Signals.	19/04/1917	19/04/1917

Type	Description	Date	Date
Miscellaneous	Infantry Works Report-Wednesday 11th April 1917		
Operation(al) Order(s)	120th Infantry Brigade Order No. 92		
Miscellaneous			
Operation(al) Order(s)	120th Infantry Brigade Order No. 93	17/04/1917	17/04/1917
Miscellaneous	11th R. Lanc. R.	19/04/1917	19/04/1917
Miscellaneous	120th Infantry Brigade No. 120/462	19/04/1917	19/04/1917
Miscellaneous	120th Infantry Brigade No. 120/XXX 462	19/04/1917	19/04/1917
Miscellaneous	11th R. Lanc. R.	18/04/1917	18/04/1917
Operation(al) Order(s)	120th Infantry Brigade Order No. 94	20/04/1917	20/04/1917
Miscellaneous	Patrol Report map Reference 57c S.E.		
Miscellaneous	To The adjutant Ref 14 A & S H from O.C. B Coy	23/04/1917	23/04/1917
Miscellaneous	14th A & S H.	22/04/1917	22/04/1917
Miscellaneous	Artillery Programme	22/04/1917	22/04/1917
Miscellaneous	To Adjutant		
Miscellaneous	B Company 14th A & S H	23/04/1917	23/04/1917
Miscellaneous			
Miscellaneous	To The adjutant		
Miscellaneous			
Operation(al) Order(s)	120th Infantry Brigade Order No. 95	22/04/1917	22/04/1917
Operation(al) Order(s)	14th (S) Battn. Argyll & Sutherland Highrs Order No. 14	23/04/1917	23/04/1917
Miscellaneous	Fighting Order water Bottles to be filled	23/04/1917	23/04/1917
Operation(al) Order(s)	120th Infantry Brigade Order No. 96	25/04/1917	25/04/1917
Miscellaneous	To all Recipients of O.O. 96	23/04/1917	23/04/1917
Operation(al) Order(s)	13th Bn East Surrey Regiment Operation Order No. 48	23/04/1917	23/04/1917
Miscellaneous	R Lanc. R. H. Surr. R. High L.I. Arp & Suth'd Highrs.	21/04/1917	21/04/1917
Operation(al) Order(s)	40th Divisional Artillery Order No. 50	23/04/1917	23/04/1917
Miscellaneous	14th (S) Bn. Argyll and Sutherland Highlanders		
Miscellaneous	14th (S) Bn Argyll and Sutherland Highlander. The Following Officers Were Killed in action.	24/04/1917	24/04/1917
Miscellaneous	14th Argyll and Sutherland Highlanders		
Miscellaneous	14th (S) Bn Argyll and Sutherland Highlanders		
Miscellaneous	Artillery Table of Tasks for 24th April to accompany 40th D.A. Order No. 3		
Miscellaneous	Artillery Table of Tasks for 24th April To accompany 40th D.A. Order No. 59		
Miscellaneous	Artillery Table of Tasks for 24th April To accompany 40th D.A. Order No. 50		
Map			
Map	Situation and German Order of Battle		
Map			
Miscellaneous	Reference 120th Infantry Brigade Order No. dated 25/4/17		
Miscellaneous	C Form. Messages And Signals.		
Miscellaneous	March Table to Accompany 120th Infantry Brigade Order No. 99		
Operation(al) Order(s)	120th Infantry Brigade Order No. 90	25/04/1917	25/04/1917
Operation(al) Order(s)	120th Infantry Brigade Order No. 100	25/04/1917	25/04/1917
Operation(al) Order(s)	120th Infantry Brigade Order No. 98	24/04/1917	24/04/1917
Operation(al) Order(s)	120th Infantry Brigade Order No. 97	24/04/1917	24/04/1917
Map			
Map	Reference		
Map	Fourth Army Front map		
Map			
Map	Fourth Army Front Map Q		
Map			

Map	Fourth Army Front Map Q		
Map			
Map	Fourth Army Front Map Q		
Map			
Map	Fourth Army Front Map Q		
Map			
Miscellaneous	R. Lanc. Regt.	29/04/1917	29/04/1917
War Diary	Etricourt	01/05/1917	01/05/1917
War Diary	Gooz Eadcourt Wood	02/05/1917	06/05/1917
War Diary	Beaucamp	07/05/1917	12/05/1917
War Diary	Dessart Wood	13/05/1917	13/05/1917
War Diary	Quarry R. 31.c.	14/05/1917	16/05/1917
War Diary	Gonnelieu	20/05/1917	24/05/1917
War Diary	Quarry R 31.c.	17/05/1917	17/05/1917
War Diary	Quarry Gonnelieu	18/05/1917	18/05/1917
War Diary	Gonnelieu	19/05/1917	26/05/1917
War Diary	H.Q. W.6.d.	27/05/1917	31/05/1917
War Diary	W6d	01/06/1917	03/06/1917
War Diary	Gonnelieu	04/06/1917	11/06/1917
War Diary	Sorel-Le-Grand	12/06/1917	19/06/1917
War Diary	Sunren Rd. N end of Gouzbau Court	20/06/1917	27/06/1917
War Diary	Leftbn Villers Plooicus Oelhi	28/06/1917	30/06/1917
War Diary	Villers Plouich	01/07/1917	05/07/1917
War Diary	Bde Reserve Near Gouzeavcourt	06/07/1917	13/07/1917
War Diary	Villers Plouich	14/07/1917	21/07/1917
War Diary	Brigade Support	22/07/1917	28/07/1917
War Diary	15 Reserve	29/07/1917	31/07/1917
War Diary	Villers Plouich	01/08/1917	02/08/1917
War Diary	Gouzeacourt Wood	03/08/1917	05/08/1917
War Diary	Villers Plouich	06/08/1917	13/08/1917
War Diary	Gonmecourt Wood Deser Wood	14/08/1917	19/08/1917
War Diary	Villers-Beaucamp	20/08/1917	31/08/1917
War Diary	Villers-Plouich	01/09/1917	06/09/1917
War Diary	GouzeauCourt Wood	07/09/1917	10/09/1917
War Diary	Bde Reserve	11/09/1917	12/09/1917
War Diary	Villers Plouich	13/09/1917	18/09/1917
War Diary	XV Ravine	19/09/1917	24/09/1917
War Diary	Villers Plouich	25/09/1917	30/09/1917
War Diary	Villers Plouich	01/10/1917	01/10/1917
War Diary	Bde Reserve	02/10/1917	04/10/1917
War Diary	Sorel Le Grand	05/10/1917	05/10/1917
War Diary	Peronne	06/10/1917	09/10/1917
War Diary	Seman Court	10/10/1917	28/10/1917
War Diary	Halloy	29/10/1917	15/11/1917
War Diary	Simencourt	16/11/1917	17/11/1917
War Diary	Courcelles-Le-Comte	18/11/1917	19/11/1917
War Diary	Beaulencourt	20/11/1917	21/11/1917
War Diary	Labucquier	22/11/1917	22/11/1917
War Diary	Bourlon Wood	23/11/1917	25/11/1917
War Diary	Trescault	26/11/1917	26/11/1917
War Diary	Hendecourt	27/11/1917	30/11/1917
Miscellaneous	14th Argyll and Sutherland Highlanders		
War Diary	Hendecourt	01/12/1917	03/12/1917
War Diary	Ervillers	04/12/1917	10/12/1917
War Diary	Fontainelez Croisilles Sector	11/12/1917	18/12/1917
War Diary	Hamelincourt	19/12/1917	24/12/1917

War Diary	Fonraine le corsll Sector	25/12/1917	27/12/1917
War Diary	Boyelles	28/12/1917	31/12/1917
War Diary	Bullecourt Right Sub Sector	01/01/1918	04/01/1918
War Diary	Bullecourt	05/01/1918	05/01/1918
War Diary	Bullecourt Right Sub Sector	06/01/1918	06/01/1918
War Diary	Mory	07/01/1918	10/01/1918
War Diary	Bullecourt Right Subsection	11/01/1918	14/01/1918
War Diary	Bde Support	15/01/1918	17/01/1918
War Diary	Bullecourt Bde Support	18/01/1918	18/01/1918
War Diary	Bullecourt Right Subsector	19/01/1918	22/01/1918
War Diary	Mory Bde Reserve	23/01/1918	26/01/1918
War Diary	Bullecourt Rt. Sub. Sect	27/01/1918	31/01/1918
War Diary	Bullecourt Rt Sub Sect Bde Support	01/02/1918	03/02/1918
War Diary	Bullecourt Right Sub Sect	04/02/1918	07/02/1918
War Diary	Bullecourt Bde Supt	08/02/1918	10/02/1918
War Diary	Ervillers	11/02/1918	11/02/1918
War Diary	Hendercourt	12/02/1918	22/02/1918
War Diary	Mercatel	23/02/1918	28/02/1918
Heading	40th Division 120th Infantry Brigade. War Diary 14th Battalion Argyll & Sutherland Highlanders March 1918		
War Diary	Berles-au-Bois	01/03/1918	12/03/1918
War Diary	Hamelincourt	13/03/1918	21/03/1918
War Diary	Vaulx-Vraucourt	21/03/1918	22/03/1918
War Diary	Army Line	23/03/1918	24/03/1918
War Diary	Behagnies	25/03/1918	25/03/1918
War Diary	Douchy	26/03/1918	27/03/1918
War Diary	Warluzel	28/03/1918	29/03/1918
War Diary	Monehy Bretopn	30/03/1918	30/03/1918
War Diary	Le Na Monde	31/03/1918	31/03/1918
Miscellaneous	To all Ranks of the 40th Division.	28/03/1918	28/03/1918
Miscellaneous			
Miscellaneous	The following extract from a letter written by the Corps Commander to the Divisional Commander is forwarded for you information	28/03/1918	28/03/1918
Miscellaneous			
Miscellaneous	Officer Commanding 14th Bn. A. &. S. Highrs.	17/04/1918	17/04/1918
Miscellaneous	14th (Ser) Bn. Argyll & Sutherland Highlanders		
Miscellaneous	14th (S) Bn Argyll & Sutherland Highrs. Casualties reported 9.4.18		
Miscellaneous	14th (Ser) Bn. Argyll & Sutherland Highlanders		
Miscellaneous			
Miscellaneous	14th (Ser) Bn. Argyll & Sutherland Highlanders		
Miscellaneous	14th Bn. Argyll & Sutherland Highlanders		
Miscellaneous	Casualties		
Miscellaneous	B Company Wounded		
Miscellaneous	D Company Wounded		
Miscellaneous	Casualties		
Miscellaneous	C Company Missing		
Miscellaneous	Wounded and Missing		

100 95/2611/11

40TH DIVISION
120TH INBY BDE

14TH BN ARGYLL & SUTH'D HDRS

JUN 1916 - MAR 1918

FROM UK

TO 14 DIV 42 BDE

June
120
Vol 1. 40

XL Volume 1

WAR DIARY
or
INTELLIGENCE SUMMARY

14" (S)B" Argyll & Sutherland Highrs

Army Form C. 2118

(Erase heading not required.)

Instructions regarding War Diaries and Intelligence Summaries are contained in F. S. Regs., Part II. and the Staff Manual respectively. Title Pages will be prepared in manuscript.

Place	Date	Hour	Summary of Events and Information	Remarks and references to Appendices
BLACKDOWN	27.5.16	—	Mobilization Orders Received	
"	3.6.16	—	2/Lt W. LANDELL and Billeting party left up to HAVRE via SOUTHAMPTON.	
"	3.6.16	—	2/Lt R.N. CHAPMAN left with 120th Bn H.Q. Staff.	
"	4.6.16	—	Bn HQ left FARNBOROUGH Station for SOUTHAMPTON in two trains	
SOUTHAMPTON DOCKS	4.6.16	—	Advance party consisting of 196 Rank and File and Reg'tl Transport under Capt HOGG and 6 Subalterns left at 8 P.M. in H.T. "ONDA" – Canadian "for LE HAVRE – Troops too tired knit parts to 6 Bn North Reg't for full up–part detained B" to Bn left H.T. being invited onto contract wagons on Keds as to for sailors. Remainder of the Bn were detained in the Docks as the weather was too stormy for the small paddle steamer "Marguerite", which was detailed to carry us – Bn's carried to SSE until it stood out with Bn-x-bag	Pom Mm
do	5.6.16	—	Rest of Bn had their Kings SOUTHAMPTON –	
"	"	4.PM	Commenced to Embark on board the H.T. MARGUERITE.	
"	"	6.45	Left SOUTHAMPTON Docks having also on board a B" of Welch Reg't and other troops – very crowded – very rough passage –	cm
LE HAVRE	6.6.16	4AM	Arrived at about 4.A.M. Had to lay till up to Quay till about 8 AM on account of the embarkation prev– ious H.T. two returned to left (as 5 of 2/4) owing to difficulty in performing in getting off the Q. at Emergency placed + tanks + twenty lorries. Marched + sled at Gare de Maritimes + was temp to train to arrive + about + to be had to marks by B" to eat down – It's was applied by Buss W'ardian's Coffee Stalls Marched B2 to Gare de MERCHANDISE to entrain – Pass advance party + transport did not arrive at Gare de MARITIMES – Too hot always available for coffee –	cm
"	"	3PM	Left LE HAVRE. Had 20 minutes for tea. 11 PM had supper.	m

WAR DIARY
or
INTELLIGENCE SUMMARY

Army Form C. 2118

Vol. 1

1/4 (S/B?) Argyll & Sutherland Highlanders

(Erase heading not required.)

Place	Date	Hour	Summary of Events and Information	Remarks and references to Appendices
EQUEDE-QUES.	7.6.16	9 a.m.	Arrived and detrained at LILLERS. Marched at once to Billets at EQUEDEQUES. When B⁰ remained till 15.6.16. Lieut. Interpreter OUVRARD joined B⁰ H.Q.	
do.	15.6.16	8.30	Left EQUEDEQUES and marched to ANNEQUIN, 1ess Day billeted at SAILLY-la-BOURSE, Billets at	
		2.30	Via BETHUNE - 15 miles full marching order - nobody fell out. Village & Buildings shelled & burning	
ANNEQUIN	16.6.16	various	Left Billets and marched up to Trenches. HOHENZOLLERN Sector. attached to 46th B⁰ & 15th DIV. for instruction -	
			B⁰ H.Q. Lt Col. G. GUNN.	
			Major E.C. HILL-WHITSON ⎫ and 'C' Coy attached to 12th(S)B⁰ H.L.I.	
			Capt⁹ adjt R. DICKIE ⎭ 'A' Coy do do 7/8 do K.O.S.B.	
			'B' Coy do do do S.R.	
			'D' Coy do do 10/11 do H.L.I.	
			Casualties wounded.	
			No. 9091 Pte GOODWIN. A.H. Gunshot wound left Knee. 'A' Coy.	
HOHENZOLLERN SECTOR.	16.6.16		No. 14352 " DICKSON. J. Shrapnel do left leg. C. Coy.	
	17.6.16		Nº 13373 " M.F. HUNTER. do do — B. Coy.	
do	17.6.16		Nº 9753 McQUEEN. R. Killed. Rifle grenade. D. Coy.	
do.	18.6.16	10.20 P.M.	Casualties. Wounded 5 men ⎱ B. Coy. Wounded 12 men A Coy. ⎱ Total Killed 1	
			Killed 1 " do ⎰ ⎰ Wounded 7	
"		7.30 p.m.	Wounded. 1 man Transport detail. A Coy	
do.			do 1 Man B. Coy. + 1 8	

WAR DIARY or INTELLIGENCE SUMMARY

Army Form C. 2118

14th (S) Bn. Argyll & Sutherland H'rs

Place	Date	Hour	Summary of Events and Information	Remarks and references to Appendices
HOHENZOLLERN Sector	19.6.16.		Casualties. Killed (bomb) 1 man - B. Coy. Wounded 2 men C. Coy	6pm
ANNEQUIN.	20.6.16	10 am.	Returned here to billets from trenches in HOHENZOLLERN SECTOR. The usual shelling at edge of village (westside) occurred in tw	10pm
do.	21.6.16.		Right half Bn: Came back to trenches. 500 men in 5 parties of 100 each with officers go to trenches in HOHENZOLLERN as Engineer Working party. Billets Shelled.	4pm
do	22.6.16		Left half do do. Working parts as for previous day - Billets Shelled (4.2's) Reasallie in billets 1 Killed 4 wounded.	
			One civilian also wounded.	9pm
do to B"HQ Coys in trenches	23.		Coys go up to trenches for Coy: training. Billets Shelled	
B"HQ ANNEQUIN Coys. HOHENZOLLERN SECTOR.	24.		Coys in HOHENZOLLERN SECTOR. Bn HQ in ANNEQUIN - Billets Shelled Casualties in Bn - wounded 4 men	5pm
ditto	25.		ditto - Casualties. Killed 2 Wounded 7.	9pm
ditto	26.		Coy instruction in trenches arend. Coys return to ANNEQUIN & Billets Casualties. 2 Killed 1 wounded.	9pm

Vol. 1.   14(5) Bn Argyll & Sutherland H'rs

WAR DIARY
or
INTELLIGENCE SUMMARY

Form C. 2118

(Erase heading not required.)

Instructions regarding War Diaries and Intelligence Summaries are contained in F.S. Regs., Part II. and the Staff Manual respectively. Title Pages will be prepared in manuscript.

Place	Date	Hour	Summary of Events and Information	Remarks and references to Appendices
BRUAY.	27.9/16	2.p.m.	Arrived here having marched from ANNEQUIN.	
BRUAY	28.9	—	Cleaning up: after very muddy trench work - 2nd Lieut Keith Alexander H.L.I. joined for duty.	
	29.9	—	Baths - clothing and equipment inspections -	
BRUAY	30.	—	Coys at work in Bois des Dames. 'B' Coy.	

40 July

14 Aug 22s

Vol 2

29

Confidential

War Diary

1st (B) Bn Tag Turk'a Afghan

Volume 2 (July 1916)

WAR DIARY
or
INTELLIGENCE SUMMARY

Army Form C. 2118

(Erase heading not required.)

Place	Date	Hour	Summary of Events and Information	Remarks and references to Appendices
BRUAY	1916 July 1-3		Remained in Bivouac - train having searched R.	Bro.
	4.		2nd MILLEN. MParties duty of 2 Lt T. SHEARER took up the S.R. [marched] to BREBIS. to relieve 1st Div. less B Coy which remained at "LABUISSIERE" Grand.	Bro.
LE BREBIS (in Reserve)	5.		Relieve Bde in Trench - supporting positions - changing embarking pts.	Pto.
ditto	6.		do. Continue training, working, bombing pts.	do.
ditto	7.		do. do. do. Casualties. 2 wounded (trenches) & 1 bullet.	Pro. v
ditto	8.		do. do. do. Casualties. 1 wounded, trenches.	Bro. /
ditto	9.		do. do. do. Casualties. 1 wounded, trenches.	Beto. /
ditto	10.		do. Aspects MAROC lines - 1 wounded - (accidental bayonet)	Sentry
MAROC	11.		Took over from 13 YORKS Regt. SUPPORT Bn. Left Bn section 19.45. Situation Normal. 1301 B+ 1078 OR p.m. 119 N.J. Base which took our billets in LE BREBIS.	Repts.
do.	12.		Supplied work parties 9-14 hours cleaning ST JAMES KEEP. 30 NCO +men do + work in firing line. 149 NCO + men Repts.
do.	13.		do working on part line. Contents of hostile bombing or post line: Enemy cut their wire in front of Crassier - pierhead wire later - looking occurred - couldhut shelling on ur front. Enemy delivered for 5 mns. gard. firing nr MAROC. Kept carrying parties for material R. to ST JAMES KEEP in Reserve. Everyavailable man out on work parties in front line. Commencing 2 hrs.	Repts.
do	14.		Shelling - Enemy shelled ur guns and trenches especially QUEEN ST + LEFT SUBSECTOR. B+F shell in SUPPORT. Furnished large work parties & ImpMt FIRE TRENCHES + carrying parties S.T JAMES Redans contained our H.Qrs girds of enemy rations, berries, barb. wire, kons.	Repts.

WAR DIARY or INTELLIGENCE SUMMARY

Army Form C. 2118

Vol. I.

Place	Date	Hour	Summary of Events and Information	Remarks and references to Appendices
HAROC.	1916 15.		In Firing Line. LEFT SUBSECTOR. Shelling. Gradually & on right fire trenches. Considerable damage done to support trenches also from H.E. Shells. Casualties. The following Officers joined B.7 yesterday from 4:7 B.R 21st W.B.CRAMB, R.J.F.McCALISTER, W.M.KILGOUR, R.G.MILLER, A.C.MacCORMICK, H.M.TYSON, T.F. STEELE and M.J.DAVIS.	SFFO.
do.	16.		Took over Left Subsector Fri line from 1st K.O.R.Lancashi Regt at 12.10 a.m. Shelling - Considerable throughout the day trending turn-sure against our left front built held by "A" Coy. Capt McSnack, the enemy H.E. Shell killed 2 men causing together in KING St. Casualties. killed 3.	Offrs.
ditto	17.		" wounded 2. Bombing. Our Special Platoon bombed enemy in vicinity of South CRASSIER. Enemy shelled front & support line fairly heavily. Small reply from our artillery. Our Bombers - at South CRASSIER bombed enemy front line trenches ditto. Stokes Guns got one direct hit on enemy trench. Casualties 2 wounded. +1 wounded 18th since died."	Arty.
ditto	18		Handed over Left Subsector, TRAROC. to 13 YORKS Rgt. & Returned to Los BREBIS in reserve. Buried at HOLE in the WALL Cemetery MAROC. Casualties - 1 wounded.	do
Los BREBIS	19.		With Bn. in Reserve - Cleaned up. Received complete new series Rubber rons.	Son
do.	20		do do Officers bathed Wand Reserve & Support lines ¼ CALONNE Sector, Army secured rations to relieve 17 Welch in Reserve at BULLY GRENAY.	an

Army Form C. 2118

WAR DIARY
or
INTELLIGENCE SUMMARY

(Erase heading not required.)

Instructions regarding War Diaries and Intelligence Summaries are contained in F.S. Regs., Part II. and the Staff Manual respectively. Title Pages will be prepared in manuscript.

7

Place	Date 1916	Hour	Summary of Events and Information	Remarks and references to Appendices
LES BREBIS to SOUTH MAROC.	July 21st	p.m. 12	Plans changed. About midday received orders to take over the Right Subsector MAROC from the 20th Bn MIDDx Regt. This Subsector to be renamed "Left Subsector of CALONNE SECTION," included in MAROC SECTOR. Relief completed 19.50 hours. 'C' Coy in left Fire Line. 'D' Coy in Right. 'A' Coy in Support at Bn.H.Q. SOUTH MAROC. A Coy supplying 1 Officer, 20 men to NEUF KEEP and the same to EDGWARE KEEP. 1 Lewis Gun to each Keep. 'B' Coy Still in Grand Balif at Les BRUSIERES. No operations to report.	↓ Copy
SOUTH MAROC.	22nd		As the Bn was 1 Coy short, a Grand Check, it was found impossible to supply with parties to help support firing line & supports. These were in poor condition especially on Right & Left of No: Bn. Anyone made arrangements that NEUF + EDGWARE KEEPS should be relieved by officers + men of the Pioneer Bn Yorks Regt. This was arranged at 20 hours – Lewis Guns remained. No shelling worth reporting – what shelling there was, was nearly all on our post – Patrols visited enemy wire – found keep strong – Enemy snipers active – considerable having done on our part – principally Hotchkiss + Vickers gund guns gaps.	Ditto
Do.	23rd		Major BURN-MURDOCH with 2Lt ALEXANDER + McMILLAN and 45 other ranks rejoined the Bn, the remainder of the Coy. (B) remaining in Grand Balis at LES BRUSIERES. Billeted in Hotters in SOUTH MAROC. SOME shelling by us during the day but with what effect from the enemy – on TMs (60 lb) had in + Stokes Retaliated, Enemy Shelled our huts, against Firing line + trenches. Trenches were repaired and considerable wiring done infront of Fire Line + Support. Much Sniping on the enemy guns Constantly, rifle fire, another force sniper. Enemy Sniper up PUIT 16 Structure a nuisance - put a Lewis on him - kept him quiet. No casualties. 3 Patrols sent across no man's land, failed to gather any of enemy, who Stillo Fight to his trenches + does not appear to care to come outside his line.	Ditto

WAR DIARY or INTELLIGENCE SUMMARY

Army Form C. 2118

Place	Date 1916	Hour	Summary of Events and Information	Remarks and references to Appendices
SOUTH BARICOL	24.	1 am	Lt RUNCIMAN leading a patrol (volunteer) of 4 other ranks pushed 15 yards through a zig zag avenue in enemy wire — (which was found to be very thin) — opposite our right. Returning he was wounded in the left shoulder & body. His patrol put up a Lot Rifle Grenade fire to fight him in. Lt Col WEATHERALL being particularly interested. He found no scouts — Shillelaghs, Saws & Bows & torches in their first being received by sailors. He continued up to point. A small mine has fired by no. 1 tunnelling Coy under South side of SOUTH CRASSIER in retaliation for enemy. During the day an enemy T.M. firing at our left was observed by our Artillery who promptly fired several rounds at it. Successfully otherwise trench evident but unimportant. Sniping by enemy active — Rifle fire by him again very slack — appears he is careless in keeping his front line at night —	fires
	25.		Our left Coy shelled for an hour at midday — One man lit — one gun wrecked. Our Howitzers 4.5's fired around DOUBLE CRASSIER during evening — Casualty (one) man to hrs to 18 Laws — luckily without suffering any casualties. Our 8 coy shelled front 10 mus to 18 Laws — luckily without suffering any casualties. to coy also hit not to severity.	ones.
	26.		Our Howitzers strewed Hanfill — Patrols found the enemy very quiet in his trenches — Coordinated with large Rifle Grenades — (Pippens). Patrols out during the night 26/27. Scanning the enemy lines. Casualties — (i) near Lt SHEARER — Lt Ht H. ADISON (ii) under Lt DAVIS coll. man — fatally wounded on return to our line — afterwards killed. (Pt Foster 2 Coy.)	50cs.
	27.		Shells for intervittant — some aerial darts fired for enemy during. H.E. damage whose left arm A coy Jan Support. Winds & coy that for line. (The BANK & S. CRASSIER —	fires

1875. Wt. W593/826 1,000,000 4/15 J.B.C. & A. A.D.S.S./Forms/C.2118.

WAR DIARY or INTELLIGENCE SUMMARY

Army Form C. 2118

(Erase heading not required.)

Place	Date	Hour	Summary of Events and Information	Remarks and references to Appendices
SOUTH MAROC	July 28		Enemy shelled our left from 14 to 17 hr with lang HE during considerable damage - as guns retaliated. Sent over some STOKES & Rifle Grenades. Enemy replied R. Grenades & Aerial darts. Intermittent shelling on both sides till evening when gun fire on both sides became very hot at times in vicinity of CROISIERS rd to N-t.S. of Fosse: A BARRAGE fell from the Enemy trenches landed on our Right Coy; trenches burst with heavy on it packed up. The first enemy Aeroplane seen by us for a week came over - about 12 Bocho aeroplanes (also Croix) enemy kits - some returned at once others appeared to have some of Recce which is is believed bivouac by the B' billet. In 9. & Billets by S. MAROC Ch was Paris not in no mans land - helped special Report. Reminder of B' Coy 2/ ment B. from Corps Guard at LA BRUSSIERE. B's received for draft at R.A.O.S.	Resps 1
"	29	"	Enemy covered / bombarded front line with T.Ms KWs long S Arial bombs: stores HE. Enemy also shelled billets with KWs long - 4 Casualties in guard house dugt - Casualties 84d - "B" Coy from Support relieved "D" Coy night the line.	App 1
"	30	"	Enemy on 29" & 30" been more active generally 18Bws - letting done his usual rest a change of the enemy in front had been noted the Lens 78 hav been enforced. The R.I. Rts relieved Connaughts at 18 hrs by the 1st WELCH Regt and attend to billets in S. MAROC near Church.	
S MAROC in Support near Church	31	"	Cleaning clothes equipment and billets	Resp 3 other Ranks - 1 accidentally Casualties

Pages 5-6-7-8-9.
Bat. July 1 — 31st 1916. — WAR DIARY. — 14th(S)B" A.I.F. 4 up 14th(S)B" A.I.F. 4 up
VOLUME. I

Place	Date. From	Date. To	Casualties. Officers.	Casualties. Other Ranks.	Reinforcements. Officers	Reinforcements. Other Ranks.	Notable Engagements. &c.
BRUAY.	1st	4	24/7/16. Wounded 2/Lt K.S. RUNCIMAN.	Killed 4. Wounded 14.	4/7/16. 2/Lt T. SHEARER " R. MILLEN. Lent 9 Aug 6th Scottish Rifles.	28/4/16. 4 O/R.	NIL.
Les BREBIS	4	11					
North MAROC (in Support)	11	15					
ditto Left Fire Line	15	18					
Les BREBIS	18	21			18/7/16. 2/Lt N.B. CRAMP " R.J.F. McALISTER. " N.W. KILGOUR " R.G. MILLER " A.S. McCORMICK " A.A.M. TYSON " T.F. STEELE " M.J. DAVIS from 4th(R) B" A.I.F. S.H.		
South MAROC Two left @ Calon N & Bueres	21	30					
S. MAROC (in Billets) (in Support) Shift time.	30	31.					

P. Lieut.-StaffOr Major
14. A.I.S.H.
21/7/16

Kent

Vol 3

WAR DIARY

10th (S) Bn Argyll & Suthd Highrs

August 1916

Volume 3

WAR DIARY
or
INTELLIGENCE SUMMARY

Army Form C. 2118

Place	Date	Hour	Summary of Events and Information	Remarks and references to Appendices
S. MAROC	Aug 1.		In reserve - Clean up Billets. Taken over from 10th Welch - Shelling intermittent. Casualties 2 wounded	—
"	2.		In reserve - Billets shing shelled + reinforced - visit 91st Field Regt on Loos Ecto (Echoes?) - Hostile + desultory shelling.	—
"	3.		do. Preparing for tomorrow night. CO. arriving complete with the BREGOIS. Very heavy gun fire on our front during night about 2 A.M. to 1 hour -	—
"	4.		Go forward during the evening + relieve 21st Middlx Regt. No 2 Sect secti. LOOS.	—
LOOS	5.		Relief completed A.M. A + B coys in firing line - 'C' in support + 'D' in reserve. Enemy was fairly quiet - find no T.M's or Stokes in our sector No 2. Which extends from JEHKYN St on the right to Bryan 36 inclusive half way between HARRISONS and HART'S Craters - some shelling on both sides - battery firing.	—
LOOS	6.		Patrols in 5/6" ground heavy in front of A coy appear to be holding # + entertaint to advance but joined the leads of their saps - Casualty 1 killed (sniper)	—
—	X		Considerable Shelling - grenades + T.M.'s in bout of enemy - commencing 2 p.m. continuous with return also trying to meet his T.M.'s or Stokes in our midst + retaliate. Difficulty in getting gunners to do so.	—
LOOS	7.		5:30 a.m. a few T.M's at intervals - with grenades + aerial darts and a few trench projectiles as yet unconfirmed. at 6:30 T.M., a trench mortar fire became very hot	—

WAR DIARY or INTELLIGENCE SUMMARY

Army Form C. 2118

Place	Date	Hour	Summary of Events and Information	Remarks and references to Appendices
LOOS No 2 Sector	7. (Continued)		and again, aeroplane + minenwerfer big gun retaliation was not forthcoming – The "Scrape" continued short of the day and late the heavy shell fire received also in the vicinity of the ENCLOSURE. also a LOSS – a large shell bursting in the gable. Had & Churches & what remained of Tab Row (Bn H.Q.) at HATCHETTS – Lt. T.M. (?) fire was ruined. Chiefly at no 'B' Coy – in the vicinity of HARRISONS CRATER. The Coy. suffered heavily – Casualties in the Bn. line – 1 killed 8 wounded our guns put down shells on behind HARRISONS CRATER –	Ditto
LOOS	8.		Throwing rifle & Grenades – Bns again accused of Grenades, the same being thrown over – & [?] small shelling of the Support trench lines. During the morning about 4 PM heavy shelled the support + Haven lines – Casualties 1 killed 1 wounded. The 115th R. F. to 1st Battn arrived the British Army Zealand for presentation of the British officers who attended – when the guns were reported.	Ditto
LOOS	9.		That portion of A Coy & most of HATCHETT relieved by Knings Own R.R.2 marched back to S.E. MAROC. C Coy closed in to relieve K.O.Y.L.I. took up in HAYPARK & Right R. CARFAX Rd. – D Coy relieved at 10 am by CONNAUGHTS – B + remain. of A Coy relieved during the night by 5 R.I. Regt. Relief Completed at 12.40 AM on 10th – Marched into Billets S.E HAYDC. in Support & Left MAROC.	Ditto
S.E MAROC	10.		Cleaning up – Refour in Billets –	Ditto
-	11.		Ditto. Received orders to march to DOBSERNAST huts. 6 Relieve 13 Yorks Regt.	Ditto

Army Form C. 2118

WAR DIARY
or
INTELLIGENCE SUMMARY

(Erase heading not required.)

14 A.F.H.

Instructions regarding War Diaries and Intelligence Summaries are contained in F.S. Regs., Part II. and the Staff Manual respectively. Title Pages will be prepared in manuscript.

Place	Date	Hour	Summary of Events and Information	Remarks and references to Appendices
S.E. MAROC	12.	6.30 p.m.	2 Support Coy ordered to MAROC. Except C. Coy in SOUTH St. 9 am. C. Coy relieved. Remainder to S.E. MAROC.	Supp.
		6.30 p.m.	Relief commenced. 13 Yorks Regt. taking over from us in S.E. MAROC. - H.Q.S.H. to Les BREBIS	
les BREBIS	13.		Clean up. Baths & Billets. B⁹. Supplies 450 men & R⁸ of workparties. 12.30 am. Baths. Rivers met by N.E. as noted above. B⁹ Ch. wrk. parade at Cinema house at 11. a.m.	1 Rome -
do	14.	-	1 move to B.44. Clean up. Refitting - drill, musketry + some training -	Sup
do	15.	4 p.m.	do - 1 p.m. Shelling commenced by enemy of this Town - at works Rd	
		3 p.m.	Shelling came & actly 1 hr. 1st shell abt 8 in. but returned in to air S'wen both. 2 then quickly followed - Killed a Lieut. in Chimneycot in Coy. Would two men - Shelling then continued neartly 5.9's around within 150 yds of school area very considerable damage - & two in hunts Etc.	Supp.
		5 p.m.	aft ½ hour lull - commenced again fretting an hr. 1 Off. Wounded. P. Present when & where 17 hit ab Revve to CALONNE richt.	
Bo do	16.	-	2 went. R.H 9 am when Relief commenced to BOLLY GRENAY. at BOLLY GRENAY. Capt. Pollock + 317 YSR both 100 then went on castle buying took party attached A.M.E for period when B⁹ in Revoir - large workparties impart. Clean up Billets	Supp. Quarters now attached

1875. Wt. W 593/826. 1,000,000. 4/15. J.B.C. & A. A.D.S.S./Forms/C. 2118.

WAR DIARY or INTELLIGENCE SUMMARY

Army Form C. 2118

14 Sept 14

13

Place	Date	Hour	Summary of Events and Information	Remarks and references to Appendices
BULLY GRENAY	Aug 16		Cleaning up Billets & inspecting Same — Supply limber patrol marched the village link - as a test - returned about 11 P.M.	Same
	17	9. P.M.		
do.	18.	—	Continue inspection of Billets - Supply limber patrol - experienced.	P.M.
do.	19.		Continue cleaning & improving Billets. Received Repeat 12 loads from cellars to repair dumps - Recon. done to return to K.O.R. trenches in K.O.R. Lancs. Left B.S. Right B.S. CALONNE on 20. Commencing 2 P.M. Capt. Ames attended.	do.
do.	20.	8.30	Commenced relief of 11 K.O.R. Lanc. Regt. in Left Subsection CALONNE. Coys. from Right to Left. 'A'. 'C'. 'D' in firing line 'B' in support. Gas was sent on by the Bns. on our right at about 10.30 P.M. The enemy retaliated heavily & shot our guns above replied - Enemy fire slackened and centre by a left Coy. & did damage to about 250° of trenches & forgaps - Everything quiet & enemy having stopped a real attack was about to be launched by us. Where as our object was to draw fire from Rev we were not into the trenches. A report on answers when evidence of something seen on fires lines 'Shape' 1 km. Bn. Op. returns were attached —	do.
CALONNE Left Subsection				do.
CALONNE L. Sub. Sec.	21.	=	Patrol good and repairing damage done - patrolling at night to see that of enemys wire cut with a view to making a demolition raid on the Trench at my of the 23/24. Casualties. D/1. M.T. Davis & Lieut. Trimble. 1 Sgt. Accidentally wounded by my Patrol	15353 Pt Wooten B. 9931 J.W.C. McDonald .D 13567 F Hutton A Sgt J.R Clarke. A 19215 Aster —

WAR DIARY or INTELLIGENCE SUMMARY

Army Form C. 2118

Place	Date	Hour	Summary of Events and Information	Remarks and references to Appendices
Colonne L.Sub.Sect.	Aug 22	—	Turning good damage done by enemy shell fire. Enemy shelled front of the position 24 hours. Made little good - improved communication dug outs. Carried out needed material. Sub Sector hunted tank after 10.15 pm on N.H.L.P. No Right Coy trenches a rail of enemy's line. The raid party succeeded & captured 1 prisoner 3 killed. Saw 10 others. He had 1 NCO killed & 4 from (6 men) wounded. Enemy meanwhile hurried front of village keeping up ZNZ hours.	8am
	23		Continued working good litter. & damage to fire line & bygone. Also prepared for fresh raid during night. 3 several attempts were the wall. 1½ & 2 am on right & left. Spl a men out of a hole at 9" against Sapp at Enemy fire line. Object to capture some of enemy. 1 & 3 apl point.	8am
			to capture any of enemy & explode Bangalore Torpedo & draw attention off the other 2 attempts. Casually 1 wounded	8am 12.00 pm O.S. out D
			Received order to be relieved by 11.K.R.R Lancashire front Territories : & to relieve Newport & relieve 13 East Surrey Regt at 'C'B: Colonne Setweer. All the Parties returned safely but failed in 2, 3 & went any enemy- No 1 out	
D.	24.		Close enemy & hear him talking but a thick belt of wire prevented breaching, present. Now for patrol at the enemy.	8am 12.00 pl C.H. Peck. C. Oy.
			Casually 11 Lancer driver died.	

WAR DIARY
or
INTELLIGENCE SUMMARY

Army Form C. 2118

Place	Date	Hour	Summary of Events and Information	Remarks and references to Appendices
CALONNE (Support) ("C" Bn)	24. (Cont'd)		Relieved 13th E. SURREY Regt. supplies the CALONNE Defences after having been relieved by 1st K.O.R. Lancs in left Sub. Sector. Cleared up and settled into Billets. Supplies front parties. (220).	Ses-
do.	25.		Continued working on Defences supplying front parties. & 2 N.C.O's + working party + 2310 R.E.	Ses-
do.	26.		Same programme as for 25th.	An
do.	27.		Same programme as for 26th. Leaky bomb during the night in our post. General Press 63rd Divn Casual wound.	Str
do.	28.		Supplying Carrying & working parties. Inspecting billets. Opening WESTHAM LANE. Casualties 1 wounded. Received news of it relieved by 1st Royal Fusiliers on 30th at 12 noon. Roumania declares war on Germany.	Atts.
do.	29.		No guns fired for 10.20 a.m. billets on 4.20, C. + 4.26a. Continue same programme as for 28th. See about CALONNE latrine supply. Not paper so sanitary supplied.	Atts.
do.	30.		Commence relief at 12 noon. go to PETIT SAINS. 60th Div. 19th 13th Corps in CALONNE. Relief Completed 3.P.M. Heavy 1st shower weather. Found the billets not up to standard. Men overcrowded. Roofs doors + windows leaky.	Wn
do.	31.		Dried clothing as weather had improved. Arranged Temporary billets.	Atth

Volume 1.
pp. 10 to 15
inclusive.

WAR DIARY
14th (S) Bn Argyll & Sutherland Hdrs.

DATE	Casualties		Engagements & Raids.	Points of interest.
	Killed	Wounded		
Aug 1—31.	4.	1 Off. 23 Oth ranks.	23/4th Raid on enemy line — This was done in silence without R.A. preparation — No prisoner were found in the Sap raided — party returned having lost men to Pt. any prisoners — Place: Ypres-CANAL INNER. 9th cancelled —	No. Sp320 2nd Lieut J.W. Weatherill received the Military Medal. 8th Aug 1916.

Lieut-Kuton begin
14 A&S.H.

Army Form C. 2118
Vol 1. p 16.

WAR DIARY
or
INTELLIGENCE SUMMARY
(Erase heading not required.)

Instructions regarding War Diaries and Intelligence
Summaries are contained in F. S. Regs., Part II.
and the Staff Manual respectively. Title Pages
will be prepared in manuscript.

Place	Date 1916	Hour	Summary of Events and Information	Remarks and references to Appendices
PETIT-SAINS	Sep 1.		Cleaning up - improved billets - Erecting beds & repairing leaks etc -	Capt. bapi.
do	Sep 2		Bn. Hot baths at the Public's - Inspection for A.& C. in afternoon. Improved Billets.	2 Ors. bapi.
do	Sep 3		Roth: Cleaning up. Some held in bath. at edge of village.	Pte. bapi.
do	Sep 4		Also received to relieve 13. Bn. Yorks Regt at HAROC. Left sub sector between 5' Sept. Commencing 8 am.	
do & HAROC.	Sep 5.		Marched into HAROC. Left Subsector. Relief completed by 11.30 am. of 13' Yorks.R. 12 O' & 1.B. 44. Entrenched. Relief improvement during the day.	
			No shelling of importance - Much work to be done in trenches. Especially after late 8 days Rain - Right S/S	Pte. bapi.
Left Subsector do	Sep 6.		Seriously & shells band out & Report or Enemys lines, Saps & - or Enemys Patrols between the 2 O.K.A S/S 1 & 2 & 5 Rifle Gnr. 20 - Quiet day. Casualties. 1 Killed.	2 Ors. bapi.
	Sep 7.		Right S/S. Patrols visited Enemys Trees. Compost Und by us to N/W army of DOUVE CROSSIER. On guns fired 20 HE or German trenches S of DOUVE CROSSIER S - Cuckoosh barrage one Enemy front 6 TMs which fell short of our frontline - evidence MBS barrage of stopped them - Enemy fired Westward between 4 pm & 7.30 pm were TMs - 77s against our front line app. 5.2. = Our Stokes Guns retaliated. Immediate wire barrage EM 9 PM. Killed. 1. Wounded. 1.	Capt. bapi.

WAR DIARY or INTELLIGENCE SUMMARY

Army Form C. 2118
Vol 1 p 17

Place: MARoC Left S.S.

Date	Hour	Summary of Events and Information	Remarks
1916 Sept 8	9 a.m.	Enemy fires at Sniper St. with Rifle Grenades. Our TMs fired on Enemy S.P. & CRASSIER.	Rars Grgs
	10.	Enemy searched for our TM in King St. – which continued fire at Enemy trenches.	
	2.4.30	Enemy sent over Emn 5;9 H.E. with King St. (? aimed at TMs) Casualty 3 (wounded), 1 since died.	
	5 p.m.		
9th	2.45 a.m.	A bombing raid was made with a 20 lb. bomb against an Enemy Sniping post on the South CRASSIER. Enemy sentry was to some extent.	Rifle grgs
		Known about 15 ft from plum. Plans about a house; the bp place was turned sudden. At Enemy Sentry was heard to cough & after he had challenged our men (1 NCO 1 man) to come out kinards them & must have been blown up in the explosion.	
	Later	Enemy'd bn'ls tried improvements effected. Was put up & patrols carried out.	
	4.20	Large enemy Umn'd in by Tunnelled Coy. L.S. CRASSIER.	5
	6 p.m.	Aft. H Bombing Platn relieved & CRASSIERS by KING'S OWN Bombing Platn.	
		Enemy sent over some 5.9's at our TMs – LIVERPOOL St. neighbourhood. Aerial Rifle Grenades not B'ay reft relieved by "A" Coy. C boy a rapid relieved by "D" oy.	Rars hrs
		Enemy sent over one round T.M's. A Double CRASSIER strings two grenades. Fires from the source with charge of shelling. Barrel airpoteant & report Engt. 2 Casualties. St JAMES St Hen'd treated by T.M's parted kill. Some shrapnel. Enemy snipers active.	1 as Pte C/o 1/7 Manson Moss. C/o R. Tenwell.
10th			
11th		Demo'd sent relieved today by 11 King's Own Rt. at 2.30 p.m. Enemy sent over some Rifle-Grgs. & men Snipers active. TM's and at the DOUBLE CRASSIER was active. TM's sent over into EXCTAX end & Queen St area. Casualties 1 killed 2 wounded.	Rars hrs

WAR DIARY or INTELLIGENCE SUMMARY

Army Form C. 2118

Vol I p 18

Place	Date	Hour	Summary of Events and Information	Remarks and references to Appendices
MAROC L. Sap.	11 Sept		Our patrols hourly searched enemy line to begin of gap. Three searched the same where kept watch at point of the Enemy TRIANGLE where line had been broken. Corporation were attempted for enemy for CRATER Sap. Wire escaped in Police Aut. came on.	See App
NE.MAROC. Support.	12.		Relieved by 11 Kings & 1st R.Lancs. Commencing at 11.a.m. & Zeppelin with supp of 2 men in Keep two platoons 2/1st McMullan & 30 Others Reserve in TRAVERS' KEEP and 2/1st KILGOUR & 30 other Reserve in St JAMES' KEEP. Three Keeps on relief. Cuts sent up write. One T.M. Whitecharge & Shelling. Supplied 127 rounds to 1/2 Funnelling Coy - Permanent parties. Buried in support. Casualties 2 wounded.	See App 32.0.000
NE MAROC.	13.	-	Supplied every relieved parties - Cleared up and improved trenches - putting in Saps. Having the evening the enemy heavily shelled the tomb parts in O.G.1. St JAMES Keep to half an hour accurate & heavy bombardment by H.E. King large. Casualties 1 killed 1 wounded. Local interchange of shelling - Enemy quiet.	See App
NE MAROC.	14.	-	St JAMES KEEP shelled again during the evening. Casualties nil - so parties at present only work in O.G.1. During the night continued improving Belloy.	See App
			Later. R DOUBLE CRASSIER. 2 men wounded - Bowen.	

Army Form C. 2118

Vol I p 19

WAR DIARY
or
INTELLIGENCE SUMMARY
(Erase heading not required.)

Place	Date	Hour	Summary of Events and Information	Remarks and references to Appendices
N.E. MAROC Support Tr.	Sept 1916 15.	—	Continued improving billets. "B" Coy platoons which have been supplying garrisons at ST JAMES & TRAVERS Keeps are relieved by platoons from "C" Coy under 2nd Lt NICOL and 2nd Lt McDONALD respectively. Guard the night.	ops rgr
do	16.		Intensely cold. About 1.30 am 16th. There was heavy fire on the night patrol heading to the South of the DOUBLE CRASSIER. A raid was suspected to be made by the E. SURREY Regt but this did not take place. The tng & Norts Cloaks has long light. As the CRASSIER as protect platoon was relieved by 1st of the KINGS OWN.	ops rgr
do	17.		Continued improving billets. Supply dump lookpost to Piccadilly lookout to fine new Bn Hq special bombardment in SIKKIM side – usual retaliation of artillery. Enemy continue to fire by Fosse 5 dump.	ops rgr
do	18		Relieved Bn A.C. Obvly brun Regt S.M. & Co Qtr Mr & Coy SM. Supplying lookparties. Portland to report at of the common.	ops rgr
do	19.		Relieved in N.E. MAROC site in Support by the 10th 18 Welch Regt 119th Inf Bde. Completed by being (7 pm). Sent up on cold billets around the Church. HQ same Les BRÉBIS place. En Chellrie	ops rgr

1875 Wt. W593/826 1,000,000 4/15 J.B.C. & A. A.D.S.S./Forms/C. 2118.

WAR DIARY
or
INTELLIGENCE SUMMARY

Army Form C. 2118

Vol I. p. 20

Place	Date Sept.	Hour	Summary of Events and Information	Remarks and references to Appendices
Les BREBIS	20.		Bⁿ in Reserve. Carrying into position, clearing up.	
do.	21.		do.	
			76th Hy Bde. Trained as 14 Bis. LOOS Salient. Arrived in time for the heavy Battle. Specialists' parties Lept. Battn. in turn.	
do. to 14 B/S left Bⁿ	22.		Commenced Relief Scheme. From our left Bⁿ position 14 B/S for Boyau 52 & Right of BOYAU 64 (Enclosure) on left. This is where the ATTACK PIT. Bⁿ on Right. Cⁿ in centre. Aⁿ on left. Dⁿ in Support. Relief completed by midnight. 7 th. P¹ Bⁿ King's Ow. R¹ Reg¹. Our 7.1/5 howitzers firing from 6.30 p.m. till 7 p.m. Rec¹ no damage to enemy fire on 2"& 7.75 as per shot. Recent P to no – An extra weeks land took reopening adv¹ enemy observed to already very bad trenches	
14 B/S (left)	23	7 am	The general condition of the trenches was BC was deplorable. C.O. left to attend a point of position at ROOLOGUS Ones about a week – Major HILL will soon assume command.	
do.	24.		Enemy sent one Rundows N of POSTN ALLEY and on the front line – air Forrest Lane – behind ATTACK PIT. Drive this large of N.G.90 Laid. Battn. went out at night ground enemy his familiar trench. Casualties (Cap¹ Ja⁵. Hogg cond A.m). Killed by Snipe before Boyau 63.64 at 6.30 am. and Co. Serg¹ Treuland Bar. For LUPH also. Done along Neocar Line. Sh⁵. Neelond Twenty km left near FULLUPH.	Killed Cap¹ James Hogg 783. P¹ h. BLACKWOOD
do.	25.		Supper did so meet one on patrols especially informed of Cheese Pit. Cap¹ Hogg was buried at PHILOSOPHY. 3 Ph. Min attempt. Combulein, Dickhamer Trauman their are on in rear Casualties 1 wounded at Maspingate	

Army Form C. 2118

Vol I p 21

WAR DIARY
or
INTELLIGENCE SUMMARY

(Erase heading not required.)

Instructions regarding War Diaries and Intelligence Summaries are contained in F.S. Regs., Part II. and the Staff Manual respectively. Title Pages will be prepared in manuscript.

Place	Date 1916	Hour	Summary of Events and Information	Remarks and references to Appendices
14 B/S (14th)	Sept 26		Relieved by 11/16 East Surreys and took their place in support in no. cup "A" in GUN wood. D cup & 65 Rates kept in right. B cup & Antrin safe kept in left centre. C cup in 10th Avenue in left to POSEN ALLEY. Received information of large enemy bin. massing for counter-attack on trenches. Made dispositions in case of attack for Nth & Nth East. Quiet night. Supplied carr working parties to R.E. &c.	sun
	27.		Quiet day. Supplying working parties – Clearing up – R.E. Cuinchy, stores. pushed on to TUTOIRE. N W Per. line – improved gas shells kept used by the enemy. Considerable movement of enemy of British lines, O. Ser. occupying KOLLOCH - HARPIN + HOHEN ZOLLERN – lies.	Sun. min.
do.	28		Quiet day. Same as 27th. Cap. Riddell [?] gunnery C. coy in relieved by Cap. Pollock + goes to HAZINGARBE to take charge of details of after day. Rain heavily.	Rain heavy.
do.	29.		Quiet day. Same at 28th. Brush- and clamp. Supplied large working parties. Awaiting relief (relieval) for 30th	
do.	30.		Relieved by 11 Kings Bn. R. L. Reg. at 1.30 p.m. who came for Right B. in front of his Bn. at 1.30. To be accommenced to relieve 13th East Surreys in left Bn. front, 120 B. 14 B/S, E. Surreys going into reserve at HAZINGARBE. Fine day – Quiet in morning.	sun hazy.

Volume 4.
pp. 16 to 21

Vol 4

W.A.R. DIARY FOR:
— 14th ARGYLL & SUTHERLAND Highlanders —

SEPT. 1916.

Date.	Casualties. Officers.	Other Ranks.	Places Held.	Points of Interest.
24th Sept.	Killed. Captain James HOGG. "A" Coy. Wounded NIL.	KILLED. Sept. 6. 12573 Pte N WADDELL 7. 8950 Sgt D.G. MUNRO 9. 13816 Pte J.G. LEITCH (Died of wounds) 11. 9921 PteG N. FOLFORD 13. 9072 " P. McGREGOR 24. 9803 " N. BLACKWOOD. WOUNDED 9900 Pte R. CADDIS 10052 " J. MAXWELL 12586 " J. MORRISON 12277. " C. BUIST 13272 L/c M. McMILLAN 14066 Pte W. LENNIE " A.N. THAIN 9090 " W.J. ANDERSON 12857. " N. GOLDIE 9601. " P. HEEPS 9032. CSM. E RAMSAY KILLED. 7. WOUNDED. 11.	Petit-Marais 2h 1-5d MAROC 8h K-19d Les BRIQUES 29. 6. 22 14 BIS 22 15 cEnE.	9.Sep. A bombing raid was made against a trench in enemy support post in the SOUTH CRASSIER at MAROC. The post was lightly damaged but a useful charge. Patrol returned safely after inflicting damage to enemy Rang ba. Front with a rifle. 24. Death of Capt. James Hogg. This officer was killed by a Sph bullet in the head. This occurred at about 6.30 am. Captn Hogg was going forward to trenches & looked over the front line parapet between Pegasus 62 and 64 in 14 BIS. Near it the enemy had been vigilant through the morning burst - second bit not above the parapet for a second before he was killed. The time being behind him made him have a field here the Nets.

Killed, 1
Wounded, NIL

30 Sept 1916

(signed) Lieut - L Allan Major
14 A & S H

WAR DIARY   OCTOBER 59

Vol 5

W. 15517—M. 141. 250,000. 1/16. L.S.&Co. Forms/W 3091/2.   Army Form W. 3091.

Cover for Documents.

Nature of Enclosures.

14th (5) Arg + Suth'd
Highrs

Notes, or Letters written.

VOLUME 5

Army Form C. 2118

Page 1.

WAR DIARY
INTELLIGENCE SUMMARY

October 1916

(Erase heading not required.)

Instructions regarding War Diaries and Intelligence Summaries are contained in F. S. Regs., Part II. and the Staff Manual respectively. Title Pages will be prepared in manuscript.

Place	Date	Hour	Summary of Events and Information	Remarks and references to Appendices
14 BIS SECTOR Left Bn frontage	Oct.1. 1916		Very quiet. Twice during the day our T.M's heavily bombarded the hostile trenches round POSTE 14 BIS. The only retaliation was about two dozen light shell of the "whizzbang" type near BOYAU 52 and on the support trenches near POSEN ALLEY. RUM RATION reintroduced. Return to GREENWICH time. Major E.C. HILL WHITSON in command of the battalion.	H.H.M.T. PARSONS
"	Oct.2		Very similar to yesterday, except that Oct.1. was dry whereas today it drizzled steadily all day. From 9 A.M. onwards. Shelling etc was limited to only apparent activity was an occasional T.M. bombardment of hostile trenches round POSTE 14 BIS. The enemy retaliated weakly, with a few aerial darts and rifle grenades. During the early stages of the night (8.0 PM) a patrol (2Lt A. McMILLAN and 6.O.R) penetrated the German wire but had to be recalled owing to a distinct corps demonstration. This consisted of bursts of rapid fire with rifles, machine guns, and T.M's at intervals during the night. Colonel G.GUNN returned and assumed command of the 120th Inf. Bde. the following morning.	H.H.M.T.

WAR DIARY or INTELLIGENCE SUMMARY

Army Form C. 2118
Page 2

Place	Date	Hour	Summary of Events and Information	Remarks and references to Appendices
148.15 SECTOR	1916 Oct 3		A little rain in the morning - cleared up later. Considerable amount of repair work done to the trenches which had fallen away severely owing to the rain; Quiet on the whole front with the same exception as on the two preceding days. (a)(p) demonstration as before.	WMT
Moved to huts at MAZINGARBE	Oct 4		Relieved by 13th E. SURREYS - operation orders attached. The battalion moved into huts at MAZINGARBE for four days in reserve. Billets very comfortable - electric light. Heavy rain during latter half of march.	WMT
"	Oct 5		Day spent in making arrangement for baths; charge of clothing etc. Urgent call for 150 men for a carrying fatigue lasting from 12.0 noon to 6.20 P.M. (time of departure and return of batch to billets). (a)(p) demonstration of previous night's culminated in a series of raids on the top postage on the night Oct 5/6 at 5.0 P.M. under cover of smoke and gas	WMT
"	Oct 6		Day spent in a dreary billet routine. Large working party out in evening	WMT
	Oct 7		Rained heavily in evening. Arrangements for relief accepted next 1The Train. M. Gun section relieved 13th E. SURREY ditto in same sector as before. 2nd Lt BIGGART went home on special leave. Capt. W.G.T. KEDDIE went to hospital.	WMT

Army Form C. 2118

Page 3

WAR DIARY
or
INTELLIGENCE SUMMARY
(Erase heading not required.)

Instructions regarding War Diaries and Intelligence Summaries are contained in F. S. Regs., Part II. and the Staff Manual respectively. Title Pages will be prepared in manuscript.

Place	Date	Hour	Summary of Events and Information	Remarks and references to Appendices
Moved to 14 Bis sector. Left battalion frontage.	Oct 8		Battalion moved up the line and relieved 13th E. Surreys in same sector as before. Operation order attached. Found trenches inundating owing to recent rain but not so bad as was expected. Hostile snipers more active than during previous tour - relief suspected. Bright moon prevented patrolling. Major E.C. HIGH WHITSON went to hospital; Major H. BURN-MURDOCH assumed command. [initials]	Casualty 1 wounded see appendix A
"	Oct 9		Very quiet day. At night owing to moon-light the enemy wire much less active. Two parties under 2Lts W.R. CRAMB and H.A.M. TYSON laid bangalore guides strings to the German wire on either side of Sap H.2.5.B.48.66. [initials]	Map 36 c N.W. 3 FRANCE
"	Oct 10		Bright moon light night. Very quiet. Slight T.M. activity on our part near Posts 14 Bis. This was repeated later in the evening. About 8.25 P.M. bangalore parties under 2Lt W.R. CRAMB successfully exploded two torpedoes near Sap H.2.5.B.48.66. A raiding party, led by 2Lt A.C. MACCORMICK, encountered strong opposition from rifle fire and bombs. A bombing fight ensued and eventually our party withdrew bringing all casualties. Full detail contained in operation order no. 28 attached and appendix B (report by O.C. to brigade) [initials]	APPENDIX B Report on raid Casualties 2nd Lt A.C. MACCORMICK killed (A) 3 O.R. killed 10 O.R wounded One canceled 1 O.R wounded died out "

Army Form C. 2118

Page 4

WAR DIARY
or
INTELLIGENCE SUMMARY
(Erase heading not required.)

Place	Date	Hour	Summary of Events and Information	Remarks and references to Appendices
14 B.'s sector	Oct. 11		Quiet day spent chiefly in arranging for the coming relief. Half of our ^n gunners was relieved by the 21st MIDDLESEX ditto — the remaining half were relieved on Oct. 12 by the 11th K.O.R.L. m. gunners. MMT	
MOVED to SUPPORT BN. HULLUCH	Oct. 12		Relieved by the 21st MIDDLESEX (121st Bde) in 14th 14 B.'s sector. Took over from 2nd DEVONS (23rd Bde) in 10th AVENUE (POSEN ALLEY to WINGS WAY) as Support battalion to the HULLUCH sector. Last party to be relieved arrived about 5.30 p.m; the rest of the battalion less A Coy, were relieved before 10.0. A.M. A Coy. was relieved by the 11th K.O.R.L. who took over the right battalion (HULLUCH SECTOR) frontage plus the frontage held by A Coy (Boyaux 64-61). Operation order attached. MMT	
SUPPORT B.N. HULLUCH	Oct. 13		Dry and very clear. A few small carrying and working parties were ordered during the day. Time spent in cleaning up, making up deficiencies, inspection etc. Stand to at 5.15 p.m. Major H. BURN MURDOCH left for a course of instruction at ALDERSHOT. CAPT. J.D. MACKIE assumed command. MMT	
"	Oct. 14		Much the same as yesterday. Stand to, working parties, weather conditions as on Oct. 13. Some T.M. activity over west of the salient. MMT	

WAR DIARY or INTELLIGENCE SUMMARY

Army Form C. 2118
Page 5

Place	Date	Hour	Summary of Events and Information	Remarks and references to Appendices
SUPPORT BN. HULLUCH	Oct 15		Same routine as on two previous days. W/M 7	
"	Oct 16		ditto	W/M 7
"	Oct 17		Preparation for relief. Machine gun section relieved E. SURREY ditto in advance. Day - very cold. CAPT. W.G.T. KEDDIE returned from (casualties 2 killed (R)) W/M 7	
MOVED TO LEFT BN. HULLUCH	Oct 18		The battalion was relieved in support by 11 K.O.R.L. and moved up to relieve 13 E. SURREYS in Left battalion HULLUCH. Found trenches in bad state owing to rain and T.M. activity. Hostile T.M's were active immediately after the relief was completed. Order of companies from right to left C, D with coaster supt, B with left (N) supt, A (oy) in support. Operation order attached. An aerial dart exploded on one gas gas cylinders and slightly gassed one man. W/M 7	Killed 2 O.R. (B) gassed (slightly) 1 O.R.
"	Oct 19		Quiet day on the whole. Hund T.M. activity in vicinity of crater seps and GREEN CURVE. On trenches suffered accordingly. All work concentrated on much needed trench repair; duck boards, etc W/M 7	2 O.R wounded
"	Oct 20		Trenches in very bad condition. Weather very cold. German T.M's active chiefly, medium at 11.00 A.M. and heavy just before dusk 4.15 - 5.30 P.M approx. An alert on most of the day. W/M 7 2dLt T.C. ANNAN from 9th A $ S Hrs joined the battalion.	

1875 W. W593/826 1,000,000 4/15 J.B.C. & A. A.D.S.S./Forms/C. 2118.

Army Form C. 2118

Page 6

WAR DIARY
or
INTELLIGENCE SUMMARY
(Erase heading not required.)

Instructions regarding War Diaries and Intelligence Summaries are contained in F.S. Regs., Part II. and the Staff Manual respectively. Title Pages will be prepared in manuscript.

Place	Date	Hour	Summary of Events and Information	Remarks and references to Appendices
HULLUCH LEFT Bn.	Oct. 21		Dry - very cold. Situation as preceding day. Men alert on far most of the day. Capt. A. Pollock was attached to the 121st B.Sc. for instruction in Staff work. Companies busy with trench repair. The following officers joined the battalion. 2Lts. M.G.S. KERR from 8th A.A.S. Hqs, A.S. DUNCAN from 8th A.A.S. Hqs, and W. HAMILTON from 7th A.A. Hqs. MMJ	Wounded 4 O.R. (B)
	Oct. 22		Major I.M. WATSON (A.+S. Hr) joined the battalion and assumed command. Moderately cold, - wind helped to dry up the trenches. Hostile T.M.s very active against the 1/4 H.L.I. on our right (who made a raid in the evening). Situation normal except for slightly increased rifle & M.G. activity. Men alert on to a few hours. 2Lt. R.W.B. MacDONALD and 1.O.R. examined the hostile wire with a view to the placing of a mobile charge. MMJ	Oct. 23 Casualties 3 O.R. Killed 1 O.R. wounded
	Oct. 23		Dry - came on to rain about 9·0 P.M. Situation quiet on our front-; T.M. activity against the battalion on our right. Position was undermeath for placing a mobile charge and the project was abandoned. MMJ	
	Oct. 24		Situation same as preceeding day. Preparation for move. 2nd Lieut. W. LAWSON went to hospital MMJ	Casualty Wounded 1.O.R.
	Oct. 25		Battalion was relieved by the 8th Bn. The Queen's 72nd Inf. Bde. and occupied billets in B area LES BREBIS. Last party to leave 95th Area at 2·0 P.M. Operation order attached. MMJ	

Army Form C. 2118

Page 2

WAR DIARY
or
INTELLIGENCE SUMMARY
(Erase heading not required.)

Instructions regarding War Diaries and Intelligence Summaries are contained in F. S. Regs., Part II. and the Staff Manual respectively. Title Pages will be prepared in manuscript.

Place	Date	Hour	Summary of Events and Information	Remarks and references to Appendices
LES BREBIS	Oct. 26		Day spent entirely in preparation for the move. At noon Brigadier General C.J.N.D. Willoughby presented the military medal to No. 9533 Sgt. Robert FLEMING and No. 12032. Pte. HUGH McGUFFIN for gallant conduct during the recent raid (see appendix C1). 2nd Lieut. D.H.W. ARNOT rejoined the battalion from the bombing school FOUQUERES. The battalion billets from 7.0 AM to 4.30 P.M. and were made up. Major I.H. WATSON became D.A.Q.M.G. of the 14th Division, CAPT. J.D. MACKIE assumed command.	APPENDIX C1.
MOVED to BRUAY	Oct. 27		Battalion marched off from LES BREBIS at 9.30 A.M. and reached BRUAY (Area A) at about 1.30 P.M. Weather on but roads very muddy - rained in afternoon. OPERATION order attached.	
MOVED to MONCHY-BRETON	Oct. 28		Battalion marched from BRUAY (9.15 A.M.) to MONCHY-BRETON (operation order attached) which we reached about 1.30 P.M. Billets north found in town and farm stove houses.	
	Oct. 29		Battalion was to from MONCHY BRETON to TERNAS which we reached about 2.0 P.M. Billets rather crowded - considerable difficulty experienced	

WAR DIARY or INTELLIGENCE SUMMARY

(Erase heading not required.)

Army Form C. 2118

Page 8

Place	Date	Hour	Summary of Events and Information	Remarks and references to Appendices
MOVE TO TERNAS.	Oct 29		in fitting A Coy into billets. Orders to the men were verbal. It rained steadily for most of the way and the roads were in very bad condition. Colonel A. GUNN resumed command of the battalion on returning from leave. MMT.	
TERNAS.	Oct 30		Day spent in cleaning up, drill, and training. At 12.45 P.M. Brig Gen C.S.W.D. Willoughby presented the military won ribbon to 2 Lieut. George Alan Campbell Smith for gallant conduct during the recent raid (APPENDIX C2) The wearing parts and all the battalion officers were present. Weather showery. Capt. W.S.T. KEDDIE and 2nd Lt. W.R. CRAAB went to hospital. MMT	appendix C2
"	Oct 31		Day spent in drill etc. All the new box helmets of the battalion were tested in gas. Night marching in the evening. Showery. MMTyson	

APPENDIX A.

Summary of casualties in fourteen bn. Arg. & Suthd. Highrs
during October 1916.

Date	No.	Rank	Name	Coy.	Buried at
9.10.16	S/13266	Pte	COLLINS. J	A	wounded (B)
10.10.16	S/9018	L/Cpl	BELL. J A	A	wounded (C)
10/11.10.16	12389	Cpl	SIBBALD. H	D	wounded (A)
10/11.10.16		2nd Lieut	A.C. MACCORMICK	C	killed (A) PHILOSOPHE
"	9674	Pte	PATERSON. A.G.	C	wounded (A)
"	9150	Pte	CARSON G	A	wounded (A)
"	12328	L.Cpl	METCALFE. W.	A	wounded (A)
"	9530	Pte	LECKIE. A. H	C	wounded (A) died of wounds 11-10-16 BARLIN
"	12452	Pte	HUDSON. H.	A	wounded (A)
"	990	L/Sgt	WALKER. A.	A	wounded (A)
"	13501	Pte	BRAND. WM	D	wounded (A)
"	12655	Pte	WHITE. A.W.	D	wounded (A)
"	13186	Pte	LONEY. T G	B	killed (A) PHILOSOPHE
"	9695	L/Cpl	PEARS. J L	C	killed (A) PHILOSOPHE
"	12446	Pte	MC.GREGOR. J.	C	killed (A) PHILOSOPHE
"	13291	L/Cpl	STURGEON. W. A.	A	wounded (A)
"	14297	L/Cpl	GILLESPIE. J.A.D.	A	wounded (A)
"		Pte	SCOTT R.M	A	accidentally burned
12.10.16	13867	L/Cpl	ROSS F.C.	D	wounded (B)
14.10.16	S/9664	Pte	IMRIE. D.	B	wounded (B)
"	12593	Pte	WILSON. H.	C	killed (B) PHILOSOPHE
16.10.16	13990	Pte	DUNNACHIE. W.	A	killed (B) PHILOSOPHE
"	9474	Cpl	GRIFFITHS. F.	B	killed (B) PHILOSOPHE
18.10.16	9926	Pte	MURRAY. J.S.	B	killed (B) PHILOSOPHE
"	13658	Pte	SMITH W.S.	B	gassed
"	13891				

APPENDIX A
Page 2

List of casualties to 14 A.I.F. Hrs
during October 1916 continued:

Date	No.	Rank	Name	Company	
19.10.16	9014	Pte	SHAW. F.H	B	wounded (B)
"	13355	Pte	KERR. H.D	D	wounded (B)
21.10.16	9112	Sgt	FISHER. M.	D	wounded (B)
"	9016	Sgt	STUART. L.L.	D	wounded (B)
"	9973	L/Sgt	LESLIE. W.	D	wounded (B)
"	9234	L/Cpl	KERR. J.	C	wounded (B)
23.10.16	9094	Pte	ANDERSON. W.J.	B	killed (B) — PHILOSOPHE
	9131	Pte	ARCHIBALD. J.H.	B	killed (B) — PHILOSOPHE
	9542	Pte	COWIE. W.	B	killed (B) — PHILOSOPHE
	10100	Cpl	SMITH. W.	B	wounded (B) rejoined 24/10/16
24.10.16	8981	Pte	McKINLEY. R.	B	wounded (L)

Secret   War Diary   Copy No. 11

Operation Orders No 28
By Major H. Bruce Murdoch,
Comndg 1st/5th Bn A&S Highlanders

9th October 1916

1. A Minor Operation will be carried out on the night of 10th/11th October 1916.

Object

2. Object. (1) To secure identification by prisoners.
          (2) To kill as many others as possible.
          (3) Destruction of dugouts or emplacements by Mobile charges.

Troops

3. 2nd Lieut. A. C. MacCormick (O.C. Raiders) with 2 Sergeants and 18 other ranks to be detailed by OC "C" Company will provide raiding party (divided into "A" and "B" groups).
Covering party of one N.C.O. and 6 men will be detailed by OC "A" Company, and will be under the command of 2nd Lieut. C.A.C. Smith.
Two Bangalore parties each consisting of 1 N.C.O. 4 carriers, and 2 bayonet men will be detailed by OC. "A" Company. One R.E. per party.

Artillery Co-operation

4. Artillery will be in readiness to open intense fire on enemy's support trench from H 25 b 33.15 to H 25 b 42.40, and on H 19 d 54.00.
Fire to be opened on direct signal from Infantry, if required.

Action to be taken by Bangalore Parties

5. Two Bangalore Parties will go out from our wire at a point prepared near Poëme 63. No 1 Party will lay Bangalore in enemy wire at H.25.b.50.42. about 60 yards S of Sap at H.25.b.50.55.
No 2 Party will lay Bangalore at H.25.b.50.60. about 30 yards N of Sap.
Placing of each Bangalore to be immediately reported to 2nd Lieut. MacCormick at F.T. opposite point of exit.

Action to be taken by Raiding Party

6. Immediately on report of both bangalores being laid, raiding party will go out from same exit point, and assemble in a suitable position between two Bangalores.
Bangalores to be exploded simultaneously by electric current either by OC. Raiders, or by R.E. officer on signal, by OC Raiders as may be settled by R.E. officer i/c Bangalores.
Immediately on explosions A and B groups of raiding party composed as under will rush gaps Nos. 1 and 2 respectively.
"A" Group.
    2nd Lieut. A. MacCormick.
    1 Sergeant
    5 Bombers
    1 Mobile charge carrier
    4 Bayonet men.

B. Group.
    1 Sergeant (2nd i/c Raiders).
    3 Bombers
    1 Mobile charge carrier.
    3 Bayonet men.

A Group on entering enemy trench will turn to left and bomb along to junction with sap at H.25.b.50.55. Two bombers and one Bayonet man will bomb this and return, while remainder hold trench at this point. Mobile charge will then be placed in emplacement or dugout opening off rear of same point. Group will continue northwards along F.T. bringing any prisoners, and effect junction with B. group. Both groups will then withdraw by No.2 gap.

B. Group will hold trench opposite No.2 gap, making a prisoner from any enemy in the immediate vicinity.
Mobile charge will be placed in emplacement or dug out opening off trench to enemy's rear at this point.
On being joined by A. Group, B. Group will withdraw through No.2 gap. A Group will follow.

O.C. Raiders will detail one or two bayonet men of each group beforehand to secure prisoners.

Action of Covering Party 7. Covering party will follow raiding party after 5 minutes interval and will take up position in No Man's Land central between two gaps; it will (1) take over prisoners if required bring them back to our F.T. at west point without delay (2) a remainder will remain to cover withdrawal of both groups.

Signalling 8. The S.O. will arrange a station in F.T. near Bogue 63, connecting up with A. Coy HQ.
Covering party will take out electric wire from electric bell at buggy at this point.

Medical 9. POSEN ALLEY will be used for evacuating wounded. This trench will be stopped under arrangements to be made by O.C. B. Coy from dusk until normal conditions are resumed.

Programme 10. Minus 1.30 Vickers open intermittent long distance fire on enemy's rear line along same front as artillery (see para 10) (about 500 yards beyond enemy F.T.)

Minus 30 Bangalores in position.
Minus 5 Raiding party in readiness.
ZERO Explosion of Bangalore.
F.M's open intense bombardment on enemy front line between H.25.d.33.35 and H.25.d.2.9.
A and B groups of raiding party rush trenches
Vickers cease fire.
N.B. Owing to necessity of seizing period of obscured moon, O.C. Raiders may accelerate explosion ZERO.

APPENDIX B   War Diary

14th (S) Bn. Argyll & Sutherland Highlanders.

Operation report on Raid carried out on night of
10/11th October 1916, in accordance with 120th
Infantry Brigade Operation Order No.34 of 9-10-16.

Scheme. 1. The Infantry Operations proceeded in accordance with
Battalion Operation Order No.28 of 11-10-16,
which was submitted and approved.

Moonlight. 2. A clear full moon presented a formidable obstacle
in the way of success. On the preceding night
it was possible to read small print of a newspaper
by its light. On the night of 10/11th it was
still fuller, and was shining from before dusk
until dawn. This difficulty was anticipated,
and was reported fully in writing by me on 8th
instant, and again on 9th instant, but was over-
ruled owing to military exigencies, the carrying
out of the scheme being definitely ordered by
higher authority after consideration of this
difficulty.

Arrangements 3. Necessary appliances for raid were requisitioned
for provis- in covering letter sent with Battalion Operation
ion of Orders when submitted for approval.
necessaries The R.E. were unable to provide the electric
by R.E. detonation for the bangalores for which I
requisitioned. The simultaneous explosion of
the two gaps, which was an integral part of the
scheme could not be ensured, and in spite of
careful effort was not obtained, an interval
of several minutes elapsing between explosions.
The wire-crossing mats, and knobkerries which
were asked for were promised, but were reported
to me by the R.E. as unobtainable shortly
before the operation commenced.

Arrangements 4. Shortly after 7 p.m. I received information that
for the Artillery support provided for (Battalion
Artillery Operation Order No.28. para 4) would not be
Support. available after 9-30 p.m. owing to a relief.
By this time the operations were already in progress.

Order of 5. The following is the order of actual events
events as as reported in a special prearranged code from
reported. advance station in F.T. (see Bn. Op. Order, para 8)
There being no direct wire obtainable to T.M's.,
a runner from nearest Stokes Gun was in attendance
at advance station.

P.M.
7-32. No.1. Bangalore in position.
7-42 No.2. Bangalore in position.
7-43 Bangalore parties returned.
7-59. Raiding party went out (having postponed
      ZERO to 8-20; T.M's. informed by Orderly
      who did not reach them in time.)
8-24. Left Bangalore exploded.
8-26 Right Bangalore exploded.
8-49 Raiding party reported to be returning.
9-10 Raiding party still returning bringing wounded.
9-23 Artillery called for to assist in return.
9-31 Artillery commenced.
9-35 Four or five of party still out but artillery
      not desired further.
9-46 All wounded in.   Roll-call being taken.
9-48 All reported in.

Signalling arrangements laid down in para. 8 of
Orders, were carried out by Lieut. T. J. Menzies,
(who remained in charge of Advanced Station), and
worked without hitch.

2.

Laying of Bangalores.	6.	Bangalores were successfully laid in position and in good time. 2nd Lieut. W. B. Cramb was in charge and supervised the laying in German wire. The R.E. Corporal and Sapper who led the two parties carried out their task with great coolness and efficiency. (L/Cpl. BAMBER and Sapper RAMSBOTTOM, 231st Field Company, Royal Engineers. At 7-43 when this was reported the enemy had given no indication that he had detected our operations.
Zero.	7.	O.C. Raiders asked for postponement of ZERO to 8-20. This was reported to T.Ms.
T.Ms. co-operation.	8.	The T.M. co-operation arranged (diversion to the right of attacked front) proceeded satisfactorily although diminished in volume by two nearest STOKES going out of action.
Detonation of Bangalores.	9.	The means of detonation provided by R.E. (see para 3 supra) consisted merely of two ordinary short fuzes which had to be ignited at points about 100 yards apart. Simultaneous ignition by time on synchronised watches was attempted, but could not reasonably have been expected to be obtained. No. 1 Bangalore exploded after No. 2, after an interval of not less than two minutes. Good gaps were made in enemy wire.
Action of B Group Raiding Party.	10.	B Group, (Sergt. A. McCurdie and 7 O.R.) rushed at gap immediately. Enemy was ready with bombs and heavy rifle fire from right and left of gap, and from behind parados, by which time leading men were hit and brought down in gap. The enemy were now plainly visible to right and left; some were wearing steel trench helmets. Sergt. McCurdie organised bombing attack to right and left, and a brisk bombing fight continued, many bombs being thrown by us into German trench, until word received from rear that A Group was withdrawing. The men remaining unwounded then withdrew in good order, bringing their casualties. Other losses sustained on way back
Action of A Group Raiding Party.	11.	Immediately on explosion (and before fragments all fallen) party rushed and penetrated gap. As with B Group enemy in numbers and in readiness, opened fire from trenches on both sides of gap, and also from behind parados opposite gap. 2nd Lieut. A. C. MacCormick led rush with great gallantry and determination, and was shot through the head, falling inside German parapet mortally wounded. His last action was to turn and cheer on the men immediately behind him. No.9533 Sgt. R. Fleming at once organised bombing attacks along parapet to right and left. Many bombs fell into trench and much damage to enemy personnel must have been caused. Private H. McGuffin fired at and threw a bomb at German who shot Lieut. MacCormick; German believed killed. Severe enemy rifle fire reduced A Group to four effectives, whereupon Sergt. R. Fleming and Pte. McGuffin got Lieut. MacCormick out of trench with difficulty, and commenced withdrawal. No.9461 Sergt. A. Taylor with one man remained and covered withdrawal, continuing to bomb. A Group bombers behaved with coolness and effect. In one or two cases our men contrived to catch in the air the German wooden stick bombs and throw them back on the enemy.

Covering/

3.

Covering Party.	12.	Covering party was under command of 2nd Lieut. G. A. C. Smith, about 40 yards from No. 1 Gap. Covering party assisted in withdrawal and recovery of casualties. 2nd Lieut. G. A. C. Smith kept the situation well in hand throughout with admirable coolness and courage.
Recovery of Casualties.	13.	This occupied over an hour and was conducted under heavy enemy rifle fire with most praiseworthy courage, and persistence by all ranks. Additional casualties were sustained during the process. I would mention the under-mentioned, out of many others, who returned again and again; 2nd Lieut. G. A. C. Smith, 2nd Lieut. W.B.Cramb, (who gave effective first aid in NO MAN'S LAND to a dangerously wounded man) No. 990 L/Sgt. A. Walker, (himself seriously wounded the last time), No.S/12140 L/Cpl. P. Cooper, S/9649 Pte. J.C.McFarlane, S/12032 Pte. H. McGuffin. S/8982 L/Cpl. J.G. Macdonald, (previously commended in orders) did useful work in the covering party.
Artillery Co-operation.	14.	At 9-23 when four or five wounded or unwounded were still in No Man's Land under sweeping rifle fire, I called for Artillery Co-operation, and some Howitzer fire was given at 9-31 for a short period. This temporarily subdued enemy fire and enabled return of remainder by 9-46.
Casualties.	15.	We lost 1 Officer (2nd Lieut. A. C. MacCormick) and 3 O.R. killed; 10 O.R. wounded, of whom 7 seriously. One other man was seriously wounded by Machine Gun fire in our lines to the right of attacked points during operations.
Damage inflicted on enemy.	16.	All ranks are agreed that considerable loss must have been caused to the enemy by our bombing attacks. This is corroborated by extensive whistling for stretcher bearers by enemy on both sides of attacked points. The enemy also probably sustained loss from our howitzers. As his trenches were strongly manned, shrapnel might have been even better. From the point of view of morale, the enemy opposite cannot fail to realize that his line is at no time safe from attack by troops which persisted in pressing their attack under the brilliant light conditions of last night's raid.
Enemy Tactics.	17.	In view of the enemy's preparedness for the raiding parties, it appears almost certain that, as was anticipated, the bangalore parties were plainly visible to the enemy. He appears to have good fire control and to have reserved fire for the raiders, probably with the object of securing identifications in his own trenches, which in this case was fortunately frustrated. His drill for our nightly bangalore attacks seems to be to hold strongly the firebays on either side of gap, while other men lie down behind parados opposite gap. Direct rapid rifle fire, with bombs, is opened immediately upon our rush. A combination of bangalores with subsequent shrapnel might prove a useful variety upon the present type of operation. Enemy used less M.G. fire than might have been expected. Our T.M. co-operation to right was partly designed to quell likely M.G. emplacements, which may partly account for this.
Conduct of Troops.	18.	Officers and other ranks engaged behaved admirably, and deserve the highest commendation, for (a) the bravery and persistence with which the raid was made and persisted in, under very adverse conditions, until insufficient effectives remained to continue the bombing fight. (b) /

fight. (b) the accomplishment of the difficult and dangerous task, of getting back all dead and wounded, from the enemy's trench, and No Man's Land. It is worthy of note that it was never even necessary to "call for volunteers", sufficient carriers being organised and ready to go out on their own initiative.

H Brown Murdoch
Major,
Commdg. 14th (S) Bn. Arg. & Suth'd. Highlanders.

In the Field,
11th October, 1916.

APPENDIX C 1

14th (Service) Battalion Argyll & Sutherland Highlanders.
:-:-:-:-:-:-:-:-:-:-:-:-:-:

Extract from Battalion Orders No. 83, para.4,
dated 25th October, 1916.

Military Medal.

The Corps Commander has awarded the Military Medal to the under-mentioned for the acts of gallantry stated:

(a) No.S/9533 Sergeant Robert Fleming,
    14th (S) Bn. Argyll & Sutherland Highlanders.

"Sergeant Fleming was a member of a party which raided German Trenches on the Night of 10/11th October, 1916. When the Officer in charge fell mortally wounded in the German Trench, Sergeant Fleming rallied the men and organised a bombing attack to the right and left. He assisted in recovering the Officer's body and skilfully conducted withdrawal when the raid was finished.

(b) No.S/12032 Private Hugh McGuffin,
    14th (S) Bn. Argyll & Sutherland Highlanders.

"During the night of 10/11th October, 1916, Private McGuffin was in front of one of two raiding parties entering the German trenches. He shot a German who killed the Officer in charge of the raiding parties, and afterwards helped to bring back the Officer's body from the German lines."

APPENDIX C2

14th (S) Battn. Argyll & Sutherland Highlanders.

Extract from Battalion Orders No. 85 (3),
dated 29th October, 1916.

MILITARY CROSS.

The General Officer Commanding in Chief has awarded the Military Cross to:
Second Lieutenant George Alan Campbell Smith,
    14th (S) Battn. Argyll & Sutherland Highlanders,
        for the following act of Gallantry:-

"During the night og the 10/11th October, 1916, when a raid was made on the German Trenches, 2nd Lieut. Smith commanded the covering party outisde the German wire. The raiding parties bombed the German trenches which were strongly manned, but sustained heavy casualties owing to the brilliant moonlight. The Officer in charge of the raid was killed, and 2nd Lieut. Smith took command and succeeded in withdrawing all casualties. This operation lasted over an hour but was accomplished successfully and so prevented any identifications falling into the enemy's hands. 2nd Lieut. Smith kept a difficult situation in hand with admirable coolness and indifference to danger."

SECRET   Copy No. 9

MOVE ORDERS
By Capt. J.D. Dickie.
Comdg. 1/5[?] Bn. A.& S.H.

24th Octr. 1916

1. The 120th Infantry Brigade [Group?] will march to Billets in
Area "A" on 25th October.

The 1/5[?] Bn. A.& S.H. will [parade?] at [Inghling Road?] at [time]
to-morrow. Rendezvous to be notified later.

2. Companies will move off from the parade ground in the
following order:
Headquarters, B Coy, [?] Coy, [?] Coy, Lewis Guns, followed
by First Line Transport.

3. Packs:- Packs will be dumped by Companies at Q.M. Stores at [time] to-morrow,
ready for loading.
All steering [?] [?] will be carried in the haversack
until further orders.
[Section?] commanders are responsible that packs contain
only articles enumerated in [the list?] [?] [?], no transport
available so [?] [?] for all [?] where this is [?]
the owner of the pack will have to carry it himself.
All officers packs must [?] at Q.M. Stores at [time], [?] officers [?]
will be responsible for the loading of [?].

4. [?] T.J. Menzies will [?] the [?] and will obtain final
instructions at the [Quartermasters?] [?] before starting out.

5. [Company?] commanders & [?] Officers will satisfy [?] that
[?] are absent before the Battalion moves off and will report to
this effect to the Adjutant when the Battalion parades at [?].

6. [?] to [?] and billeting party will meet the S.M.[?] [?]
at Cross Roads [?] [?] at [time] to act as [?].

7. Sick parade will be at [?].

8. Bivouacs will be in bivvis by 5 [?] & [?] and [?]
will be at [?].

* A loading party of [?] and under per [?] [?] will be
at Q.M. Stores at [time].
Every pack must bear Company letter of Owner.

                                        Capt. Dickie, Capt. [?]
                                        Adjutant
                                        1/5 [S] Bn. A.& S.H.

Copy   No. 1   A, B, C, D & H.Q. Coys.
       6   Quartermaster
       7   Transport Officer
       8   Billeting Officer
       9   War Diary
               File

SECRET

Move Orders.
By Capt. J. D. Mackie
Comdg. 14th (S) Bn. A. & S. H's

No. 1. 120th Infantry Brigade Group will march to Bruay on 27th October 1916.
The 14th A. & S. H's, will march off in the following order.
Headquarter Company (less Lewis Guns).
"A" Coy.
"B" "
"C" "
"D" "
Lewis Guns
First Line Transport, and Baggage wagons will march in Rear of the Battalion.
All movements will be by Platoons until orders to close up are given.
1st Platoon of H.Q. Coy will march off at 9.30 am.
O.C. Companies are responsible for moving off in the above order, and at proper intervals.

No. 2 Route.   Divisional Bombing Ground – Fosse No. 2 – Petit Sains – Hersin – Barlin – Ruitz – Bruay.
Lieut. W. J. Meagher will reconnoitre the Route, and report. He will obtain instructions at Orderly Room.

No. 3 Billeting Parties.   2nd Lieut. D. Nicol, and Billeting Party, with cycles will meet the Staff Captain at the Cross Roads at Petit Sains (R. 2. b. 4. 7).
The Billeting Party will meet the Battalion on arrival at Cross Roads at Bruay (J. 16. a. 6. 7) to-morrow.

No. 4. Loading.   O.C. Companies will arrange to have packs, and blankets, in bundles of 10, properly labelled securely stacked at Q.M. Stores at 6.30 a.m. to-morrow, ready for loading.
O.C. Coys, including H.Q. Coy will detail loading parties of 1 N.C.O. and 5 men, to parade at Q.M. Stores at 8 a.m.
2nd Lieut. Hamilton will be in charge of these parties, and superintend loading.
When loading is completed, parties will join their respective Companies, and on arrival at billets in Bruay will connect off loading.
The Officer i/c Brigade Signal Section will arrange to have his Blankets at Q.M. Stores, ready for loading at 7.30 a.m. to-morrow.

No. 5. Meals.   Companies will arrange to have Tea ready for the men at the long halt in the middle of the day's march. One hour's notice will be given before this HALT.
O.C. H.Q. Coy. will hand over to Coys to-night tea & sugar ration for this meal, and Coys will send 1 Tank to H.Q. Coy.

De Mob Dress.   Fighting Order, with Haversack on shoulder straps, waterproof sheet rolled, and fixed on the belt under Haversack, Steel Helmet fixed on Haversack, and Mess tin fastened to belt under waterproof sheet.

No. 7. Discipline.   Special attention will be paid by Coy & Specialist Officers that Sections of Fours are properly dressed and covered off & that no straggling is allowed.

Robt Dickie Captain
Adjutant
14th (S) Bn. A. & S. H's

Secret   Copy No. 7

Operation Order No. 51
By Major J.M. Watson
Commanding 14th (S) Bn. A.& S. Hrs.
                                                                23rd Oct. 1916

No. 1 Relief

The 120th Infantry Brigade will be relieved by the 72nd Infantry Brigade in the Hulluch Sector on 24th October 1916.

The 14th (S) Bn. A.& S. Hrs. will be relieved in the Left Front Sub Section by the 8th Bn. "The Queens".

No. 2 Guides

Guides will be furnished by the 14th (S) Bn. A.& S. Highrs. as follows.

24th October 1916: 1 Guide per company, 1 from Battalion Headquarters, and one from each of the following specialist sections: Signallers, Snipers, Bombers, and Lewis Gunners, will meet Advance Parties of the 8th Bn. "The Queens" at Junction of Le Rutoire Alley and 10th Avenue at 3pm.

25th October 1916: 4 Guides per Company, and 1 from Battalion Headquarters will meet the incoming Platoons of the 8th Bn. "The Queens" at Junction of Le Rutoire Alley and 10th Avenue at 11 a.m.

No. 3 Order of Relief

The following will be the order of the Relief, and Routes to be used.

1. "C" Coy 14th A.& S. Hrs. will be relieved by "C" 8th Bn "The Queens" in Right Front
2. "D"   "   "   "   "A"   "   "   Centre Front
3. "B"   "   "   "   "B"   "   "   Left Front
4. "A"   "   "   "   "D"   "   "   Reserve

Relieving Platoons for Nos. 1, 2, and 4 will proceed via Hay Alley and on relief these Companies will come out via Essex Lane, 10th Avenue, Northern Up, Cross Roads, Mazingarbe Church, thence to Les Brebis.

Relieving Platoons for No. 3 will proceed via Wings Way and on relief this Company will come out via Wings Way, 10th Avenue, Northern Up, Cross Roads, Mazingarbe Church, thence to Les Brebis.

All movements will be by Platoons, at not less than 200 yards distance interval.

No. 4 Billets

The Quartermaster, and 2nd Lieut D. Nicol, with Billeting Party will report to the Town Major, Les Brebis at 8.30 p.m. on 23rd instant.

No. 5 Trench Stores &c

All Trench Stores, Leg Cocks, Air Packs, and Gum Boots will be handed over on relief and receipts taken.

Copies of lists of Trench Stores handed over will be sent to Orderly Room as soon as completed.

Company and Specialist Officers will obtain certificates that the trenches are handed over in a clean and sanitary condition.

No. 6 Completion of Relief

Completion of Relief will be reported by wire to Battn. Headquarters.

On relief the Battalion will occupy Billets in B Area, Les Brebis.

Copy No. 1 to 5 "A", "B", "C", "D", and HQ Coys
     6. O.C. 8th Bn. "The Queens"
     7. War Diary
     8. File.

Robt. Dickie Captain
Adjutant
14th (S) Bn. A.& S. Highrs.

Secret.   Copy No. 9

Operation Order No. 30,
By Capt. J. D. Mackie.
Comdg. 11th (S) Bn. A. & S. Hrs.

17th October 1916.

No. 1. Relief: 11th (S) Bn. A. & S. Hrs. will be relieved in Brigade Support, HULLUCH
Sector, on 18th instant, and on relief by 11th Kings Own (R.L.) Regt. will
relieve 13th East Surrey Regt. in Left Sub Section.

Specialists:— i. The Lewis Guns of 11th A.&S.Hrs. will be relieved to-day by
the Lewis Guns of the 11th Bn. Kings Own (R.L.) Regt., and on
relief will relieve the Lewis Guns of the 13th (S) Bn.
East Surrey Regt. in the Left Front Sub Section.
ii. All arrangements to be completed between Battalion
Lewis Guns Officers direct.
ii. Bombers. } Will relieve with Bn. HQ.
iii. Signallers. }

No. 2. Dispositions: Companies of the 11th A. & S. Hrs. will be relieved by Companies of the
11th (S) Bn. Kings Own (R.L.) Regt. as follows:—
'A' Coy. 11th (S) Bn. A.&S. Hrs. will be relieved by 'B' Coy 11th Kings Own R.L.Regt.
'D'   'D'
'B'   'A'
'C'   'C'

Guides:— The usual guides will be provided by the Companies
to meet Companies of the 11th Kings Own (R.L.) Regt. as follows:— at 4.30. am.
'A' Coy. 11th A.&S. Hrs. to meet 'B' Coy. Kings Own and 'C' Coy. A.&S. Hrs.
to meet 'D' Coy. Kings Own, at junction of POSEN ALLEY and 9th AVENUE
'B' Coy. A.&S.H. to meet 'D' Coy. Kings Own, and 'D' Coy. A.&S. Hrs. to meet
'C' Coy. Kings Own at junction of VERDUN ALLEY and 9th AVENUE.

The 11th A.&S. Hrs. will relieve the 13th (S) Bn. East Surrey Regt. in the following
order.
'A' Coy. 11 A.&S. Hrs.   —   'A' Coy. 13th East Surrey Regt. in Reserve.
'B'   'B'   " in Left Front.
'C'   'C'   " Centre Front.
'D'   'D'   " Right Front.

Guides:— The usual guides from the 13th East Surrey Regt. will meet
Platoons of 11th A.&S. Hrs. at 12 noon as follows.
From 'A' Coy. 13th East Surrey Regt. to meet 'A' Coy. 11 A.&S. Hrs.
Junction Essex LANE and Reserve TRENCH.
'B' " 13th East Surrey Regt. to meet 'B' Coy. 11 A.&S.H. } Junction of HAY
'C'   'C'   } ALLEY and RESERVE
                                                           } TRENCH.
'D'   'D'   } Junction of ESSEX LA.
                                                           } and RESERVE TRENCH.

No. 3. Advance   The R.S.M. and 1 N.C.O. per Coy. from the 11th A.&S.H. Regt. will report at Batten.
Parties.   Headquarters, 14 A. & S.H., at 8 a.m. on 18th inst. to take over Trench Stores.
1 N.C.O. per Coy. 11th A.&S. Hrs. will report at Batten. H.Q. 13th East Surrey Regt.
at 8.30 a.m. and the R.S.M. 11th A.&S. Hrs. will report at the same place at
10.30 a.m. to take over Trench Stores.

No. 4. Returns.   Signed copies of Trench Stores handed over & taken over will be
sent to Orderly Room as soon as completed. Certificates that Trenches
are handed and taken over in a clean and sanitary condition
will also be forwarded to Orderly Room.

No. 5. Completion   Completion of relief will be sent by wire to Battalion Orderly
of Relief.   Room.
                                        Robt. Drape. Captain.
Copy. Nos. 1–5: OC A. B. C. D & H.Q. Coy.   Adjutant.
       6. OC. 11th Kings Own R.L. Regt.   11 (S) Bn. A. & S. Hrs.
       7. " 13th East Surrey Regt.
       8 War Diary.
       9 File.

Secret.   Copy No. 9.

Operation Order No. 14
By Lieut. Col. _____ H. Bem-Murdoch
Commdg. 11th (S) Bn. (A.S.) S. Rgt.
                                        11th October 1916.

No. 1.   Reliefs of Battalions of the 20th Infantry
               Brigade by Battalions of the 21st Infantry Brigade
               will be carried out on the 12th instant, and reliefs
               of Battalions of the 21st Infantry Brigade by the
               Battalions of the 20th Infantry Brigade will be
               carried out on the same date.

No. 2. Relief The 11th (S) S. S. Highland Hoe. Class T company in the front
               line (B & C) will be relieved by two (2) Companies
               of 21st Middlesex Regt, as follows:-
               "B" & "C" Companies 11th A.& S.H. will be relieved by
               "C" Company 21st Middlesex Regt.
               "B" Coy 11th A.& S.H. by "D" Coy. 21st Mdsx Regt.

No. 3. Advance 3 N.C.O's from 21st Middx Regt. will report at Head-
      Parties quarters 11th A.& S.H. at 9.30 a.m. tomorrow to take
               over Trench Stores.

No. 4. Guides. 8 Guides (4 from "B" Coy, 2 from "C" Coy, and
                2 from "D" Coy) 11th A.& S.H. will meet "C" & "D"
                Coy. 21st Middx. Regt. at Junction of Railway Alley
                and Reserve Line at 6 a.m.

No. 5. Relief. "A" Coy 11th A.& S.H. will be relieved by the 11th Kings Own
                (R.L.) Regt, after relief of 2nd New Yorks Regt by the 1st Kings
                Own (R.L.) Regt, in the Right Subsection Hallesch. Arrangements for
                guides will be notified later.

No. 6. Move.   On relief, Companies will move off by Platoons via
                Posen Alley and 10th Avenue, and will relieve 2nd Devon Regt.
                in Brigade Support, Hallesch Section, as follows:-
                "B" Coy. 11th A.& S. Hrs., on Left
                "C"   "   "   "   . Left Centre
                "D"   "   "   "   . Right Centre
                "A"   "   "   "   . Right

No. 7. Guides. Guides 1 per platoon for B, C, & D, and 1 for "A" Coy. Details,
                from 2nd Devon Regiment, will be at Junction of Posen
                Alley and 10th Avenue at 9.30 a.m. tomorrow.

No. 8. Lewis Guns. The Battalion Lewis Guns, will be relieved partly by
                the Lewis Guns of the 21st Middx. Regt, and partly
                by the Lewis Guns of the 11th Kings Own (R.L.) Regt.
                On relief they will proceed via Posen Alley and 10th Avenue
                to relieve the Lewis Guns of the 2nd Devon Regt. in
                Brigade Support, Hallesch.

No. 9. Advance 2nd Lt. P.U.C. Smith, and N.C.O. per company, will proceed
      Parties. to Headquarters 2nd Devon Regt. to take over trench stores.
                Guides will meet this party at the Junction of Posen
                Alley and 10th Avenue at 6 a.m.

No. 10. Billets.   First Line Transport, and Quartermasters Stores will remain
                          at LES BREBIS.

No. 11. Trench   Copy of list of Trench Stores handed, and taken over
        Stores.   will be submitted to Orderly Room. So soon as completed.
                          "C" & "D" Companies, 11th K.O.R.L. Rgt, will hand over the Stores
                          in their own Company frontage separately.

No. 12 Completion   Completion of relief will be wired to Orderly Room,
       of Relief.   and report sent by runner when Companies have
                          taken over in Brigade Support, HULLUCH.

                                                          Robt. Dickie. CAPTAIN.
                                                                  Adjutant.
                                                          14th (S) Bn. A. & S. Hrs.

          No. 1 – 5. O.C. "A", "B", "C", "D" & H.Q. Coys
               6 .. 11th King's Own (Royal Lancs) Regt.
               7 .. 21st Middlesex Regt.
               8 .. 2nd Leinster Regt.
               9 .. War Diary.
              10 .. File.

Plus 5. T.P/s drop to deliberate fire, same target.
15. T.P/s. open intense bombardment, on same target
Raiding party withdraws
25. T.P/s cease fire.
ZERO hour will be 8 p.m. unless cancelled as above.

CODE 11 POKER.

Operations cancelled - DRAW POKER
ZERO - Poker hand
Operations suspended - LONG POKER
Resume Normal Conditions - Hot POKER
Artillery will open fire - Poker hand

Maps &c. 12. Trench map being sent showing approx. to enemy trenches at attacking point. O.C. RAIDERS will rely on air photos and instruct party by keeping from them.

Rob Dickie Captain
                 Argyll & Sutherland Highlanders

Copy No 1. H.Q. 120 Inf Brigade
      2. Left Group Artillery
      3. O.C. 120th M.G. Coy.
      4. 120th T.M. Battery
      5.
      6. O.C. 11 Coy
      7.
      8.
      9.
     10.

Secret

Copy No. 8

Operation Orders No. 37.
By Major E. C. Hele-Whilson,
Comdg 14th (S) Bn. A & S. Hrs.

7th October 1916.

No. 1. Relief. The 14th (S) Bn. A & S. Hrs. will relieve the 13th (S) Bn. East Surrey Regiment, in the Left Front Sub section, 14 BIS, on 8th instant.

No. 2. Advance Party. The R.S.M. and 1 N.C.O. per company, 14th A & S. Hrs. will leave Mazingarbe at 8am, and report at Headquarters, 13th East Surrey Regt. to take over Trench Stores. Return of Trench Stores taken over must be sent to Orderly Room so soon as completed.

No. 3. Lewis Guns. The Lewis Guns of the 14th A & S. Hrs. will relieve the Lewis Guns of the 13th East Surrey Regt. to-day. Arrangements will be completed between Battalion Lewis Gun Officers direct.

No. 4. Huts. Company and Specialist Officers will arrange for inspection of Huts, and render a certificate to Orderly Room that they are in a clean condition.
Lieut. H. Landell will arrange for handing over Huts, and obtaining a certificate that they are in a clean and sanitary condition.

No. 5. Guides. No Guides will be provided by 13th East Surrey Regiment.

No. 6. Keeps. One Officer, and 25 Other Ranks of 11th King's Own (R.L.) Regt will report at Headquarters, 14th A & S. H. at 6pm to-day to take over ~~Trench Stores~~ Keeps. O.C. "C" Coy. will be responsible for handing over these Keeps, and on relief the present Garrison will ~~rejoin~~ their company, and proceed with them to-morrow.

No. 7. Dispositions. Companies will move off by Platoons, at 200 yards interval commencing at 7.30am in the following order. Signallers, Bombing Platoon, "A" Coy, "D" Coy, "C" Coy, and "B" Coy, and will relieve Coys. of the 13th East Surrey Regt as follows:-

"A" Coy. 14th A & S. Hrs. will relieve "D" Coy. 13th East Surrey Regt on Left Front
"D"   "   "   "   "   "   "B" "   "   "   "   " in Centre.
"C"   "   "   "   "   "   "A" "   "   "   "   " on Right Front.
"B"   "   "   "   "   "   "B" "   "   "   "   " in Reserve.

No. 8. Routes:- For the purpose of relief, Routes are allotted as follows:-
14th (S) Bn. A & S. Hrs.   CHALK PIT ALLEY.   IN.
13th (S) Bn. East Surrey Regt.   POSEN ALLEY.   OUT.

No. 9. Completion of Relief. Completion of Relief will be reported at once to Orderly Room by wire.

Robt. Dickie Capt.
Adjutant.
14th (S) Bn. A & S. Highrs.

Copy No. 1-5.   O.C. "A" "B" "C" "D" & H.Q. Coy.
         6.   O.C. 13th (S) Bn. East Surrey Regt.
         7.   O.C. 11th (S) Bn. King's Own (R.L.) Regt.
         8.   War Diary.
         9.   File.

Secret.   War Diary   Copy No. 7

Operation Order No. 26
By Major R.C. Hill-Whitson,
Commanding 14th (S) Bn. A.&S. Hrs.

3rd October 1916

No. 1. Relief. The 14th (S) Bn. A.&S. Hrs. will be relieved in Command in the left front Sub Section 11 Bis. on 4th instant by the 13th East Surrey Regiment.

No. 2. Advance Parties. The R.S.M., and one N.C.O. per company from 13th East Surrey Regiment will report at 14th A.&S. Hrs. Headquarters to take over Trench Stores. The party will leave MAZINGARBE at 7 a.m.

No. 3. Billets. Lieut. W. Landell will report to-night to Headquarters, East Surrey Regiment to arrange the taking over of billets.
One N.C.O. per platoon will report to Lieut. W. Landell at Battalion Orderly Room, MAZINGARBE at 10 a.m. to-morrow, to arrange distribution of billets, and to meet their platoon when coming in.

No. 4. Lewis Guns. The Lewis Guns of 14th A.&S. Hrs. will be relieved to-day by the Lewis Guns of the 13th East Surrey Regiment. All arrangements to be completed between Battalion Lewis Gun Officers direct.

No. 5. Guides. No Guides will be provided by the 14th A.&S. Hrs.

No. 6. Distribution
Companies will be relieved in the following order.
"A" Coy. 14 A.&S. Hrs. will be relieved by "D" Coy. 13th East Surrey Regt. on Left front.
"D"   "   "   "   "   "   "B"   "   "   "   "   Centre.
"B"   "   "   "   "   "   "A"   "   "   "   "   Right front
"C"   "   "   "   "   "   "C"   "   "   "   "   in Reserve

No. 7. Mode. On relief, platoons will move off at not less than 200 yards intervals, and will occupy billets vacated by the 13th East Surrey Regt. in MAZINGARBE.

No. 8. Routes. For the purpose of Relief, routes are allotted as follows:-
13th East Surrey Regiment:- CHALK PIT ALLEY   "IN"
14th A.&S. Highlanders:- POSEN ALLEY –
                         K5 AVENUE – NORTHAMPTON "OUT"
Company commanders & Specialist Officers will take special care to prevent men using unauthorised routes, or exposing themselves.

No. 9. Keeps. 2nd Lieut. R.C. Miller, with 2 N.C.O's & 23 O.R. from "C" Company will report at East Surrey H.Q., MAZINGARBE at 11 a.m. to-morrow, to take over KEEPS.

No. 10. Certificate. Certificate will be obtained from relieving Unit, and sent to Orderly Room that all trenches taken over are in a clean & sanitary condition.

No. 11. Trench Stores. Return of Trench Stores handed over will be sent to Orderly Room as soon as possible.

No. 12. Completion of Relief. Completion of relief will be reported by wire.

No. 13. Arrival in Billets. Company Commanders & Specialist Officers will report when their men have arrived in billets.

                                        Robt. Dickie. Captain.
                                        Adjutant
                                        14th (S) Bn. A.&S. Hrs

Copy. No. 1 – 5. O.C. "A" "B" "C" "D" & "H.Q." Coy
         6. O.C. 13th (S) Bn East Surrey Regt.
         7. War Diary.
         8. File.

14th Bn ARG & SUTH'D HIGH'RS

Army Form C. 2118

WAR DIARY
or
INTELLIGENCE SUMMARY
(Erase heading not required.)

November 1916

Place	Date 1916	Hour	Summary of Events and Information	Remarks and references to Appendices
TERNAS	Nov.1.		Ordinary billet work, gas helmet drill, squad drill etc. Tactical exercise on the use of machine guns near MAISNIL ST. POL attended by C.O, Coy Commanders, L.G.O, and other Officers in the morning. The following Officers joined the battalion: Major J. MOORHOUSE (second in command), and 2/Lts. A. MACMILLAN, D.C. PRESTON, T. RUSHTON, H.W. HAMILTON, and R. ATHEY. 2M/L T.Shearer att'd to Hq 120th Inf'y Bde as acerated Staff Captain.	HARRINGTON
Moved to PETIT-BOURET	Nov.2.		Battalion marched from TERNAS about 9:15 A.M — start delayed owing to rain. Rained continuously all the way — reached PETIT-BOURET via SIBIVILLE and FREVENT. Billets very crowded.	MMT
"	Nov.3.		Dry. Morning occupied in saluting and squad drill. A small party marched into FREVENT in the afternoon. Remainder occupied in team work or playing football.	MMT
Moved to WAVANS and BEAUVOIR-RIVIÈRE	Nov.4.		Battalion marched from PETIT BOURET (8.45 A.M) via the outskirts of FREVENT, BONNIÈRES, VILLERS-L'HÔPITAL, to billets in WAVANS and BEAUVOIR-RIVIÈRE which were reached about 1:0 P.M.	MMT

Army Form C. 2118

WAR DIARY
INTELLIGENCE SUMMARY
(Erase heading not required.)

November 1916

Instructions regarding War Diaries and Intelligence Summaries are contained in F. S. Regs., Part II. and the Staff Manual respectively. Title Pages will be prepared in manuscript.

Place	Date	Hour	Summary of Events and Information	Remarks and references to Appendices
Moved to RIBEAUCOURT	Nov. 5		Battalion marched via MAIZICOURT, PROUVILLE and BEAUMETZ to RIBEAUCOURT. Billets rather poor. Snipers and machine gunners return from H.Q. Coy. to their respective companies. Capt. W.G.T. KEDDIE and 2Lt. W.B. CRAMB returned from hospital.	
"	Nov. 6		Rest in RIBEAUCOURT. Drills, inspections etc. in morning. Companies practised the attack under open warfare conditions in the afternoon. Rained in showers most of the morning.	
"	Nov. 7		Rained practically all day — no field work possible.	
"	Nov. 8		Rained at intervals throughout the day. Attack practised on fields in morning — lecture in afternoon. Night operations — a practice relief under open warfare conditions. The battalion relieved the 11th K.O.R.L. 2Lt. W.S. LAWSON rejoined from hospital.	
"	Nov. 9		Dry. Ordinary drill followed by practice attack. Capt. J.D. MACKIE rejoined from hospital.	

Army Form C. 2118

November 1916

WAR DIARY
or
INTELLIGENCE SUMMARY
(Erase heading not required.)

Instructions regarding War Diaries and Intelligence Summaries are contained in F.S. Regs., Part II. and the Staff Manual respectively. Title Pages will be prepared in manuscript.

Place	Date	Hour	Summary of Events and Information	Remarks and references to Appendices
RIBEAUCOURT	Nov.10		Preparation for a moet attack practised by whole brigade starting from VACQUERIE 9.45 A.M. and operating over fields in the direction of RIBEAUCOURT. Operations ceased before 12 noon. 2dLt. A.A.H. GILLESPIE joined the battalion	
Moved to BONNEVILLE	Nov.11	1.30 P.M.	Battalion marched from RIBEAUCOURT 9.45 A.M. and arrived at BONNEVILLE. Route BARLETTE, BENEUIL, MONTRELET, Billets in the whole good - straw obtainable. Rained slightly later. 2dLt. R.A. LAW joined the battalion. 2dLt. R.G. Mills went to hospital. Division transferred to XIII Corps.	
Moved to DOULLENS	Nov.12		Battalion left BONNEVILLE at 9.45 A.M. and marched via BEAUVAL to DOULLENS. Outskirts of the town reached by 12.10 P.M. Billets good on the whole. Capt. A. POLLOCK rejoined battalion from attachment to 121 Inf. Bde. and took over command of D. Coy. 2dLt. A.A.C. SMITH went to hospital. Advanced parts reconnoitred line near HERUTERNE.	
DOULLENS	Nov.13		Rest in billets at DOULLENS - cleaning up, baths etc.	
Moved to THIEVRES	Nov.14		Bn. left DOULLENS (9.30 A.M.) and proceeded via AUTHIEULE, AMPLIER, and ORVILLE to THIEVRES which was reached about 11.45 A.M. Lt. Col. G. Gunn proceeded today to the fourth army school of instruction, Major S. MOORHOUSE assumed command.	at coy. gym

WAR DIARY or INTELLIGENCE SUMMARY

Army Form C. 2118

(Erase heading not required.)

Instructions regarding War Diaries and Intelligence Summaries are contained in F.S. Regs., Part II. and the Staff Manual respectively. Title Pages will be prepared in manuscript.

November 1916

Place	Date	Hour	Summary of Events and Information	Remarks and references to Appendices
THIEVRES	Nov. 15		Draft of 34 O.R. arrived. Lieut. W.P. LEIGHT 12th Inf. Batt. attached to 2nd Divn - part of the Batt. employed under instructions of HEUREUSE.	(App 7)
	Nov.		Draft of 5 NCOs joined the Battalion. Company Drill and Bayonet fighting. Fort details continued. Capt. to Battn.	
			Transferred to the 2nd Batt. detailed to report and were 2nd Lt. G.E. COLEMAN and 250 O.R. proceeded to REQUETOIRE and were attached to the R.E. on a special fort. 2nd Lt. W.P. LEIGHT	(App 7)
			went to hospital.	
	Nov 17		Various other Battalion Employment work and MARIEUX-VAUCHELLES-FUTEAU.	(App 7)
	Nov 18		Support during raid 3/4 Inf Br. 38 Suff. Unit Battalion Employment.	(App 7)
			Some improvement in Defence of ILLIERS and RUBEMPRE	(App 7)
			Co-op with 124th Bde in attempt to extend line.	
	Nov 20		Attack practice in NORTH. 2nd Lt. W.P. LEIGHT had 10 a.m. & proceeded to a R.B. Gunnery School	(App 7)
	Nov 21		Railway Classes Leaving via HUMBERCISE FM - ARCHES - HALLOY With rest of Divn. During the day actually Regimental canteen opened	

Army Form C. 2118

WAR DIARY
or
INTELLIGENCE SUMMARY

(Erase heading not required.)

Instructions regarding War Diaries and Intelligence Summaries are contained in F.S. Regs., Part II. and the Staff Manual respectively. Title Pages will be prepared in manuscript.

November 1915

Place	Date	Hour	Summary of Events and Information	Remarks and references to Appendices
Moved to huts at AMPLIER	Nov 2		Battalion marched from THIEVRES and arrived at huts in AMPLIER. Capt J.B. MACDONALD rejoined from 40 I.B.D. and assumed command of "B" Coy.	
AMPLIER to MONTRELET	Nov 3		Bn. marched via AUTHEUILE - DOULLENS EPREDEL to MONTRELET. Billets got - tolerable.	
Nov 4 to VAUDRICOURT	Nov 4		Bn. marched via BERNEUIL, DOMART, FORENCLOT, BONNEVILLE, VAUDRICOURT, arrived and remained at 2.0 p.m. Billets here - found reasonable accommodation made late.	
	Nov 5		Pretty receipt of no inspection of doctors; no progress in anything general and little Field work provided for, except munition to be bound. Capts J.C. URQUHART [24/4/16], 2nd Lt A.C. JAMES [24/11/16] to the 2/L A.J.T. BARTILON [8/9/16] joined Bn as reinforcements. Lieut Chamill passed to Hospital.	
	Nov 6		Commencement of a system of training. Specialist M.G's as a rule, and to receive special training, whilst rifle and musketry leave suspended.	

Army Form C. 2118

WAR DIARY
or
INTELLIGENCE SUMMARY
(Erase heading not required.)

Place	Date	Hour	Summary of Events and Information	Remarks and references to Appendices
Vaucourt	28/11/15		Carried out Sectional Training	
"	29/11/15		Do	
"	30/11/15		Do	

Ashworth Major.
Cdg. 14th A/F & Bde. Amm.

WAR DIARY

INTELLIGENCE SUMMARY — DECEMBER 1916

Vol 7

14th A&SH

Place	Date	Hour	Summary of Events and Information	Remarks and references to Appendices
YAUCOURT	1 Dec		Carried out Divisional Training	Wors/Wish
	2 "		"	Wish
	3 "		Divine Service with Divisional Band – Battalion Bathed	Wish
	4 "		Started second week of Divisional Training	Wish
	5 "		Battalion Sports – Brigadier General C.S.W. Willoughby presents best "C" Coy won 4 out of 5 events including the handling of Arms Competition. Capt'n P. Mackie proceeded to "No 2 Sch" of Instruction to take over the duties of 2d in Command to Col. G. Gunn	Wish
	6 "		Divisional Training	Wish
	7 "		" 2/Lt D. Biggart returns to Duty	Wish
	8 "		"	Wish
	9 "		"	Wish
	10 "		Divine Service – A draft of 202 O.R. arrives from Base	Wish
	11 "		Battalion bathed. Rain during evening – 2/Lt R. Kay went to Hopkins Court	Wish
	12 "		Snow and sleet during the day. No feet work parties – Draft paraded for Musketry by Companies – Capt'n J.R. MacDonald went to hospital – Lt C. Clarke proceeds to 4th Army School of Musketry as instructor	Wish

WAR DIARY or INTELLIGENCE SUMMARY

Army Form C. 2118

DECEMBER 1916

Place	Date	Hour	Summary of Events and Information	Remarks and references to Appendices
YACOURT	13 Dec		First day of Move to Camp III. Transport (complete) proceeded to St. SAUVEUR by Road. Draft Parades by Companies proceeded to St. SAUVEUR.	Work
Woot to Camp III	14"		Battalion marched to EAUCOURT via PONT REMY – Insufficient Billets. Transport proceeded from St Sauveur to Vaux sur Somme	Work
	15 "		Battalion entrained at PONT REMY & trained to BUIRE – sur – ANCRE & marches to from there to Camp III via DERNANCOURT. Transport proceeded from Vaux sur Somme to Camp III. Rained heavily during the day making marching very heavy – Draft of 50 men arrived –	
Camp No III	16 "		Large fatigue parties were occupied in cleaning up the Camp –	Work
	17 "		Divine Service – Battalion on Duty – Fatigues were supplies for work on Roads under Bde arrangements	Work
			2/Lts T.F Steele & R.G Miller proceeded to join the R.F.C.	
	18 "		Large fatigue parties occupied on Camp improvement	Work
	19 "		Work as per Battalion Programme – Fatigue parties shovelling away mud – Very Cold – Snow during afternoon & Evening	Work
	20	-	cleared on previous day.	Work
	21	-	Raine – very Cold . took Chiefs indoors. Divisional General inspected Bde Tour als nd visit the Battalion work –	Work

Army Form C. 2118

WAR DIARY
or
INTELLIGENCE SUMMARY
(Erase heading not required.)

DECEMBER

Instructions regarding War Diaries and Intelligence Summaries are contained in F.S. Regs., Part II. and the Staff Manual respectively. Title Pages will be prepared in manuscript.

Place	Date	Hour	Summary of Events and Information	Remarks and references to Appendices
CAMP III	22		"C" Coy Xmas Dinner – Mrs. Macdonald & D. Smith were attached to Hosp. Capt Smith returned to duty	
	23		"D" & "B" Coy Dinners. Concert. Rain & strong wind blast	
	24		Church Parade. Capt Miller relieves duty Coy and Coy. Commander visits the Balm ?ter.	
	25		Christmas Day. C.O. Capt C. Stoance parties proceeds to the trench work.	
Move to Trenches.	26		Bn. left for trenches proceeding from Camp III to MAUREPAS HALTE by Motor Lorries then across country to trenches. Bn. were right Batln. right North Bouchavesnes	MAP REF. BOUCH-AVESNES
North BOUCHAV-ESNES	27		and immediately on our right were the French. The trenches we occupied had just lately been taken over from the French. Owing to our front not the line being slightly in the hollow the trenches were in a very bad state. Parts of the front line were impassable causing C.Os to wipe in such a condition that troops causing gaps which are could not walk much. (In some places waist deep in mud.) both traffic was over the top.	
	28			
	29			
	30		During the whole of stay Rain fell nearly every day which made all special work in the trenches absolutely impossible. Owing to the fact that the front of the line is as follows, the trenches of station was the very bad. Even on the top, the going was very slow and painful	

Army Form C. 2118

WAR DIARY
or
INTELLIGENCE SUMMARY — DECEMBER

(Erase heading not required.)

Instructions regarding War Diaries and Intelligence Summaries are contained in F.S. Regs., Part II. and the Staff Manual respectively. Title Pages will be prepared in manuscript.

Place	Date	Hour	Summary of Events and Information	Remarks and references to Appendices
Trenches NORTH BOUCHAVESNES	26-30		Were being considerably held up by force on sticking in the mud. Dug outs were very scarce and any that were were in bad. There is little to report during this space as there was little work were occupation of the trenches was impossible. Bn was relieved by the 7 Suffolk Regt. and went back to Camp 21 by ANDOYER PLACE (where lin. bus provided & men into hands over.) Bn. H.Q. & on reaching MAUREPAS RAVINE lorries were waiting	Casualties 3 Killed 4 Wounded
	31st		which conveyed the Bn. to the Camp. During this space on the trenches very few men were taken up. Bn. went up about 600 strong but on reaching the line owing to the bad state & lack of accommodation, about 40 per Coy were returned to details at CAMP 20. (under 2/Lt. W. LONDON) — Transport during the 5 days were at EQUESSEN B about 2 miles N.E. of Camp 20 - Many men went sick with trench feet etc. but the performance of the Bn. under the trying circumstances was very creditable. There was shelling intermittently by day & night chiefly on back area	Killed M/qqq St. Bertrann 8/A (D) 4265 L/Cpl Ronome W (R) 9039 Pte 9 Jurker (a) Wounded 1/1938 Cpl Sweeny c (c) 194 a.c.m. Sutherland H (c) 8858 Pte Ronone R (c) 7202 Pte 17802 Trump R (E)

Army Form C. 2118

WAR DIARY
or
INTELLIGENCE SUMMARY — DECEMBER
(Erase heading not required.)

Instructions regarding War Diaries and Intelligence Summaries are contained in F.S. Regs., Part II. and the Staff Manual respectively. Title Pages will be prepared in manuscript.

Place	Date	Hour	Summary of Events and Information	Remarks and references to Appendices
Moyet to Camp 21			which left the front line moderately quiet. There was some sniping at dawn dusk as to when we are in the habit of going on top of their trenches about that time.	

Alwoshilde Major
Commanding 14th Bn Argyll & Sutherland Hrs

1875 Wt. W593/826 1,000,000 4/15 T.R.C. & A. A.D.S.S./Forms/C. 2118.

14 A F S H — (Brown (H))

Army Form C. 2118

14 (S) Bn. A. & S. Hrs. **WAR DIARY**
or
INTELLIGENCE SUMMARY January 1917.
(Erase heading not required.)

Vol 8

Place	Date 1917	Hour	Summary of Events and Information	Remarks and references to Appendices
CAMP 20 on the SUZANNE-MARICOURT road	Jan 1.	—	Battalion was relieved in BOUCHAVESNES Sector (Right Bn. frontage) on night of 31st/1st and proceeded to Camp 20 on SUZANNE-MARICOURT road. Day spent in cleaning up and rest.	(HAM Tyson)
Camp 20	Jan 2.		Cleaning up and rest.	(Appx 1)
do	Jan 3.		Military honours published in London Gazette of Jan 2. 1917 :— Military Cross Capt. J.D. Mackie. Distinguished Conduct Medal No.S/9875 Sgt. G.O. Anderson. has transferred with a direct commission to the 13th Bn. The London Highlanders. 2nd Lt. T. Shearer proceeded to 120 Bde. H.Q. to take up appointment of Asst. Staff Captain. 2nd Lt. HAM Tyson rejoined the battalion from Bde. H.Q.	
Moved to Support trenches RANCOURT	Jan 4.		Battalion relieved 17th Welsh Regt. in the Support Bn. trenches RANCOURT Sector. Relief complete about 1.30 P.M. Accommodation for 600 rifles very limited.	(Appx 1) (Appx 2)
	Jan 5.		About the whole battalion employed on working and carrying parties — dug out construction under R.E.'s.	(Appx 2)

Army Form C. 2118

WAR DIARY
or
INTELLIGENCE SUMMARY January 1917.

(Erase heading not required.)

Instructions regarding War Diaries and Intelligence Summaries are contained in F.S. Regs., Part II. and the Staff Manual respectively. Title Pages will be prepared in manuscript.

Place	Date	Hour	Summary of Events and Information	Remarks and references to Appendices
Support Bn RANCOURT	Jan. 6		Same as Jan. 5. Working parties as usual. The whole battalion is below weather. Day but ground sodden underfoot. Authority given to the following officers to wear the badges of undermentioned rank pending notification in London Gazette :- Major S. MOORHOUSE Lt. Col. while commanding a battalion Capt. J.D. MACKIE Major while acting Second in Command.	
do.	Jan 7		Draft of 14 O.R. joined the battalion.	
Right Bn RANCOURT	Jan. 8		Battalion relieved 11th K.O.R.L. as right battalion RANCOURT section. Weather very cold.	
do.	Jan 9		Artillery activity above normal on both sides. 1 O.R. Died of wounds, S.O.R. wounded.	
do.	Jan 10		Artillery again active. S.O.R. wounded, 1 Shellshock. Major H. BURN-MURDOCH returned from Senior Officers' course at ALDERSHOT and took over command of 120 INF. BDE. details at Camp 20 (close to Camp 24).	
do.	Jan 11		Nowt except for artillery activity.	

1875 Wt. W593/826 1,000,000 4/15 J.B.C. & A. A.D.S.S./Forms/C.2118.

WAR DIARY

or

INTELLIGENCE SUMMARY JANUARY 1917

Army Form C. 2118

(Erase heading not required.)

Place	Date	Hour	Summary of Events and Information	Remarks and references to Appendices
RANCOURT to CAMP 21	Jan. 12		Battalion relieved by 12th SUFFOLKS, 121 Inf. Bde., and marched on foot to MOISLAINS HALTE and thence to CAMP 21 by Light Rail. Last parts arrived about 2.0 P.M. on 13th.	
Camp 21	Jan 13		Rest in Camp 21. Fatigue round camp.	
	Jan 14		Working parties round camp. 2/Lt. A. MACMILLAN (of B Coy) went to hospital	
	Jan 15		do.	
	Jan 16		Capt. J.D. Mackie took over command of D Coy; Major Burn Murdoch second in command. 2/Lt. W. LANDELL went to hospital. Attached in French trenches at SUZANNE	
	Jan 17		Showered (about two inches) during the night of the 16/17 Jan. 2/Lt. A.A.H. GILLESPIE went to hospital	
	Jan 18		Bn. relieved 19th Bn. R.W.F. (119 Inf. Bde.) in Reserve Battalion, BOUCHAVESNES. North section. Battalion H.Q. at ASQUITH FLATS shared with Support Battalion (14 H.L.I.). Three companies in RAVINE below (west) of ASQUITH FLATS; fourth company (D) at A.26.D (ALBERT 40,000). Relief complete about 1.30 P.M. Capt. & A.C. SMITH went to hospital	

WAR DIARY
or
INTELLIGENCE SUMMARY

JANUARY 1917

Army Form C. 2118

(Erase heading not required.)

Place	Date	Hour	Summary of Events and Information	Remarks and references to Appendices
Reserve Bn. BOUCHAVESNES NORTH (Bn. section)	Jan 19		Large parties required to carry out dug-out parties. Battalion now employed in improving existing accommodation which was too small even for the Bn. less one Coy.	
ASQUITH FLATS.	Jan 20		Continuing improvement of dug-outs and improvement of area generally.	
do.	Jan 21		Same as previous day. Major H. BURN-MURDOCH appointed Camp Commandant of ANDOVER PLACE. 2dt W.B.CRAMB is struck off the strength on attachment (on probation) to R.F.C.	
Move to Rt. Bn. BOUCHAVESNES NORTH	Jan 22		Bn. relieved 11th K.O.R.L. in right battalion BOUCHAVESNES NORTH sector. Relief complete about 9.0 P.M. Strength to the two front companies each 70 rifles, support Coy. + Bn. H.Q. = 70 rifles, Reserve Company 190 rifles. Reserve Coy. (D) at ANDOVER PLACE provided all carrying parties etc. Lt.Col. J.MOORHOUSE went to hospital - Major BURN-MURDOCH assumed command.	Change of command.
do.	Jan 23		Quiet. Ground exceedingly heavy owing to about six days continual frost. Trenches dry. Location soil somewhat made digging and wiring very difficult.	
do	Jan 24		Quiet, very cold. Internal relief on night of 24/25 C & D Coys. changing places with A and B.	

WAR DIARY
or
INTELLIGENCE SUMMARY JANUARY 1917

Army Form C. 2118

(Erase heading not required.)

Place	Date	Hour	Summary of Events and Information	Remarks and references to Appendices
Right Bn. BOUCHAVESNES North Section	Jan. 25		Situation very quiet. Freezing hard.	
Move down the line to Camp 124	Jan. 26		Battalion relieved early in the night by the 1st Bn. WORCESTERSHIRE Regt. 24 Inf. Bde. Relief complete about 9.0 P.M. Around still covered with the snow that fell on the night of the 16/17th and it froze hard every night of our eight day tour. Marched down by company on to as MAUREPAS HALTE and thence proceeded by tram a ten as Camp 124 on the BRAY-CORBIE road. Arrived at Camp 124 about 12.30 A.M. on the morning of the 27th. Accommodation bad. Cold intense. No Casualties during their tour of the trenches.	
Moved from Camp 124 to CORBIE	Jan 27		Proceeded by tram from Camp 124 (11:30 A.M) to CORBIE which was reached about 1.0 P.M. Accommodation limited and only moderately good. On arrival at CORBIE the battalion received the following draft which had joined details on Jan. 22nd 2d/Lts. S.B.N. COUPAR: D. MacLULLOCH: R.S. FORBES: J. MORISON: W.F. WALKER: and 108 O.R	

Army Form C. 2118

WAR DIARY
or
INTELLIGENCE SUMMARY
(Erase heading not required.)

JANUARY 1914.

Place	Date	Hour	Summary of Events and Information	Remarks and references to Appendices
CORBIE	Jan 28		Church Parade in morning. Hotel de Ville. 2Lt. G. McCROW took over command of D Coy from 27th inst. Capt. J.D. MACKIE acting 2nd in command. 2Lt. W. KNOX joined the battalion. C.S.M (a/R.S.M) E.E. BRETT appointed to a permanent commission in the Border Regt. as 2Lt. and posted to the 7th Bn.	
"	Jan 29		Commencement of training under a new group system. Inspection of draft.	
do.	Jan 30		Company training.	
do	Jan 31		Battalion bathed. 2Lt. A. MACMILLAN (B Coy) returned from hospital	

(signature)

APPENDIX.

Casualties for Jan. 1917.

3.1.17	10391	Pte. T. Martin	S.I.W. (cleaning rifle)
9.1.17	No. 9081	L/c. E. Allan	Wounded.
	6667 "	W. McIntosh	Died of wounds
	40738 "	J. Quinn	Wounded
	16554 "	McKillop	Wounded
	11432 "	J. Peel	Wounded
	40723 "	J. Jardine	Wounded

10/1/17	16491	Cpl. Halliday	Wounded
	12460	Pte. P. A. Edwards	"
	12398 "	J. Petrie	"
	11396 "	D. Edgar	"
	9088 "	J. Bradley	"
	8854 Sgt.	A. H. Robertson	"

H.H.M. Tyson 2Lt.
14 A.& S.H.

31.1.17.

WAR DIARY or **INTELLIGENCE SUMMARY**

Army Form C. 2118

February 1917

Place	Date	Hour	Summary of Events and Information	Remarks and references to Appendices
CORBIE	Feb 1st		Military Medal presented by acting Brigadier to 12004 Pte. J. McIvor. (vide Appendix A.) Col. freak - Front System.	Appen S/A(1)
	2nd		Short route march - Col.	
	3rd		Cold - nerve took under group System.	
	4th		Divine Service at Hotel de Ville - Band, Service, amusement arrangements reformed. (vide Bn. Ors. 2 of 4/2/17).	
	5th		Major A.D. Carmichael (Black Watch) took over Command of the Bn. from Major H. Burn Murdoch, MC, Capt J.D. Mackie MC remained with Bn. HQ. as 2nd in Command. 2nd Lt M.G.S. Kerr took on duties of Transport Officer from 2nd Lt J.Y. Grier admitted to hospital.	
	6th		2nd Lt K.S. Runciman joined the Bn. 16 OR joined the Bn. Cold. Front System	
	7th		Capt A Pollock, 2nd Lt J.S. Robertson admitted to hospital.	
	8th		Battalion bathes at Divisional Baths - Capt C.H. Niles, 2nd Lt A. Mac-Millan (B.Co.) admitted to hospital	
	9th		Lecture by Div. Gas Officer.	

Army Form C. 2118

WAR DIARY
or
INTELLIGENCE SUMMARY

(Erase heading not required.)

February 1917

Instructions regarding War Diaries and Intelligence Summaries are contained in F.S. Regs., Part II. and the Staff Manual respectively. Title Pages will be prepared in manuscript.

Place	Date	Hour	Summary of Events and Information	Remarks and references to Appendices
CORBIE	Feb 10		Preparations for move to BRAY. Weather fair	Wed
	11		LEFT CORBIE 3.15 p.m. and marched to BRAY (arrived 7 p.m.) Billets on the whole good.	Wed
BRAY	12th		General improvement of billets. "C" Coy detached for duty to LE PLATEAU. Fatigues about BRAY.	Wed
	13th		Capt J.R. Macdonald to strength (transferred to Gen. List) Lt. J.J. Menzies invalided to U.K. Struck off strength 14.11.16 back fatigues round BRAY. Weather fair.	Wed
	14th		Battalion Concert. Lt. R.A.B. MacDonald admitted to Hopkins	Wed
	15th		"C" Coy temporarily drawn from their billets owing to a fire in LE	
	16th		PLATEAU Amm. Dump. 2 O.R. wounds (See Append. No. A.S. Battalion to takes to BRAY. Capt. G.A.C. Smith returned from hospital and took over "A" Coy.	APPENDIX II
	17th		Capt C.J. Miller returned from Hospital. Round slightly	Wed
	18th		Divine Service. Heavy unloading fatigues at BRAY TOUBIERE	Wed
	19th		Dump. over to LE PLATEAU being generally closed. Wet. Wed Thaw & wet. Heavy fatigues	Wed

Army Form C. 2118

WAR DIARY
or
INTELLIGENCE SUMMARY
(Erase heading not required.)

February 1917

Instructions regarding War Diaries and Intelligence Summaries are contained in F. S. Regs., Part II. and the Staff Manual respectively. Title Pages will be prepared in manuscript.

Place	Date	Hour	Summary of Events and Information	Remarks and references to Appendices
BRAY	Feb 20		Heavy snow, slightly wet. Heavy fatigues. Fatigues loading at LE PLATEAU - fair, wet.	Work
	21st		do. do. - fair, rain -	Work
	22nd		do. -	Work
	23rd		Battalion bathed at BRAY. Fatigue of 200 at LE PLATEAU, work. Move to Camp III by Coy. Move complete 5.40 p.m. Transport remained at BRAY. Camp duty stale.	
Camp III	25		Divine Service. Inoculation "A" Coy. Fatigues round camp.	Rest
	26th		Inoculation "B" Coy. Weekly instruction for Officers & NCOs. Fair. Battalion fatigue round camp.	Rest
	27th		Inoculation "C" Coy. Local fatigues.	Rest
	28th		Draft of 54 ORs arrived. Inoculation "D" Coy. Capt Urquhart reported from base. Took over "A" Coy - weather fair.	Work

A. Carmichael Major
Cmdg 14 (S) Bn. 14 A.& S. Hrs.

1st March 1917

I.
Appendix A.

D.R.O. No 925 is published —

The Corps Commander has awarded the military medal to :-
  No 12006 Pte John McIvor.
14 (S/Bn. A. & S. Highlanders — for the following act of gallantry :-

"During the period Decr. 26th Dec. 31st/16 Pte McIvor showed conspicuous bravery and devotion to duty as stretcher bearer, but particulars on the morning of 29th Decr. while conducting a sick man to the R.A.P. On account of the state of the trenches he was obliged to take him over the top. The man eventually collapsed and had to be carried by Pte McIvor on his back. It was now daylight, and the enemy seeing them opened M.G. fire on them. Pte McIvor persisted in his task and succeeded in bringing the man to the R.A.P. Although Pte McIvor was advised to remain there by the M.O. he returned to the trenches and there continued his work thus setting a splendid example to all under trying conditions."

[signature]

II.
2. Or. Casualties at LE PLATEAU.
    16th FEB 1917.
    1/05/. 9397 Pte. Y Oswald
     12057 "   M. Cameron.

[signature]

Secret   Copy No. 7.
                No 2.

Move Orders.
By Major A. D. Carmichael
Comdg 14th (S) Bn Arg & Suth Hdrs.   9th February 1917.

No 1. The 40th Division will relieve the 8th Division in the Rancourt Sector on 11/12th February and will become the left Division of the XV Corps.

No 2. During the 10th and 11th the 120th Infantry Brigade will relieve the 3 Battalions of the 121st Infantry Brigade working at Bray &c.

No 3. The 14th A.S.H. will leave Corbie and be at starting point ¼ mile North of R in Corbie at 3.15 pm on 11th February. Destination Bray, to relieve 13th Yorks Regt.

<u>Detached Company</u> O.C. "C" Company will proceed to Le Plateau on the morning of 12th February and report there in accordance with separate instructions already issued to him.

<u>Billeting Party.</u> Billeting party under 2nd Lieut R. S. Forbes will leave Orderly Room at 9.30 am on 10th inst and report in accordance with separate orders already issued to him.

No 4. Distance between Companies and Transport already laid down will be maintained, marching order will ~~be worn~~ be worn.

<u>Blankets.</u> Blankets rolled tightly in bundles of 10 and properly labelled will be stacked by Coys at Quartermaster's Stores on 11th inst as follows:—

   H.Q. Company 12 noon.
   "A" do 12-10 pm.
   "B" do 12-20 pm.
   "C" do 12-30 pm.
   "D" do 12-40 pm.

O.C. Coys are responsible that blankets are sent under properly organised parties at the times specified.

O.C. Coys will personally inspect billets before their Coys move off and render a certificate to Orderly Room by 2 pm that they have been left in a clean and sanitary condition.

O.C. Coy on duty on 11th inst will detail rear party of 1 Officer and 10 men to ensure that billeting area is left clean and tidy, this Officer will report to Town Major when the Battalion has moved off and will render a certificate to him to be forwarded to Brigade, that billets have been left in clean and good order.

           (Sgd) Robt Dick, Capt
           Adj. 14th (S) Bn Arg & Suth Hdrs.

Secret

Move Orders No 3.
By Major A.L. Carmichael
Comdg 14th (S) Bn Argyll & Suth'd Highrs.

Copy No 12

23rd February, 1917

No 1.   The 14th Argyll & Sutherland Highlanders will be relieved on 24th February 1917 by 18th Welsh Regt, and on completion of relief will march to Camp III.

No 2.   Billeting parties of 4 other ranks per company under 2nd Lieut., A. Macmillan "D" Company will report to Camp Commandant at 8-30 am on 24th inst.

No 3. (a)   Officers Valises will be stacked in covered entrance to Orderly Room at 10 am.   The Q.M. will detail the special loading party for duty at that time.

(b).   Mess Boxes will be packed ready for loading at the various messes at 10 am.

(c).   Blankets properly rolled in bundles of 10 and labelled will be stacked by Companies at Battalion H.Q as follows:-
   H.Q. 8-45 am : "A" Coy 8-55 am : "B" Coy 9-5 am :
   "D" Coy 9-15 am :

No 4.   All details of work will be handed over and care must be taken that no work is interrupted.

No 5.   O.C. Companies will personally inspect billets &c, before their companies move off and will obtain a certificate from the relieving unit that the billets have been taken over in a clean and sanitary condition.   2nd Lieut. K.S. Forbes will be in charge of rear party of 8 other ranks from the Company on duty and he will render the usual certificate to Orderly Room as soon as possible.

No 6.   O.C. Companies will report to Orderly Room on arrival in Camp III.

Copy No 1 - "A" Company
      2 - "B"
      3 - "C"
      4 - "D"
      5 - H.Q.
      6 - Commanding Officer
      7 - Quartermaster
      8 - Transport Officer
      9 - L.G. Officer
     10 - Medical Officer
     11 - War Diary
     12 - File.

Rob Dickie Capt,
Adj. 14th (S) Bn Argyll & Suth'd Hdrs.

WAR DIARY of INTELLIGENCE SUMMARY

Army Form C. 2118

1/4th A & S H
March 1917. Vol 10
120/40

Place	Date 1917	Hour	Summary of Events and Information	Remarks and references to Appendices
Camp III on BRAY-MEAULTE road	March 1	—	Improvement of camp. Instruction for regimental stretcher demonstration at Camp 20 to selected N.C.O's.	HPMcTyer
do	2		Battalion tested with the French anti-frostbite balm	(HPM)
"	3		Capt. J.D. MACKIE, M.C. resumed command of D Coy. 2dLt. T. SHEARER returned from 120th Bde. H.Q. 2dLt. Alistair Mac Millan (D Coy) proceeded to 120th Bde. H.Q. for instruction in A. & Q. duties (commanding officers' course). Draft of 11 O.R. joined the battalion. Snow fell during night 4/5th	HPMT
"	4			HPMT
"	5		Advanced party reconnoitred the new battalion sector. Very cold.	HPMT
"	6		Preparations for the move.	HPMT
March to Camp 19	7		Battalion marched to camp 19 about two kilos. E. of SUZANNE which was evacuated to us by the 17th Welsh Regt at 3.0 P.M. Very cold.	HPMT
March to ROAD WOOD	8		Battalion left Camp 19 and relieved 4th KINGS (Liverpool Regt) of the 98th Bde, 33rd Divn. in SUPPORT BATTALION, BETHUNE ROAD sector, at ROAD WOOD, one mile S.W. of BOUCHAVESNES. Three companies and Bn. Hd. Qrs. Relief complete about 7.0 P.M. One company in close support 400 yards rear the front line (see S. of R/wood)	HPMT 10

Army Form C. 2118

WAR DIARY
or
INTELLIGENCE SUMMARY
(Erase heading not required.)

March 1917

Instructions regarding War Diaries and Intelligence Summaries are contained in F.S. Regs., Part II. and the Staff Manual respectively. Title Pages will be prepared in manuscript.

Place	Date March	Hour	Summary of Events and Information	Remarks and references to Appendices
ROAD WOOD	9		Carrying parties and clearing of rubbish while area covered with several weeks' accumulation of refuse. Several tons of rubbish burned or buried. Weather frosty.	(HMT)
Moved to left battalion frontage	10		Relieved 13th E. Surrey Regt. in left sub-sector BETHUNE ROAD section. Reserve Coy. in dug outs on BETHUNE ROAD, one platoon in strong point 100 yds. due E. of QUARRY (on BETHUNE ROAD. S. of BOUCHAVESNES). Three companies in front line Bn. H.Q. at MARJORIE (at W. end of QUARRY). Thawing. deft and centre Coy. isolated by day - large gaps (about 200 yds) between companies. 1 O.R. wounded	(HMT)
do.	11		Moderately heavy shelling, retaliation three times by our artillery. Weather thawing. Trenches mostly 6 inches deep in mud. Patrol out from each company, wiring, and improvement of Trenches	(HMT)
do.	12		Rained during night of 11/12 making communication trenches almost impassable (knee deep). Hostile artillery active over whole area. 1 O.R. killed, 3 O.R. wounded. 2/Lt D.MacLULLICH went to hospital	(HMT)
Moved to HOWITZER WOOD	13		Hostile shelling continued intermittently on whole area. Were relieved by 13 E. Surrey Regt. on night of 13/14. Heavy shelling during relief. Battalion marched down to dug outs at HOWITZER WOOD about midway between	(HMT)

1875 Wt. W593/826 1,000,000 4/15 J.B.C. & A. A.D.S.S./Forms/C. 2118.

Army Form C. 2118

WAR DIARY
or
INTELLIGENCE SUMMARY
(Erase heading not required.)

March 1917

Place	Date 1917	Hour	Summary of Events and Information	Remarks and references to Appendices
March 16 HOWITZER WOOD	13th		HEM. and CIERY. Last platoon reached destination about 7.0 A.M. on the 14th. 3.0.R. killed by stray shell which landed on Bn. H.Q. and also killed the Earl Surrey R.S.M. 10.R. wounded	(MMT)
"	14		Cleaning up equipment. Foot baths	(MMT)
	15		do — Part of hostile front line opposite VIIIth Divn. on our left evacuated.	(MMT)
Moved up again to left subsector	16		Relieved 13th E. Surreys in left sub sector as before. Relief complete 12.10 A.M. on 17th. Relief conducted entirely on the top. Patrols which went out at intervals during night from all companies reported German still in occupation of their front line. Heavy shelling on left coy front during night 16/17.	(MMT)
	17		Morning and afternoon quiet. At 4.0 P.M. the 1st R.I.R. (8th Divn) on our left reported that the German front line opposite them was not occupied. Telephone communication had broken down with our left coy, we were informed by a runner could we satisfy that on the top our left coy was informed	(MMT)

1875 Wt. W593/826 1,000,000 4/15 T.R.C. & A. A.D.S.S./Forms/C. 2118.

Army Form C. 2118

WAR DIARY
or
INTELLIGENCE SUMMARY

(Erase heading not required.)

Instructions regarding War Diaries and Intelligence Summaries are contained in F. S. Regs., Part II. and the Staff Manual respectively. Title Pages will be prepared in manuscript.

Place	Date	Hour	Summary of Events and Information	Remarks and references to Appendices
Most Co [German] reserve trench			and our Coys. advanced in echelon from the left and occupied hostile front line without opposition. Further advance was made during the night and at dawn three coys. (A.B.D) consolidated the German reserve line (BROUSSE TRENCH - MERMAN TRENCH) and [pushed] patrols out in front aorn the TORTILLE RIVER. Progress during the night was very slow owing to the broken ground, numerous barbed wire fences, and the unusual darkness which made it difficult to keep in touch with flanking units. (MMT) Battalion consolidated above mentioned trench line. Patrols reported no sign of the enemy except on occasional attempt at sniping from long range. 2Lt. T. Shaw appointed O.C. 120th Pde. Sub-ammo stores. 2Lt. Morison accidentally wounded, 10 O.R. wounded. (MMT)	
Advanced	19		Battalion H.Q. moved from MARJORIE 4.0 P.M to DETVA SUPPORT TRENCH (original German close support trench). A. and D. coys moved from BROUSSE TR. to an outpost position beyond the NURLU PERONNE road about 300x E. of AZECOURT-LE-HAUT. Major H. BURN-MURDOCH	

1875 Wt. W593/826 1,000,000 1/15 T.R.C.&A. A.D.S.S./Forms/C. 2118.

WAR DIARY
or
INTELLIGENCE SUMMARY
(Erase heading not required.)

Army Form C. 2118

Instructions regarding War Diaries and Intelligence Summaries are contained in F. S. Regs., Part II. and the Staff Manual respectively. Title Pages will be prepared in manuscript.

Place	Date	Hour	Summary of Events and Information	Remarks and references to Appendices
	20		appointed outpost commander. Rained and snowed most of the night 19/20th.	1.O.R. wounded (HMMT)
Advanced outpost line at DRIENCOURT TEMPLEUX-LA-FOSSE			B and C Coys. moved up from BROUSSE TRENCH line through A and D Coys. and occupied an outpost line from DRIENCOURT to TEMPLEUX-LA-FOSSE. A and D Coys. consolidated their line on the NURLU-PERONNE road making it the line of resistance. Bn. H.Q. was established in the QUARRY at W. end of AZINCOURT-LE-HAUT.	(HMMT)
Moved down to dugouts E. of HAUT-ALLAINES.	21		Battalion relieved by 14 H.L.I. and marched down to dug outs accommodation about 500x. S.E. of HAUT-ALLAINES CHURCH. C Coy. shelled when being relieved at TEMPLEUX-LA-FOSSE.	1.O.R Killed 2.O.R. wounded (HMMT)
	22		Large bathing on road repair. Major A.D. CARMICHAEL granted authority to assume temporary rank of Lt. Colonel while commanding a battalion.	(HMMT)

1875 Wt. W593/826 1,000,000 4/15 T.B.C. & A. A.D.S.S./Forms/C. 2118.

WAR DIARY or INTELLIGENCE SUMMARY

Army Form C. 2118

(Erase heading not required.)

Place	Date	Hour	Summary of Events and Information	Remarks and references to Appendices
	23		Every available man on road repair	(HAMZ)
	24		do.	(HAMZ)
Mond G LINGER CAMP near CURLU	25		Battalion marched from HAVT-ALLAINES to LINGER CAMP 200 x N.Q CURLU Church. Accomodation in NISSEN huts very wanted	(HAMZ)
	26		Every available officer and men working on construction of new full gauge railway track to PERONNE. Commenced work at MAUREPAS RAVINE 8.0 A.M. Hours 8.0 - 12. Noon. ½ hour for meal. 12.30 to 4.20 P.M. Capt. G.A.C. SMITH (5.3.17 to 26.3.17) and 2dt. A. MACMILLAN (17.2.17 to 27.3.17) returned from attachment to 120th INF. BDE. H.Q. 2dt. T. SHEARER returned from 120th INF. BDE. H.Q.	
	27		Every available officer and men at work on railway. Weather very wet. Major M.E. ROUSE joined the battalion and took over the duties of 2d in command.	(HAMZ)
	28		ditto.	(HAMZ)

Army Form C. 2118

WAR DIARY
or
INTELLIGENCE SUMMARY
(Erase heading not required.)

Instructions regarding War Diaries and Intelligence Summaries are contained in F.S. Regs., Part II. and the Staff Manual respectively. Title Pages will be prepared in manuscript.

March 1917

Place	Date	Hour	Summary of Events and Information	Remarks and references to Appendices
	29		Same as above. Rained.	
	30		Same as above. Major H. BURN-MURDOCH went to hospital. Rained most of the day.	
	31		Same as above. G.O.C. 120th Inf. Bde. inspected the battalion huts. Weather fine until 4.0 p.m. Heavy rain later.	JHMT

Onderwished Lt. Col.
Comdy M. s A.S. pm.

WAR DIARY
INTELLIGENCE SUMMARY

Army Form C. 2118

APPENDIX A.

(Erase heading not required.)

Place	Date	Hour	No.	Rank	Summary of Events and Information	Remarks and references to Appendices
					Casualties during March 1917.	
	10.3.17		12580	Cpl.	HENDERSON. A. — Wounded. C.	
	12		7274	Sgt.	JOHNSTONE. J. — Wounded. B.	
	"		9903	Pte.	JAMIESON. N.E. — Wounded. C. — Died of wounds.	
	"		9534	Pte.	JACKSON. J. — Killed C.	
	"		40557	Pte.	CLIXBY. F. — Wounded A. — Died of wounds	
	12		~~~~	Pte.	~~~~~~~~~~	
	13		13238	Pte.	McTAGGART. D. — Wounded C	
	14		12585	A/Cpl.	McKINNON. N. — Killed C	
	"		12664	Pte.	BURGESS. R.H. — Killed C	
	"		12744	Pte.	WITHERINGTON. J. — Killed C	
	17		~~~~	2 LIEUT.	J. MORISON. ~~~~~~~~~~~	
	18		7121	Pte.	— Wounded - accidentally	
					MILLER. H. — Wounded - C	
	19		6078	Pte.	HASTINGS. J.R. — Wounded C	
	21		9441	A/Cpl.	BRUCE. D. — Killed C	
	"		12109	Pte.	TODD. J. — Wounded C	
	"		12854	Pte.	THOMSON. A. — Wounded C	

Army Form C. 2118

WAR DIARY
or
INTELLIGENCE SUMMARY

APPENDIX B

(Erase heading not required.)

Place	Date	Hour	Summary of Events and Information	Remarks and references to Appendices
			The following is a copy of a letter from the 231st FIELD Coy. R.E. referring to the work done by the working parties of this Battalion on the 22, 23, and 24 inst. "14th Argyll and Sutherland Highlanders. Officers of the 231st Field Company wish to express their appreciation of the work done by the officers and men of the above battalion during the period they formed working parties to repairing roads and filling craters under their supervision. The work was well and rapidly carried out after a period of considerable fatigue during our advance. Signed J. H. Johnson Major R.E. O/C 231 Fld.Coy. Royal Engineers 29 March 1917.	

Index..................

SUBJECT.

No.	Contents.	Date.
	War Diary 1st A. & S. Abn. April 1917.	

14th Argyll & Sutherland Army Form C. 2118
April 1917   Vol X

WAR DIARY
or
INTELLIGENCE SUMMARY
(Erase heading not required.)

Instructions regarding War Diaries and Intelligence Summaries are contained in F.S. Regs., Part II. and the Staff Manual respectively. Title Pages will be prepared in manuscript.

Place	Date	Hour	Summary of Events and Information	Remarks and references to Appendices
Linspburg	1st		Battalion working on Railway. 2/Lt Nachulich returned to the Bn. from Hospital R.S.A.	
"	2nd		Battalion work on Railway. Bn received a gift of tobacco from Baztic Bng Dundee. R.S.A.	
"	3rd		Battalion working on Railway.	
"	4th		Battalion working on Railway. Lt Blake went to Hospital R.S.A.	
"	5th		Battalion working on Railway. Lt Kilgour took over duties of Intelligence Officer from 2/Lt Tyson. 2/Lt R.M.Nish took over duties of Intelligence Officer from 2/Lt Tyson. 2/Lt Tyson returned to duty with 'B' Coy. R.S.A.	
"	6th		Battalion working on Railway. Left WO & Stodhe and Mr 935 SM A.C. Murdoch. Ry. MRO para 761 of 3.4.17. (see Appendix B). R.S.A. Appendix B.	
"	7th		Battalion working on Railway. Sgts Burn-Murdoch and 2/Lt Nicholson returned to the Bn. from Hospital R.S.A.	
"	8th		Battalion working on Railway. R.S.A.	
"	9th		Battalion working on Railway. 2/Lt W.Knox and Walker with 4 O.R. rejoined the Battalion from 40th Div. School R.S.A.	
"	10th		Battalion working on Railway. R.S.A.	

WAR DIARY
or
INTELLIGENCE SUMMARY

(Erase heading not required.)

Army Form C. 2118

Instructions regarding War Diaries and Intelligence Summaries are contained in F.S. Regs., Part II. and the Staff Manual respectively. Title Pages will be prepared in manuscript.

April 1917.

Place	Date	Hour	Summary of Events and Information	Remarks and references to Appendices
Lupu camp	11th		Battalion working on railway. Capt J.D. Mackie M.C. returned from leave and took over command and payment of "D" Coy. from Lt G.W. Kofour. Capt Pollok rejoined the Batt from hospital. R.A.S.I.	
"	12th		Batt working on railway. 28 O.R. rejoined the Batt from hospital and the Base Depot. R.A.S.I.	Battalion 12 Off. 478 O.R. 2/Lt/477.
"	13th		Battalion working on railway. Capt Pollok proceeded to take over the duties of Town Major at EQUANCOURT. R.A.S.I.	
"	14th		Battalion working on railway. A Batt concert was held in Lupin Camp. R.A.S.I. Preparations for the concert.	
"	15th		Battalion working on railway. Work finished by 1pm. The afternoon & Col Carmichael were made the following day. 2/Lt D. Weir went to hospital. R.A.S.I. proceeded to Senior Officers course at Thiencourt. 2/Lt D. Weir went to hospital. R.A.S.I.	
"	16th		2/Lt L. Truman took over duties as Battalion Lewis Gun Officer. The Battalion moved off from Lupin Camp at 10 am and marched to ETRICOURT to repair Hut Division. The Battalion was in Brigade Reserve. R.A.S.I.	120th Inf. Bde. O N.O.R.
ETRICOURT	17th		The Bn arrived in Billets about 4.30pm R.A.S.I. Battalion worked on the Billets - improving and extending the accommodation. Capt Smith rejoined the Batt from Brigade Bombing School. 2/Lt R.A.M. Lyon went to 120th Bde H.Q. to take over duties at Intelligence Officer. R.A.S.I.	
"	18th		Arrived in Billets. The Battalion moved into Brigade Support at EQUANCOURT supplied a working party to 229th R.E. at 7.30pm. 7 Officers and 200 O.R. supplied to work on Line of Resistance. R.A.S.I.	
EQUANCOURT	19th		Improvement & extension of Billets at EQUANCOURT. Officers and 200 O.R. supplied to 229th R.E. to work on Bn. of Resistance. Rural Cadre in case of attack. R.A.S.I.	

1875 Wt. W593/826 1,000,000 4/15 I.R.C. & A. A.F. S./Forms/C. 2118.

Army Form C. 2118

WAR DIARY
or
INTELLIGENCE SUMMARY
(Erase heading not required.)

April 1917.

Place	Date	Hour	Summary of Events and Information	Remarks and references to Appendices
EQUANCOURT.	20th.		Battalion moved to huts in DESSART WOOD. Bn. in Reserve to operations indicated in 130th. Inf. Bde. Order No 94. RMQ. "B" Coubany took over Bluing points in Q27a & Q27c	
DESSART WOOD	21st.		Battalion improved camp & dump area R.M.Q.	
	22nd.		The battalion relieved the 11th Bn (K.O) Royal Lancaster Regt. in the left out-post. "B" Coubany marched off by platoon from DESSART WOOD about 830pm. B'boubany took over the position in the front line while D'boubany were in close support. 21 B/gnt took out a patrol which remained in the German trench and found it plainly held and well wired. In this operation 2/B'boubany was out with a covering party. 2/Lieuenant D'by pushed forward & his platoon and established & found post on the right 2/Lt Laws with his platoon did the same on the left of 2/Lt. Ruxelan and so linked up with "B" boy on the left. A & C boys into B/Kd were in the N.W. Corner of GOUZEACOURT WOOD.	
	23rd.		Bn. holding the line. Operation orders regarding the attack on the following day were received. The plans of S.A.A. Bombs Picks and shovels moving up from the Brigade Dumps – These were issued to Coubanies were drawn from the early part of the night. The bontany Commanders got their orders and spent the night making preparations. The two Coubanies at GOUZEACOURT WOOD moved up (2pm) the lifts then laid a barrage by the Germans delayed this. and all Coubanies were in position by 3.55 am. The Barrage started at 4.15am and the Bn attacked close under the Barrage on the order D boy – B boy – A boy. C boy.	

Army Form C. 2118.

WAR DIARY
or
INTELLIGENCE SUMMARY.
(Erase heading not required.)

Instructions regarding War Diaries and Intelligence Summaries are contained in F. S. Regs., Part II. and the Staff Manual respectively. Title pages will be prepared in manuscript.

Place	Date	Hour	Summary of Events and Information	Remarks and references to Appendices
S.W. and S. of BEAVCAMP	1917 April 24th	4.15 a.m.	Artillery barrage began and continued as in programme, until 6.15 a.m. in progressive stages. The first objective was enemy front trench from about Q.18.b.6.3. to Q.17.b.8.8. (Map references all to 57 C N.E. 1/20,000.) Trench was protected by strong wire which had not been cut at all by artillery. D Coy under Capt. J.D. Mackie M.C. tacked through wire with cutters, whilst leading two companies had been fully equipped. This was done under heavy fire both from trench immediately in front and from heavy enfilade fire on left. The enemy also put up a prompt barrage within a few minutes of our own. It is evident that they were experienced and on the alert. A number of casualties were sustained at this point. When the wire had been thus passed the enemy trench was rushed and a number of prisoners taken, estimated at 30, after a short but sharp bombing fight.	
		4.45 a.m.	Second objective BEAVCAMP village. After taking the first objective, D Coy went straight on to village of BEAVCAMP, closely followed by B Coy under Capt. C.W.H. MILLER. Comparatively slight opposition was met with in the village itself, the heavy enemy fire being encountered on the far side (N) of the village, and especially from the left of the whole area attacked, on both sides of the village, from throughout an area in Q.11.d. and Q.11.b. where the enemy had numerous detached trenches, a shell holes, from which he kept up m.g. and rifle fire... the battalion	

Army Form C. 2118.

WAR DIARY
or
INTELLIGENCE SUMMARY.
(Erase heading not required.)

Place	Date	Hour	Summary of Events and Information	Remarks and references to Appendices
BEAUCAMP	April 24th 1917	5.15 a.m.	Final objective: high ground N. side of BEAUCAMP. On emerging on the N. side of BEAUCAMP, the battalion at once came under heavy m.g. and rifle fire. Of D. Coy. 2nd Lt. K. S. RUNCIMAN went forward to assist in establishing a L.G. post. He was wounded on returning to his Platoon but carried on steadying and cheering his men. He afterwards succumbed to his wounds. Captain J. D. MACKIE, M.C., 2nd Lt. W. F. WALKER and 2nd Lt. R. H. LAW were all hit during this stage; so also were many senior N.C.O.s and men. Corp. JOHNSTON took command of this coy. at the time. D. Coy. B. Coy. the Commander, Capt. C.W.H. MILLER was knocked out wounded. 2nd Lieut. D BIGGART was wounded but carried on in command until he had been thrice hit and had to withdraw owing to faintness. 2nd Lieut. D W HUMPHREYS was wounded in the stomach on far side of village and ultimately died there. On emerging from village D Coy took up its position and B Coy the left. We knocked out an enemy M.G. on the right.	
		9.45 a.m.	Action of supporting companies (A & C). While the leading coys. took BEAUCAMP and endeavoured to establish themselves on the final objectives, A & C. coys. followed close behind as supports Reserve coys. respectively each having full complement of porters and shovels for purposes	

Army Form C. 2118.

WAR DIARY
or
INTELLIGENCE SUMMARY.
(Erase heading not required.)

Instructions regarding War Diaries and Intelligence Summaries are contained in F.S. Regs., Part II. and the Staff Manual respectively. Title pages will be prepared in manuscript.

Place	Date 1917	Hour	Summary of Events and Information	Remarks and references to Appendices
BEAUCAMP	April 24	5.30 a.m.	consolidating the positions gained. They came under deadly enfilade fire from their left from the area previously referred to. A and C Coys swung to the left to deal with this flank. They had to pass through a barrage of the same range as Until the leading companies had penetrated. Lieut W. LAWSON and 2nd Lt R.S. FORBES were both killed while gallantly leading their men on here. Capt A. POLLOCK was dangerously wounded. At this stage Pte W PITCHER did excellent work as a runner. 2/LT TATHEY was wounded at this stage. Capt H URQUHART A Coy under Capt J URQUHART was on the right of this flank movement. Lieut G.H.F. BARTHOLOMEW, was killed by a sniper while in the W. edge of the village. for the remainder of this operation who was beside him took command of the company and a number of snipers	
		6.30 a.m.	C Coy under Capt W.G.T. KEDDIE, having accounted for a m-g and a number of snipers on the left of the Left flank, formed up in sunken road about Q.18.d.1.9 leaving a L-G out in front to cover the taking up of this position. About the same time A Coy withdrew from the W. of BEAUCAMP to a position immediately S of the village. Touch was established with C Coy and a position dug in, by latter. Shell Hole approximately Q.18.b.2.9 to Q.18.d.5.9. This was carried out under heavy enemy shelling. During this stage of the operations, the following of C Coy did great work:-	

Place	Date 1917	Hour	Summary of Events and Information	Remarks and references to Appendices
BEAUCAMP	Nov 24	6.30 a.m.	2nd Lieut. D RUSHTON, Sjt. D LAMBIE (killed) Sjt R FLEMING (wounded) Capt P COUPER (killed), 2nd Lieut SHAW, 11th King's Own (R.L.) Regt, who was in command of a Lewis gun of that unit in position of our front to immediate left of attack area, gallantly went out from the sunken road above mentioned under fire to attend to one of our wounded lying in a shell hole. A Coy before taking up its position above described suffered many casualties in and near BEAUCAMP from enemy M.G. and also from the snipers enfilading from the left. Sergt MacNEIL collected shovels in the village for the subsequent consolidation of line behind the village. During the attack 2nd Lt W.W. KILGOUR, Signalling Officer, pushed out from Bn HQ. in Q.17.d. and after repeated and determined efforts succeeded in establishing telephonic communication with Capt. KEDDIE in advanced trench in Q.18.d. This was done in face of dangerous fire from enemy mgs & snipers who commanded all the area lying between the two points and also under considerable enemy shelling in the rge on Q.17.b.1.6. Three wiremen were knocked out but more went up until the line had been established. It remained working throughout the day and until about 10 pm when it was cut by shelling.	
		8.0 a.m.		

Army Form C. 2118.

WAR DIARY
or
INTELLIGENCE SUMMARY.
(Erase heading not required.)

Instructions regarding War Diaries and Intelligence Summaries are contained in F. S. Regs., Part II. and the Staff Manual respectively. Title pages will be prepared in manuscript.

Place	Date	Hour	Summary of Events and Information	Remarks and references to Appendices
BEAUCAMP	April 24th 1917	7.30 am	A preliminary report on the situation was brought to Bn. HQ by Lieut G.W. McCROW of D Coy. him the advanced trench at great personal risk in passing through the dangerous area described. While he remained at Bn. HQ this Officer dressed the wounds of men wounded there by enemy 77 mm shells & hastily embussed the wounded men.	
		7.0 am	With the object of strengthening the line opposite the critical left flank of the attack one Coy. of the support Bn. (11th Kings Own) was brought up to the consolidated trench round about Bn. HQ. They advanced across the open in artillery formation and although in broad daylight the enemy artillery did not open until just as they were dropping into the trench where however some casualties were sustained.	
		9.0 am	After the telephone was established fuller information was received of the location of the advanced enemy mgs & snipers who had held up our left flank. At 9.0 am. our artillery opened on the region Q.11.d central with the immediate result of turning out about 25% of the enemy from the region. They were mostly shot down by our L.G. & rifle fire from sunken road. About this time Lt/Cpl. J.W.CRAWFORD went out and got D. Coy. back to join what was now the main body of the battalion in advanced trench in Q.18.b and 2 under fire.	

Army Form C. 2118.

WAR DIARY
or
INTELLIGENCE SUMMARY.
(Erase heading not required.)

Instructions regarding War Diaries and Intelligence Summaries are contained in F. S. Regs., Part II. and the Staff Manual respectively. Title pages will be prepared in manuscript.

Place	Date 1917	Hour	Summary of Events and Information	Remarks and references to Appendices
BEAUCAMP	April 24th	12 noon	About 12 noon three strong patrols were pushed out through the village from advanced trench, under 2nd Lt. T.C. ANNAN, 2nd Lt. A. TAYLOR, and 2nd Lt. D. RUSHTON. On the far side of the village they came under heavy fire. 2nd Lt. Mc CURDIE was killed and 2nd Lt. RUSHTON wounded. The village itself was found not to be held by the enemy.	
		2 pm	At 2pm patrols were again sent out to BEAUCAMP but it was found that a number of the enemy had filtered back into the village and were at this time holding it. The enemy bombarded throughout the day their old trench immediately behind our advanced trench in P.18.b and d., leaving comparatively unmolested the position which had wisely been taken up by Capt. W.F.T. KEDDIE and Lieut. G.M.T. BARTHOLOMEW. The Stretcher-bearers, who had been reinforced by the Batt. Band as reserve S.B. did fine work throughout the operations.	
		9 pm	At night, the survivors of D and B coys went back to old German trench behind an advanced trench with A & C coys remained in advanced trench. This was consolidated by deepening the narrow trenches between shell-holes and adding parapet and fire step. 2nd Lt. T.C. ANNAN and Capt. J. FLETT went out during night and brought in B Coy wounded.	

WAR DIARY
or
INTELLIGENCE SUMMARY.

(Erase heading not required.)

Army Form C. 2118.

Instructions regarding War Diaries and Intelligence Summaries are contained in F. S. Regs., Part II. and the Staff Manual respectively. Title pages will be prepared in manuscript.

Place	Date	Hour	Summary of Events and Information	Remarks and references to Appendices
BEAUCAMP	April 24 1917	11 p.m.	At 11 p.m. the 20th Division on the immediate left of our line attacked and took the line Q.11.3.9.1 – road – BILHEM, with the assistance of about one hour barrage. This had the result of bringing heavy enemy barrage on BEAUCAMP and old enemy trenches in Q.18.a and b.	
	April 25th	1 a.m.	Before dawn on 25th April, the battalion was relieved by the 11th King's Own (R.L.) Regt. in advanced trench. The enemy partners commanding our left flank being now in the hands of the 20th Div. a detachment of the 11th KING'S OWN went forward shortly after relief and secured all the objectives. "BEAUCAMP" was earmarked by this battalion and two machine guns captured in BEAUCAMP by the 11th KING'S OWN respectively.	
Beaucamp Wood		3.55 a.m.	On being relieved by the 11th KING'S OWN Pte Leo (A. Coy) with B Company Reserve in BOUZEAUCOURT WOOD. A Company threw to the Quadralateral trench beside advanced Bn. H.Q. in Q.23.c. During the day they were at the Cross Roads in collecting any men amount had parties were organised for collecting any men amount wounded and also burying the dead. Lt G W McCRAW – 2/Lt CHISHOLM, Lt G.H.E BARTHOLOMEW, 2/Lt Lt W KILGOR – 2/Lt CHISHOLM. By 2/Lt RUSHTON & 2/Lt W KNOX all took charge of parties. By the 11th KING'S OWN certified R.L. Regt. area had been hurried greatly in the R.H.A. having suffered greatly in the R.H.A.	

Army Form C. 2118.

WAR DIARY
or
INTELLIGENCE SUMMARY.
(Erase heading not required.)

April 1917.

Instructions regarding War Diaries and Intelligence Summaries are contained in F. S. Regs., Part II. and the Staff Manual respectively. Title pages will be prepared in manuscript.

Place	Date	Hour	Summary of Events and Information	Remarks and references to Appendices
BOIZLEAUCOURT WOOD	26th		The whole Bn was in the wood except "B" Company which had been ordered to assist N/10 B Batt'n the night before. The Germans made most of the day and at 9 oclock the Bn was relieved and marched off by Companies to billets in ETRICOURT where they arrived about 12 midnight. R.H.A.	
	27th		The Bn was resting for the most part of the day. Rolls were called. The Bn was reorganized. The men killed and wounded were taken in belongings of the men killed and wounded were taken hard for dispatch. 96 blanks reported the Bn from hospital R.H.A.	
	28th		The Bn were cleaning up and Companies reorganizing. In the evening there was a band arranged with the 40th Divisional Band present. It was held at 7.30 in the open air in ETRICOURT. R.H.A.	
	29th		Church parade for the Bn was held in the open behind Bn H.Q. in ETRICOURT - The Divisional Band played at the Service. R.H.A.	
	30.		Company parades and further reorganising of Platoons R.H.A.	

APPENDIX "B"

Extract from Battalion Order No 59 para 2 of 6th April, 1917.

No.2 ACTS OF COURAGE:- The General Officer commanding 4th Army wishes to express his appreciation of the following acts of acts of courage, performed during the bombing of an ammunition railhead by hostile aircraft on 16th February, 1917.

No.1 T/Captain W.G.T.Keddie, Argyll and Sutherland Highlanders, was in charge of a party which, in face of considerable danger from bursting shells successfully removed a quantity of dangerous chemical stores. The success of the work was materially due to the initiative and courage displayed by Captain Keddie(R.O.para 761 of 3/4/17).

2 No.S/9359 Sgt. A.C.Murdoch, Argyll and Sutherland Highlanders by his exertions and coolness, both by removing men to a place of greater safety, and then by organizing them for the work they had to do, was responsible for saving a dangerous situation. (R.O. 761 of 3/4/17.)

Certified a true copy,

[signature]

2nd Lieut.
A/Adjutant 14th (S) Bn. Argyll and Sutherland Highlanders.

Secret   15 April 1917.

14th (S). Bn. Arg Suth. Highlanders
                              Order No 13   Copy No 13

Reference 1/40 000, 62 C.
          1/40 000, 57 C.

1. The 120th Inf. Brigade less 14th H.L.I. will rejoin 40th Division on 16th April 17. The 14th A.S.H. will march to ETRICOURT.

2. Distances already laid down will be maintained. Cookers will march with Companies. Each Company will put one tank at disposal of O.C. Hqrs. Company, who will arrange for the rations required by his Coy. on the march being handed to the respective Q.M.S.'s tonight.

3. A halt of one hour will be made at 11-50 am 16th inst. for dinners.

4. Packs will be worn, leather jerkins will be carried rolled on the top of the pack.

5. Blankets rolled in bundles of 10, properly labelled & tied will be ready for loading at 9am, they will not be taken from huts till further orders are issued. Company stores & Q.M. baggage will be ready for loading by 9am. A loading party of 1 N.C.O & 5 O.R. per Company, will report to Quartermaster at his stores at 9am. Officers valises will be stacked in Q.M. stores by 8.30 am. The Q.M. will detail special loading party. Mess Kit & M.O's. stores will be ready for loading at 9am.

6. Rations for 17th will be delivered at new 1st Line Transport lines V.2.d. on 16th. Refilling point on 17th will be near Cross Roads in D.20.

7. Brigade Hqrs. will open at EQUANCOURT, at 10am on 16th inst.

8. Battalion will parade on road at 9-45am. ready to move off in the following order. Hqrs. A. B. C. D. 1st Line Transport will move in rear of Battalion

9. O.C. Companies will personally inspect the huts and lines before their Coy. moves off, and will hand a Certificate to Adjutant, at 9-45 a.m. that huts and lines have been left in a clean and sanitary condition.

10. O.C. Companies will report personally at Orderly Room, when their Companies are settled in quarters at ETRICOURT.

Rob Dickie.
Capt & Adjt.
14th (S) Batn. Argyll & Suth. Hgrs.

Copy No. 1   C.O.
      2   2nd in Command
      3   Adjutant
    4 - 7 O.C. Companies
      8   Q. Master
      9   Transport Officer
      10   Medical Officer
      11   O/c Hqrs Company
      12   File
      13   War Diary.

Secret.   D.O.   15 April 1917.

14th (S) Bn. Arg & Suth. Highlanders
Order No 13   Copy No 12

Reference 1/40,000, 62 C.
           1/40,000 57 C.

1. The 120th Infy Brigade less 14th H.L.I. will rejoin 40th Division on 16th April 17. The 14th A. & S. H. will march to ETRICOURT.

2. Distances already laid down will be maintained. Cookers will march with Companies. Each Company will put one tank at disposal of O.C. Hqrs. Company, who will arrange for the rations required by his Coy. on the march, being handed to the respective C.Q.M.S.s tonight.

3. A halt of one hour will be made at 11-50 am 16th inst. for dinners.

4. Packs will be worn; leather jerkins will be carried rolled on the top of the pack.

5. Blankets rolled in bundles of 10, properly labelled & tied will be ready for loading at 7am, they will not be taken from huts till further orders are issued. Company Stores & Q.M. baggage will be ready for loading by 7am. A loading party of 1 N.C.O. & 5 O.R. per Company will report to Quartermaster at his stores at 7am. Officers valises will be stacked in Q.M. stores by 8.30am. The Q.M. will detail special loading party. Mess Kit & M.O.s stores will be ready for loading at 9am.

6. Rations for 17th will be delivered at new 1st Line Transport lines V.2.d. on 16th. Refilling point on 17th will be near Cross Roads in D 20.

7. Brigade Hqrs. will open at EQUANCOURT at 10am on 16th inst.

8. Battalion will parade on road at 9-45am ready to move off in the following order. Hqrs. A. B. C. D. 1st Line Transport will move in rear of Battalion

SECRET. COPY NO. 9

120th INFANTRY BRIGADE ORDER NO. 91.

Ref. 1/40,000.62.c.
1/40,000.57.c.

15/4/1917.

1. The 120th Infantry Brigade less 14th H.L.I. will rejoin 40th Division on 16th April.

2. Movements on 16th instant will be carried out in accordance with attached table.

3. Distances already laid down will be maintained. Cookers will march with Companies.

4. Four additional baggage wagons per Battalion have been allotted to carry blankets.
Baggage wagons will report as follows :-
4 each to 11th R. Lanc. R. and 13th E. Surr. R., and 2 to 14th A.& S.H. on afternoon of today, 15th instant.
Remaining wagons at 7.30 a.m., 16th instant.

5. Packs will be worn. Leather jerkins will be carried rolled on the top of the pack.

6. A halt of one hour will be made at 11.50 a.m., 16th inst, for dinners.

7. Rations for 17th will be delivered at new 1st Line Transport lines, v.2.d., on 16th.

8. Refilling point on 17th will be near cross roads in D.20.

9. Brigade Headquarters will close at EARTHWORKS at 10 a.m. and will reopen at EQUANCOURT at the same hour.

10. A C K N O W L E D G E.

Issued through Signals
at 2 p.m.

Captain,
Brigade Major,
120th Infantry Brigade.

Copy No. 1. G.O.C.
2. Brigade Major.
3. Staff Captain.
4. File.
5. War Diary.
6. 11th R. Lanc. R.
7. 13th E. Surr. R.
8. 14th High. L. I.
9. 14th Arg.& Suth'd.Hrs.
10. 120th Machine Gun Coy.
11. 120th Trench Mortar Bty.
12. No.3 Coy., Div.Train.
13. 229th Field Coy. R.E.
14. Brigade Signals.
15. Bde. Supply Officer.
16. Camp C'dant.,
LINGER CAMP.
17. 119th Inf. Bde.
18. 121st Inf. Bde.
19. 40th Div. "G".
20. 40th Div. "Q".
21. 40th Div. Train.
22. A.P.M., 40th Div.
23. Camp Commandant,
EQUANCOURT.

Does 1st Line Transport move with Battalion?

9. O.C. Companies will personally inspect the huts and lines before their Coy. moves off, and will hand a Certificate to Adjutant at 9.45 a.m. That huts and lines have been left in a clean and sanitary condition.

10. O.C. Companies will report personally at Orderly Room when their Companies are settled in quarters at ETRICOURT.

Rob Dickie.
Capt. & Adjt.
4th (S) Battn. Arg. & Suth. Hgrs.

Copy No. 1   C.O.
      2   2nd in Command
      3   Adjutant
   4–7   O.C. Companies
      8   Q. Master
      9   Transport Officer
    10.   Medical Officer
    11   Tc Hqrs Company
    12   File
    13   War Diary.

March Table to accompany 120th Infantry Brigade Order No. 91.

UNIT.	STARTING POINT.	TIME.	ROUTE.	DESTINATION.	REMARKS.
13th E. Surr. eR.	Cross Roads. A.30.b.	9 a.m.	CLERY - ALLAINES - HAUT-ALLAINES - MOISLAIN - MARAMCOURT - ETRICOURT.	EQUANCOURT.	
11th R. Lanc. R.	Road junction H.1.d.	9-40 a.m.	do.	do.	
29th Field Coy. R.E. (less 2 sections)	do.	10-10 a.m.	do.	do.	
14th A. & S. Hrs.	Cross Roads. A.30.b.	10-10 a.m.	do.	ETRICOURT.	

"C" Form.
MESSAGES AND SIGNALS.

Army Form C. 2123.
(In books of 100).
No. of Message............

Prefix **SM** Code **FP** Words **23**

Charges to collect

Service Instructions. **FB1**

Received. From **FB1**
By

Sent, or sent out. At............ m. To............ By

Office Stamp. 9/4/14

Handed in at............ Office............ m. Received **6.8** p.m.

TO **UNCORD**

Sender's Number	Day of Month	In reply to Number	A A A
G115	19/4	Nel osé	

reference ~~120th inf bde~~ no
120/462 aaa in para 2
insert after "this cancels"
"para 3"

FROM **UNCLOSE**

PLACE & TIME

----th Inf. Bde.

INFANTRY WORKS REPORT - WEDNESDAY, 11th APRIL, 1917.

Index No.	Sector.	Nature of Work.	Proposed Location.	Work in hand.	% of work in hand completed.	Estimated No. of days to complete the whole.	Remarks.
4.	--th Bn.	Wire Entanglements on Main Line of resistance.	Whole frontage of main line.	Whole frontage.	30.	4.	12 ft. belt.
5.	do.	Front line trench main line of resistance.	As per scheme.	Posts at N.2.b.4.5. W.26.c.3.9. etc., etc.	50.	10.	2 ft. command.
6.	--th Bn.	Communication trench.	V.24.central to W.19.b.central.	V.24.central 100. to W.19.a. 0.0.		5.	Trench Boards not yet available.

----th Inf. Bde.

INFANTRY WORKS REPORT - SATURDAY, 14th APRIL, 1917.

6.							Completed. Trench boards laid.

SECRET.   COPY NO. 9

120TH INFANTRY BRIGADE ORDER NO. 92.

1. The 40th Divisional Boundary on the South will be altered as follows on night 17/18th April.
   The new boundary will be :-
   The old boundary as far east as its junction with the FINS - GOUZEAUCOURT ROAD (Q.35.d.) to Q.36.c.6.5. (road inclusive) and thence along the GOUZEAUCOURT - LE PAVE road (road exclusive).

2. From the night 17/18th April inclusive the Divisional Sector will be held on a two Brigade front.
   The inter-Brigade boundary line will be as follows :-
   Q.31.a.0.0.
   Q.27.a.0.0.
   Q.29.a.1.2.
   Q.24.a.5.C.
   R.14.a.0.5.

3. The 120th Infantry Brigade will relieve the 121st Infantry Brigade on the left Sector on the night 18/19th April.

4. On taking over the Sector the 120th Infantry Brigade will be responsible in that Sector.-
   (a) For the consolidation of an advanced line of resistance running from east edge of GOUZEAUCOURT through Q.23 central to S.E. corner of HAVRINCOURT WOOD.
   (b) For the completion of the preparation of the main line of resistance METZ en COUTURE - N.E. corner of GOUZEAUCOURT WOOD - Main Road in Q.35.d.
   (c) For the completion of the line of strong posts in support of (b).

5. 1 Battalion 121st Brigade will remain at EQUANCOURT and be at the tactical disposal of the G.O.C. 120th Brigade in case of necessity.
   This Battalion will rejoin its Brigade at ETRICOURT as soon as H.L.I. is released from work under Corps.

6. 14th A. & S.H. will probably be brought up to EQUANCOURT.

7. Further orders will be issued later.

8. A C K N O W L E D G E.

Issued through Signals
at 8-45 pm

                                                    Captain,
                                                Brigade Major,
                                            120th Infantry Brigade.

Copy No. 1. G.O.C.   13. 229th Field Coy. R.E.
        2. Brigade Major.   14. Brigade Signals.
        3. Staff Captain.   15. Bde. Supply Officer.
        4. File.   16. 40th Divn. Art.
        5. War Diary.   17. 119th Inf. Bde.
        6. 11th R. Lanc. R.   18. 121st Inf. Bde.
        7. 13th E. Surr. R.   19. 40th Div. "Q"
        8. 11th High L.I.   20. 40th Div. "G"
        9. 14th Arg. & Suth'd Highrs.   21. 40th Div. Train.
       10. 120th M.G.C.   22. A.P.M. 40th Division.
       11. 120th T.M.B.
       12. No. 3 Coy. Div. Train.

Copy No.	1.	G. O. C.
	2.	Brigade Major.
	3.	Staff Captain,
	4.	File.
	5.	War Diary.
	6.	11th R. Lncs.R.
	7.	13th E. Surr. R.
	8.	14th High. L. I.
	9.	14th Arg.& Suth'd. Highrs.
	10.	120th M.G.C.
	11.	120th T.M.B.
	12.	No.3 Coy. Div.Train.
	13.	229th Field Coy. R.E.
	14.	Brigade Signals.
	15.	Brigade Supply Officer.
	16.	40th Div. Art.
	17.	119th Infantry Brigade.
	18.	121st Infantry Brigade.
	19.	40th Div. "G".
	20.	40th Div. "Q".
	21.	40th Div. Train.
	22.	A.P.M. 40th Division.
	23.	Town Major, EQUANCOURT.

"SECRET" COPY NO. 9

120TH INFANTRY BRIGADE ORDER NO. 93.

17/4/17.

In continuation of 120th Infantry Brigade Order No. 92.-

1. On taking over the left Sector on night 17/18th April, the 120th Infantry Brigade will be disposed as follows :-
   2 Battalions holding the Line of Resistance and the Outpost Line.
   1 Battalion in Brigade Support.
   1 Battalion in Brigade Reserve.

2. The dividing line between battalions will be, Q.27.b.4.0. - Q.22.b.5.0. - Q.17.d.0.0.

3. 13th E. Surr. R. will relieve the 20th Middlesex in the right sub sector, and 11th R. Lanc. R. will relieve 20th Middlesex and one Company 21st Middlesex in the left sub sector.
   14th Arg. & Suth'd. Highrs. will be in Brigade Support at EQUANCOURT.
   20th Middlesex R. will be in Brigade Reserve at EQUANCOURT.

4. All details of relief will be arranged direct between C.Os. concerned.

5. Hour at which Arg. & Suth'd. Highrs. will move to EQUANCOURT will be notified later.
   Advanced Party should report to Town Major EQUANCOURT at 11 a.m.
   1st Line Transport and Quartermaster's Stores will remain at ETRICOURT.

6. O.C. 120th M.G. Coy. will arrange relief direct with O.C. 119th M.G. Coy.

7. Blankets of 11th R. Lanc. R. and 13th E. Surr. R. will be stored at EQUANCOURT. Accomodation will be provided by the Town Major.

8. Completion of relief will be wired to Brigade Headquarters using Code Word - BOB.

9. Command of Left Sector will pass to G.O.C. 120th Infantry Brigade on completion of relief.

10. Brigade Headquarters will remain at EQUANCOURT.

11. ACKNOWLEDGE.

Issued through Signals

Captain,
Brigade Major,
120th Infantry Brigade.

SECRET.

11th R. Lanc. R.
13th E. Surr. R.
14th Arg. & Suth'd Highrs.
20th Middlesex Regt.
120th M. G. Coy.
120th T. M. Battery.

The next stages of the Advance on HINDENBURG LINE allotted to the Division are:-

1. Capture and consolidation of the line R.26.b.5.5. - R.20.d.0.0. - 18 Ravine - Q.18.c.8.7. - TRENCHS in Q.17.a. thence to Q. 15.b.9.6. This operation will be carried out in conjunction with an attack by the 8th Division on GONNELIEU and will probably take place in a day or two.

2. The capture of VILLERS, PLOUICH and BEAUCAMP and gaining a footing on the high ground in R.14.a. and c. and R.7.c., Q.12.d.
   This operation will not take place before the 22nd instant.

3. Further Orders will be issued as soon as possible.

Captain,
Brigade Major,
120th Infantry Brigade.

19-4-17.

120th Infantry Brigade No.120/462.   S E C R E T.

   11th R. Lanc. R.
   13th E. Surr. R.
   14th Arg.& Suth'd.Hrs.
   14th High.L.I.
   120th M.G.Coy.
   120th T.M.B.
   229th F.Coy.R.E.

1.   The following extract from 40th Division Defence Orders just received is forwarded :-
" 3. Action in case of attack.
   (a) Outposts in front of the Advanced Line of Resistance will resist any partial attacks without falling back - they will be supported by local counter attacks or reinforcements as the situation demands.
   Should the enemy attack in force they will withdraw gradually on the Advanced Line of Resistance. They will be provided with S.O.S. signals.
   (b) The Advanced Line of Resistance will be held at all costs.
   (c) The Main Line of Resistance will be fully occupied immediately.
   (d) Should the enemy penetrate the Advanced Line, immediate local counter attacks will be made. Any troops taken from the garrison of the Main Line for this purpose will be replaced by moving up troops from behind.
   A minimum garrison of two Companies in each Brigade sector (excluding Machine Guns) will however always remain in the Main Line trenches.

2.   This cancels para 3 120th Inf.Brigade No.120/462, dated the 18th. 13th E. Surr. R. will not now be able to send up an additional Company to work on the Advanced Line of Resistance.
   The 2 Companies of the 2 front line Battalions garrisoning the Main Line of Resistance will now be responsible for the work on the main line, helped by the Support Battalion, 229th Field Coy., and Works Coy.

3.   A fresh scheme of work will be published tonight. For the present Outpost Coies. plus 1 Coy. of the 11th R. Lanc. R. will be responsible for the Advanced Line of Resistance. Garrison of the Main Line, Support Battalion, and 229th Field Coy R.E. will be responsible for the Main Line of resistance.

4.   In case of attack Working Parties will immediately report to the Battalion Commander in whose sub-sector they are working.

                                            Captain,
                                            Brigade Major,
                                            120th Infantry Brigade.

19/4/17.

120th Infantry Brigade No. 120/XXX 462.   SECRET.

11th R. Lanc. R.
13th E. Surr. R.
14th High. L. I.
14th Arg. & Suth'd Highrs.
120th M. G. Coy.
120th T. M. Battery.
229th Field Coy. R.E.

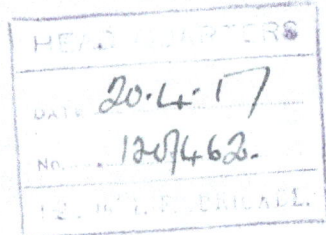

Reference 120th Infantry Brigade No. 120/462 dated 18-4-17 and 120th Infantry Brigade No. 120/462 dated 19-4-17.

For para 3 of former letter substitute :-

3. The responsibility for work in the present Sector will be:-

(a) <u>Two front line Battalions.</u>

(1) Wiring and construction of advanced line of resistance as given in 120th Infantry Brigade Order No.92 on Battalion frontage.

(2) Wiring and construction of main line of resistance on frontage of companies holding the line.

<u>Right Front Battalion.</u>   Completion of strong point in Q.27.d.
<u>Left Front Battalion.</u>   Completion of strong point in Q.26.b.

These points to be strongly wired and completed as rapidly as possible.

(b)   Battalion in Brigade Support, with Battalions holding the line, 229th Field Coy. R.E., and the Brigade Works Company. - Wiring and construction of the main line of resistance as given in 120th Infantry Brigade Order No. 92.

(c)   The amount of work completed by each Battalion during the period reported on will be given in the bi-weekly Summary :-

The % of work in hand completed, and The estimated Number of days to complete the whole, on main line of resistance, will be reported by the Battalions holding the front line.

The support battalion need not report on these two headings.

Captain,
Brigade Major,
120th Infantry Brigade.

19-4-17.

SECRET.

11th R. Lanc. R.
13th E. Surr. R.
14th High. L. I.
14th Arg. & Suth'd Highrs.
120th M. G. Coy.
120th T. M. Battery.
229th Field Coy. R.E.

---

1. The daily Works Report will not in future be sent in. From Friday 20th April inclusive, Battalions will render a bi-weekly Works Report by 4 p.m. every Tuesday and Friday.

2. The report will be rendered in tabular form, sample attached. It will not be necessary to repeat in successive reports the detail of work previously reported, reference need only be made to the Index Number of the particular piece of work on which progress is to be reported.

3. The responsibility for work in the present Sector will be as follows :-
   (a) <u>Two Front Line Battalions.</u>   Wiring and construction of advanced line of resistance as given in 120th Inf. Brigade Order No.92, on Battalion frontage.

   <u>Right Front Battalion.</u>   Completion of strong point in Q.27.d.
   <u>Left Front Battalion.</u>   Completion of strong point in Q.26.b.
   These points to be strongly wired and completed as rapidly as possible.
   Neither Battalion will send up more than one Company at a time in addition to the outpost Companies, to work on the advanced line of resistance.
   (b) <u>Battalion in Brigade Support.</u>- With 229th Field Coy. R.E., and the Brigade Works Coy. - Wiring and construction of the main line of resistance as given in 120th Inf. Brigade Order No.92.

4. Each Battalion will report in the bi-weekly Works Reports, on the work for which it is responsible.

Captain,
Brigade Major,
120th Infantry Brigade.

18/4/17.

SECRET   COPY N. 4

120th INFANTRY BRIGADE ORDER NO. 94.

20-4-17.

1.   The 40th Division will attack and occupy the following line on 21st April, 1917.

Road at R.26.b.3.3. (inclusive) - R.20.c.6.2. - FIFTEEN RAVINE - Q.18.d.1.4. - Trenches in Q.17.a. thence to join up with 20th Division.

The 8th Division on the Right will assault GONNELIEU at the same time.

2. OBJECTIVES.

(a)   The 119th Infantry Brigade.
The Spur R.26.b.3.3. - R.20.c.6.2. - FIFTEEN RAVINE all inclusive.

(b)   The 120th Infantry Brigade.
From FIFTEEN RAVINE exclusive - Q.18.d.1.4. - ROAD Junction Q.17.b.1.6. - Trenches in Q.17.a. The Posts in Q.16.c. and d. will be advanced to conform with the approximate line Q.17.b.5.5. - Q.18.a.5.5.

Touch will be maintained with Brigades.

3.   The 13th E. Surr. R. will be on the Right and the 11th R.Lanc. R. on the Left.
Dividing line between Battalions will be BULL ALLEY Q.17.d. - Q.18.a.9.0. - Q.17.d.6.7.

4.   13th E. Surr. R. will push forward patrols after dark on night 20/21st April to ascertain if the objective is held. If the objective is unoccupied posts will at once be pushed forward to consolidate, if opposition is met with at Post reported at Q.18.d.1.4. this post will be assaulted at ZERO HOUR. Not more than 6 small posts to be established on New Line. Posts already held should be further strengthened.

Right Post to be clear of Barrage on FIFTEEN RAVINE.

5.   11th R. Lanc. R. will assault and consolidate the trenches in Q.17.a. with one Company. Not more than two platoons to garrison the captured trenches by day. West of TRESCHULT, the Posts detailed in para 2 (b) above and a Post at Q.17.central will be established during night 20/21st April. Posts at Q.16.a. and Q.16.c. to be strengthened and held.

6.   O.C.120th Machine Gun Company will detail
(a) Two guns to assist 11th R. Lanc. R. One gun will be about Q.17.d.5.6. firing North. The second gun will be in Post at Q.16.b.6.6. and will fire North East.
(b)   Two guns to be in position about Q.22.central to bring indirect fire on BEAUCAMP and VILLERS PLOUICH in case of counter attack.

7.   O.C. 120th Trench Mortar Battery will detail
(a)   One Stokes Mortar to deal with Machine Gun reported about Q.18.d.1.4. under orders of O.C.13th E. Surr. R.

-2-

8. ZERO hour will be notified later.

9. (a) At ZERO hour the Artillery will put down barrage on the objectives. The line of this barrage is shown in green on attached map.
At ZERO plus * minutes the barrage will lift.
Assaulting troops will be about 200 yards from objective at ZERO and will then move up as near to the barrage as possible: as the barrage lifts assaulting troops will then advance close behind it.

(b) Time table of barrage will be issued if received.

10. The most advanced troops will light red flares when called upon to do so, by contact aeroplanes. Contact aeroplanes will be marked by black band and black streamers on each of their lower planes and will sound kloxon horns and fire red lights when calling for flares to be lit.

11. Any prisoners will be sent back without delay to Brigade Headquarters.

12. Watches will be synchonized at 6 p.m.

13. Report Centre will be established at present Headquarters of 13th E. Surr. R.
All messgaes to be sent to this point.

14. Advanced Brigade Headquarters will be open at N.W. Corner of DESART WOOD W.1.b.1.a. at 7 p.m. 20th April, 1917.

15. ACKNOWLEDGE.

Issued through Signals
at 6.15 p.m.

Captain,
Brigade Major,
120th Infantry Brigade.

Copy No. 1. 11th R. Lanc. R.
2. 13th E. Surr. R.
3. 20th Middlesex Regt.
4. Arg. & Suth'd Highrs.
5. 119th Infantry Brigade.
6. 61st Infantry Brigade.
7. 40th Division "G"
8. 178th Bde. R.F.A.
9. 40th Div. Art.

Patrol Report, morning of 2.3rd C/o 1917

Map Reference 57c S.E.

Officers Patrol consisting of 1 Officer & 12 O.R. & covering party of 1 Officer & 15 O.R. went out from our right post – Q.17.A.10.8 – at 1am & returned 3.30 am. Object of patrol was to observe if enemy occupied his front line trench & if possible to establish posts. The party failed to locate left flank of enemy trench & proceeded onwards in N.N.E direction for 600 – 700 [yds] where second line was encountered. About point Q.11.B.7.5. this line was fairly well & continuously held, puts post was located – on return – in front line at about Q.17.B.8.9. Sentry was observed & work on the post was in progress.

S P M

D.R Black 2/Lt

To The Adjutant   Ref. 57°SE
    14th a.S.H.   1/20,000
From O.C. B Coy.
___

Enclosed please find patrol report by Mr Biggart.

Post Established about the point Q11c34. The point where the King's Own were order to establish about this was not started by them, But it is now occupied by us.

Cliff Mullins Capt
O.C. B Coy

23.4.17
5-15am

14th R.I.H.

SECRET
TWELVE

Ppt at present at Q 10. d 8 4.
To be established at Q 11 c 3.4

Post to be established between
trenches in Q 17 a and left
of E Sun R.

Strong patrol to be pushed down
the trench from Q 17 a 9.9 through
Q 17 b as far east as possible.

The trench thus cleared will
be occupied and held.

22.4.'17

J H Smith Capt.
Brigade Major
129th Inf Bde

SECRET

Artillery programme

10.30 pm — 11 pm
Bombardment on trenches in Q18a+b

11 pm to 11.30 pm
Bombard BEAUCAMP

11.30 pm Cease fire

Patrol to enter BEAUCAMP
after 11.35 pm & report
as soon as possible for
information of artillery
& to establish themselves.

J. L. [illegible] Capt.

22.4.17

German wire must be cut
& posts [established] in
[line?] [against?] counter attack

To: Adjutant,
    Hertford

From: OC "D" Coy

2 Posts have been established to cover Capt Miller's right flank.

The information on the map does not square with the information received as regards sight of trenches occupied by "B" Coy.

~~~

1 Post would be about Q17B15 and the other about Q17A94.

No touch has yet been obtained with 1st Gentlemen

B Company 14th C of S H.

Reference Map 57 C S E 1/20,000

The following is the line held by this Company. Trench from Q 17 a 6.4 to Q 17 a 7.7. held by one platoon (including L.G.)

Trench from Q 17 a 6.9 to Q 11 c 0.1 held by two platoons (including 2 L.G.)

Post held at Q 11 c 3.2 (single by day double by night)

Support trench from Q 17 a 7.5 to Q 17 a 0.3 to Q 11 c 0.1 held by one platoon (including L.G.) A small party of D Coy are also in Support Trench.

Nearest post of K.R.Rs on left is about Q 10 D central.

D Coy have a post on my right with L.G. at about Q 17 central.

No change in enemy line. Situation normal.

12 noon. 23.4.17

[signature] Capt
O.C. B Coy

37
31
28
39

135

the Runciman on the
service of the next
hour. The road along
which our line of Posts
was extended is in many
places little more than
a track. and there are
a good many tracks not
shown on the map.
This partly accounts for
the failure of his
                              Jas Patrick
By Runner
5.25 AM

To, the Adjutant

Smith

The Angelians gave us no
information on going out
and our own efforts
so far failed.

Could you obtain from
our Gentleman via East
Surreys news of his
doings? I am sure our
patrols did not look in
the right direction

I am sending 2
runners to du Cour.
The way to our Gentleman's
Hdqrs — will you please
forward them via E. Surrey
Hdqrs.
Shall visit

SECRET.   COPY NO. 9.

120TH INFANTRY BRIGADE ORDER
No. 95z

22-4-17.

1. 14th Arg. & Suth'd Highrs. will relieve 11th R. Lanc. R. in the Left Sub-sector on night 22/23rd April 1917.

2. On completion of relief 11th R. Lanc. R. will withdraw to Brigade Support at DESERT WOOD.

3. 11th R. Lanc. R. will take over strong points in Q.26.a.and Q.27.c. from 14th Arg. & Suth'd Highrs. with one platoon each.

4. All details of relief will be arranged between C. Os. concerned.

5. Patrols will be pushed out by 14th Arg. & Suth'd Highrs. after relief, to reconnoitre wire running through Q.17.b. and Q.18.a. and lines of advance against village of BEAUCAMP, during hours of darkness.
    Times at which patrols will be sent out to be wired to Brigade Headquarters in sufficient time for artillery to be warned.
    Reports to be forwarded by wire.

6. 14th High. L. I. will rejoin 120th Infantry Brigade to-day 22nd instant. and will be in Brigade Reserve at ~~DESERT WOOD~~ EQUANCOURT.

7. Completion of relief will be wired to Brigade Headquarters by code word "TIM"

8. ACKNOWLEDGE.

CO. gave verbal instructions to send off Tim at 12 m.m.
R'd.
11.35 p.m.
22.4.17

Issued through signals at _____ a.m.
                                 10

Captain.
Brigade Major.
120th Infantry brigade.

Copy No. 1. G.O.C.   12. No.3 Coy D Div.Train.
        2. Brigade Major.   13. 229th F. Coy. R.E.
        3. Staff Captain.   14. Bde. Signals.
        4. File.   15. Bde. Supply Officer
        5. War Diary.   16. 40th Div. Art.
        6. 11th R. Lanc. R.   17. 119th Inf. Bde.
        7. 13th E. Surr. R.   18. 121st Inf. Bde.
        8. 14th High. L. I.   19. 40th Div. "G"
        9. 14th Arg. & Suth'd Highrs.   20. 40th Div. "Q"
       10. 120th M. G. Coy.   21. 40th Div. Train.
       11. 120th T. M. Battery   22. A.P.M. 40th Div.

14th (S) Battn. Argyll & Sutherland Highrs.
Order No 14.

Copy No
23-4-17

Ref= 57c S.E. (Ed 3A)
Artillery Sketch - Barrages.

1. **Information:** The 14th A&S Highrs will assault the hostile trench Q.18.a.0.6. and the village of BEAUCAMP on 24th inst, and occupy as final objective the line R.7. Central exclusive to Q.11.b.9.0. inclusive —

2. **Distribution.**
   Leading Company — "D"
   Second   "   B
   Support   "   A
   Reserve   "   C

   One Company of 1th K.O.R.L. Regiment will be placed under orders of O.C. 14th A&S Highrs to act as garrison of strong point in Q.17.a and to push forward posts before ZERO hour to about Q.11.c central and Q.11.c.9.5. Guides will be provided by O.C. "B" Coy 14th A&S H to meet this company at these present H.Qrs at midnight.

3. **Dress**
   Fighting Order.
   Water Bottles to be filled

4. **ASSEMBLY.**
   Companies will move out to line of Assembly and be ready by ZERO -15 minutes

5. **FLARES**
   The most advanced troops will light FLARES on being called for by Contact PATROL AEROPLANES.

6. **R.A.P.** The R.A.P. will be at Q.22.c.4.5.

7. **Communications** Battalion Headquarters at commencement of operations will be at Q.17.a.5.4

8. Prisoners will be sent back to Battalion Headquarters without delay.

9. **ZERO TIME** – ZERO TIME will be announced later – At ZERO artillery barrages will be commenced in accordance with TIME TABLE already announced.

23-4-17.

Rob Dickie
Capt. Adjt.

SECRET.
COPY No. 9

120th Infantry Brigade Order No.96.

23/4/17.

1. The 40th Division will assault the villages of VILLERS PLOUICH and BEAUCAMP and gain a footing on the heights in R.14.central, R.7.central, on the 24th April.

2. The 119th Infantry Brigade will attack on the right and the 120th Infantry Brigade on the left. Boundary between Brigades a line from R.19.a.0.7. to R.14.b.1.8.

3. OBJECTIVES.
(a) 120th Infantry Brigade.
Ravine R.14.b.2.8. (inclusive) - R.8.c.8.6. - R.7.central - Q.12.central - Q.11.b.9.0. thence to the present line.
(b). (1) The 13th E. Surr. R. will assault the hostile trench in R.13.c. and VILLERS PLOUICH from a position of assembly on the line Q.24.b.8.8. to Q.18.d.5.9. occupying and consolidating as final objective the ravine R.14.b.3.8. inclusive to R.7.central inclusive.
(2) Close touch will be maintained with the advance of 119th Infantry Brigade.
(3) Strong points will be established at R.8.c.8.6. and R.7.central and a post at R.7.d.7.6.
(c). (1) The 14th Arg.& Suth'd.Hrs. will assault the hostile trench Q.18.a. and b. and BEAUCAMP from a position of assembly Q.18.d.4.9. to Q.17.b.8.0. occupying as final objective the line R.7.central exclusive to Q.11.b.9.0. inclusive.
(2) A strong point will be established at Q.12.central.

4. (a) 14th High. L. I. will support the 13th E. Surr. R. in the attack detailed in para 3.b. above with a special view to driving home the assault on the ravine in R.8.c. of the final objective
(b) Two platoons will be detailed to report to O.C 13th E. Surr. R. and to act as moppers up for the assaulting troops of that Battalion. Mopping up parties will wear white bands.

5. (a) The 11th R. Lanc. R. less one Company will be in Brigade Reserve in the Line of Resistance GOUZEAUCOURT WOOD.
(b) One Company will be placed under the orders of O.C. 14th Arg.& Suth'd.Hrs. to act as garrison of strong point in Q.17.a. and to push forward posts before ZERO hour to about Q.11.c.central and Q.11.c.9.5.

6. O.C. 120th M.G.Company will detail the following guns :-
2 guns at Q.17.b.1.7. approximately to fire (1) BOAR COPSE - BILHEM. (2) Over BEAUCAMP to R.1.d.0.0.
2 guns at Q.17.d.5.8. approximately, to fire in sector from R.7.central to BOAR COPSE.
2 guns at Q.18.c.7.7. approximately to fire (1 gun) to R.1.d.central, (2 guns) to R.8.a. central.
2 guns at R.13.d.9.6.. to fir, approximately R.8.a.5.7. - R.8.b.9.8.
8 guns in reserve at GOUZEOURT. WOOD

7. (a) 229th Field Coy. R.E. will establish a forward dump for the night attack at Q.23.central and for the left attack at Q.17.d.4.4.
(b) The 229th Field Coy. R.E. will move to a forward position at the East end of GOUZECOURT WOOD and be prepared to send forward parties to consolidate strong points when the situation permits.

-2-

8. (a) At ZERO hour the Artillery will put down a barrage as marked in blue on attached map. At ZERO plus 6 minutes the barrage will commence to creep forward at the rate of 100 yards in 4 minutes, pausing for 10 minutes on the lines marked in red. The barrage will halt and become protective about 200 yards beyond the final objectives which are shewn by a green line on attached map.
    (b) Time table of Artillery barrages has been issued to 14th Arg.& Suth'd.Hrs. and 13th E. Surr. R.
    (c) ZERO hour will be notified later.

9. Assaulting battalions will be formed up on lines of assembly as detailed in para 3 above on White Tape at ZERO - 15 minutes, and at ZERO will move up as close to the barrage as possible.

10. <u>Contact Aeroplanes.</u> The most advanced troops will light red flares when called upon to do so by contact aeroplanes. Contact aeroplanes will be marked by a black band abd black streamer on each of their lower planes and will sound KLAXON horns and fire red lights when calling for flares.

11. Prisoners will be sent back without delay to Brigade Headquarters.

12. Supporting Companies of assaulting battalion will carry picks and shovels at the rate of 5 shovels to 1 pick.

13. O.C. 178th Brigade R.F.A. will attach an Officer to the 14th Arg.& Suth'd.Hrs. and O.C. 181 Brigade R.F.A. will attach an Officer to the 13th E. Surr. R. to act as Liaison Officers.

14. Advanced Brigade S.A.A. and Bomb Dump has been established at Q.23.b.3.4. Both battalions will draw from this dump.

15. Headquarters at the commencement of operations will be as follows :-   120th Infantry Brigade...... Q.27.c.6.2.
               11th R.Lanc. R.   Q.21.b.3.4.
               13th E. Surr. R.   Q.18.d.4.0.
               14th High. L. I.   Q.23.d.8.5.
               14th Arg.& Suth'd.Hrs.   Q.19.d.5.9.   Q.17.a.5.4
               120th M.G.Company.   Q.27.c.6.2.
Any move of Headquarters will be at once notified to Brigade Headquarters.

16. Units will send an Officer to synchronize watches at 11 p.m.

17. Brigade Headquarters will close at DESERT WOOD at 6 p.m. 23rd and will reopen at Q.27.c. at the same hour.

                                                                 Captain,
                                                     Brigade Major,
                                                120th Infantry Brigade.

Issued through signals
at   3-48 p.m.

S E C R E T.

To all recipients
of O.O. 96.

****

1. With reference to 120th Infantry Brigade Order No.96,
dated the 23rd instant.

2. Zero is 4-15 a.m. 24th April.

3. ACKNOWLEDGE.

Given personally to ~~~

Captain,
Brigade Major,
120th Infantry Brigade.

23/4/17.

13th Bn. East Surrey Regiment.   Copy No. 7

Operation Order No. 48.

Ref: 57c S.E. (ED. 3A) 1/40,000.   23/4/17.
    Artillery Sketch.- Barrages.

1. INFORMATION

The 40th Division will assault the villages of VILLERS PLOUICH and BEAUCAMP on the night 23/24 April.
119th Infantry Brigade will attack on the RIGHT.
120th   "   "   "   "   "   LEFT.

2. INTENTION.

The Battalion will assault the village of VILLERS PLOUICH and gain a footing on the high ground to the N.E.

3. OBJECTIVE.
   BATTALION BOUNDARIES.

RIGHT BOUNDARY from edge of 15 Ravine at R.19.a.0.8 to R.14.b.2.8.

LEFT BOUNDARY from Q.18.c.3.6 to R.7. Central.

As soon as the objective has been gained, the Battalion will consolidate on the line R.7. Central to the Ravine R.14.b.2.8 (both inclusive)

4. STRONG POINTS.

Strong points will be established at R.8.c.8.6 and R.7.

5. DISTRIBUTION

    RIGHT FRONT Coy   "B"
    LEFT FRONT   "   "A"
    RIGHT SUPPORT "   "D"
    LEFT SUPPORT "   "C"

O/C C & D Coys will detail two Platoons each as a carrying party. They will carry one tool per man in the proportion of three shovels to one pick.

The 14th H.L.I. will detail two Platoons to act as Moppers-up and who will be responsible for Prisoners, &c.

The division between Companies in the Front Line will be Q.18.d.2.3 - R.13.a.8.3 - R.8.c.2.7.

6. DRESS.

Fighting Order

Each man will carry 2 Sand bags.

Water bottles to be filled

O/C Coys will make the necessary arrangements to draw from Forward Dump established at Q.23.b.8.4 necessary bombs and to make ammunition up to 220 rounds per man.

(2)

7. COMMUNICATIONS.

The main line of communication will be from Cross Roads Q.23.b.8.3. along the road to VILLERS PLOUICH.

Battalion Headquarters at commencement of operations will be at Q.18.c.8.3. Subsequently in rear of last wave.

8. ZERO TIME.

At Zero hour Artillery will put down a barrage as follows.

ZERO. Barrage on line marked in BLUE.

ZERO + 6 mins. Barrage will commence to creep forward at the rate of 100 yards in 4 minutes pausing for 10 mins on lines marked in RED.

Barrage will halt and become protective about 200 yards beyond final objectives shewn by GREEN lines and continue firing until +120 mins.

9. ASSEMBLY.

Coys will move out on line of Assembly and be ready by -15 mins.

At ZERO Coys will move up as close as possible to BARRAGE.

10. FLARES.

The most advanced troops will light Flares on being called for by Contact Patrol Aeroplanes.

11. R.A.P.

The R.A.P. will be established at Q.23.c.8.3.

No 1. C.O.
2. O.C. A
3. B
4. C
5. D
6. 14th H.L.I.
7. 14th A. & S.H.
8. 17th Welsh.
9. Med. Off.
10. War Diary.
11. File.
12. Spare.

23/4/17

Adjt. 13th Bn East Surrey Regt. Lieut.

R. Lanc. R.
E. Surr. R.
High. L. I.
Arg. & Suth'd Highrs.

Herewith map showing Situation and German Order of Battle up to 10 a.m. 21-4-17.

WM Tyson 2Lt.
for Captain,
Brigade Major,
120th Infantry Brigade.

23-4-17.

Ref.Map.No. T.S.53 & 51
1/10,000 (attached).

Copy No. 36

SECRET.   40th Divisional Artillery Order No.53.

23rd April, 1917.

1. The 40th Divn. will assault the villages of VILLERS PLOUICH and BEAUCAMP and gain a footing on the heights in R.14.central and R.7.central on the 24th April.

2. Zero hour will be notified later.

3. The 119th Inf.Bde. has been ordered to attack on the right and the 120th Inf. Bde.Bde. on the left. Boundary between Brigades - a line from R.19.a.0.7 to R.14.b.1.8.

4. Objectives :-

   (a) 119th Inf. Brigade.

   The spur R.21.c.5.0 - R.21.a.1.1 - R.14.c.8.0 - trenches on spur R.14.b.3.3 - R.14.b.2.8. (exclusive.).

   (b) 120th Inf. Brigade.

   Ravine R.14.b.2.8.(inclusive) - R.8.c.8.6. R.7.central - R.12.central - R.11.b.9.0 thence to their present line.

5. 119th Inf. Brigade are establishing strong points about R.21.a.1.1. - R.20.a.8.8. - R.14.b.3.3. - R.14.b.1.2. and the 120th Infantry Bde. at R.8.c.8.6 - R.7.central. and R.12.central.

6. Patrols are being pushed down the trenches from R.14.b.3.3. towards R.15.a.3..0. to clear them of the enemy and to hold them with advanced posts.

7. (a) The attack will be supported by -

   (1) 40th Divisional Artillery.

   (2) 33rd Brigade, R.F.A.

   (3) 91st Brigade, R.F.A.

   (4) XV Corps Heavy Artillery.

   (b) The 33rd Bde. R.F.A. will support the attack of the 119th Inf Bde..
   The 40th Div.Artillery and 91st Bde.R.F.A. will support the attack of the 120th Inf. Bde. as follows :-

   181st Bde. R.F.A. and one 18-pdr battery,178th Bde.the attack on VILLERS PLOUICH.

   178th Bde.(less 1 18-pdr battery) and 91st Bde.R.F.A. the attack on BEAUCAMP.

   (c) The XVth Corps Heavy Artillery will not be affiliated to Brigades but can be called on for further support through this office.

-2-

8. At zero hour Brigades will put down barrages as per table of tasks attached.

9. (a) The O.C. 33rd Brigade, R.F.A. will detail a senior officer for the operation to report to G.O.C. 119th Infantry Brigade.

   (b) The O.C. 181st Bde. R.F.A. will be in personal touch with G.O.C. 120th Infantry Bde. for the operation and will control the artillery support for the attack on VILLERS PLOUICH.

   (c) The O.C. 178th Bde. will control the Artillery support for the attack on BEAUCAMP.

10. The most advanced troops have been ordered to light flares when called upon to do so by contact aeroplanes.

11. Watches will be synchronized at 3.30 p.m. and 6.30 p.m. 23rd April.

12. Acknowledge.

F. A. Pile

Issued at 8.00 a.m.

Major, R.A.,
Brigade Major, 40th Divisional Artillery.

Copy No.
	1.	File.
	2 & 3.	War Diary.
	4.	G.O.C. R.A.
	5.	Brigade Major.
	6.	Staff Captain.
	7 to 11.	33rd Brigade R.F.A.
	12 to 16.	91st Brigade R.F.A.
	17 to 21.	178th Brigade R.F.A.
	22 to 26.	181st Brigade, R.F.A.
	27.	40th D. A. C.
	28 to 30.	40th Divn. "G".
	31 to 33.	119th Inf. Bde.
	34 to 36.	120th Inf. Bde.
	37.	8th Divisional Artillery.
	38.	20th Divisional Artillery.
	39 to 40.	R.A. XV Corps.
	41 to 43.	H.A. XV Corps.

14th (S)Bn. Argyll and Sutherland Highlanders.

Nominal Roll of Officers, wounded in action on 24/4/17.

(1)
Captain J.D.Mackie,
" C.W.H.Miller,
" A.Pollock,
2nd Lieut. D.Biggart,
" R.Athey,
" W.F.Walker,
" R.H.Law.

Nominal Roll of Other Ranks wounded in action 24/4/17
"A"Company.

No. 12672	L/Sgt.	P.McNeill,
8973	Cpl.	D.McIntee,
9357	L/Cpl.	J.Angus,
12376	"	C.E.Forsyth
12813	"	W.L.Morrison,
11764	xxx Pte.	J.L.Benson,
40552	Pte.	J.Campbell,
40553	"	P.Carroll,
9934	"	R.Crawford,
9043. 40060	"	W.Docherty,
9047 xxxxx	"	D Norrie
17084	"	H.Edgecombe,
12204	"	J.Ewart,
9786	"	T.Goodwin,
13395	"	J.Gibb,
40734	"	J.Greenlees (Died of wounds 25/4/17).
12562	"	J.Hutton,
13525	"	J.S.Jarvie,
13688	"	J.Reilly,
13876	"	R.M.Scott,
7349	"	J.Turner,
9029	"	J.Wood,
40250	"	M. Cameron - slight (Rejoined 29.4.17).

"B" Company.

No 7692	Sgt.	A.Flockhart,
9813	"	H.O.Cockburn,
9105	"	H.Dryden,
9130 xxxxxxxxxx	L/Cpl.	C.D.M. Wallace
15873	Cpl.	W.Kerr,
8985	L/Cpl.	A.McKenzie,
14390	"	J.F.Watson,
9959	"	A.Falconer,
9301	"	J.D.Davidson,
9810	"	R.H.Patterson,
13519	Pte.	A.Brown,
12586	"	W.Blair,
8922	"	R.Aitken,
13868	"	A.L.Campbell,
9177	"	J.B.Coull,
4310	"	J.Collier,
12063	"	S.Donaldson,
8978	"	J.M.Daes,
5515	"	J.Farrow,
3275	"	J.Hendry,
9515	"	J.Herbert,
40742	"	D.Hannah,
12803	"	D.Imrie,
5923	"	A.Imrie,
43010	"	J.Kelly,
11703	"	J.Linn,

14th (S)Bn. Argyll and Sutherland Highlanders.

The following Officers were killed in action :-
on 24/4/17

Captain J.Urquhart,
2nd Lieut. D.V.Humphreys,
Lieut. W.Lawson,
2nd Lieut. R.S.Forbes,
2nd Lieut. K.S.Runciman,

The following Other Ranks were killed in action :- on 24/4/17.

"A"Company.
No. 8960 L/Sgt. A.McCurdie,
    12563 L/Cpl. L.T.Hill,
    9824 ,, T.McKinley,
    40724 Pte. J.Donnelly,
    5035 ,, J.Crawford,
    12599 ,, G.Kemp,
    8031 ,, L. Newsum,
    12995 ,, J.Reid,

"B"Company,
No 9817 Sgt. H.R.Seaward,
    9838 Cpl. J.Heriot,
    8939 ,, J.Seals,
    9684 L/Cpl. J.McKenzie,
    12355 ,, A.D.Ross,
8902 8967 Pte. G.C.Berry,
    9225 Sgt E.R.McINROY
    9148 Pte W.D.Duncan.
    8944 ,, P.Dunn,
    270036 ,, R.McCulloch,
    14304 ,, T.Mabon,
    9044 ,, A.Nicolson,
    9908 ,, W.Rust,
    3418 ,, J.Paton,
    14282 ,, A.Stark,
    5044 ,, A.B.Watson,
    12321 Sgt. J.GRAY

"C"Company,
No. 13802 L/Sgt. D.Lambie,
    12726 Cpl. W.A.Smith.
    12140 Cpl. P.Couper,
    9767 L/Cpl. J.E.Dewar,
    12129 Pte. S.Aitken,
    12108 ,, R.Bain,
    12453 ,, W.Hislop,
    15916 ,, J.N.Milne,
    15530 ,, W.Murphy,
    40182 ,, T.Thompson,

"D"Company.
No. 9197 Sgt. H.Nairn,
    9013 ,, H.N.Alexander,
    15646 L/Sgt. A.Galbraith,
    12566 Cpl. W.Weatherill,
    9842 L/Cpl. C.E.Green,
    13643 ,, A.W.Thain,
    13214 Pte. B.Campbell,
    40789 ,, R.Davis,
    14369 ,, G.Glen,
    13493 ,, T.C.Graham,
    12588 ,, A.S.Henderson,
    12753 ,, H.Hankinson,
    13384 ,, P.D.Higgins,
    12654 ,, R.Jack,
    14079 ,, T.Kempton,
    7525 ,, H.Laird,
    13401 ,, J.N.Melville,
    xxxxxxxxxxxxxxxxxxxxxx
    9120 ,, T.McDermid,
    14283 ,, A.Mair,
    14873 ,, A.McDonald,
    16262 ,, J.McPherson

14th Argyll and Sutherland Highlanders.

Nominal Roll of Other Ranks wounded in action 24/4/17.   Contd.

"D" Company.

No.	13388	Pte.	R.R.Grieve
No.	13315	L/Cpl.	A.Hiatt,
	14139	,,	G.Wanne,
	13148	,,	A.J.Loutit,
	9349	,,	R.Irvine,
	9862	Pte.	A.Auld,
	1336?	,,	W.J.Auld,
	13331	,,	G.Brden,
	13394	,,	G.Beveridge,
	14697	,,	W.G.H.Bryden *Rejoined 28/4/17.*
	~~9040~~	,,	~~J.Brown,~~ *Now reported Killed.*
	8445	,,	J.Carrigan,
	40765	,,	J.Drummond,
	14067	,,	P.Fraser,
	~~4350~~	,,	~~J.Garene~~ *Now reported Killed.*
	14308	,,	A.Hall,
	2314	,,	J.Hunter,
	40792	,,	T.Kneebone,
	19539	,,	R.Kennedy
	13582	,,	W.Lilburn,
	40763	,,	P.Moden,
	14305	,,	J.M.McIntosh,
	40803	,,	A.McInnes,
	9322	,,	T.McKee,
	9881	,,	W.Mackie,
	12316	,,	G.McQuillan,
	40796	,,	T.McIvor,
	40797	,,	D.McIvor,
	40763	,,	D.Spence,
	13651	,,	R.D.Thomson,
	9878	,,	A.D.Wilson,
	8460	,,	J.Wilson, *Rejoined 26.4.17.*
	13873	,,	J.S.Walker,
	49844	,,	R.N.Nicol
	13503	L/C	J.O.Callender. *Rejoined 28/4/17.*

The following Other Ranks were "Missing" on 24/4/17.

"A" Company.

No. ~~40590 Pte. M.Cameron,~~ *Now reported wounded Slight.*
~~10401 ,, M.McInnes, "D" Company,~~ *Now reported Killed.*

"D" Company.

No.	9069	Pte.	A.Wood,
	14261	L/Cpl.	G.D.Paterson, (Prisoner of War, Believed).
	13650	,,	R.N.Henderson,
	13301	,,	W.S.Gordon,
	~~13503~~	,,	~~J.O.Callender~~ *Now reported wounded.*
	~~9190~~	Pte.	~~W.Angus,~~ *Now reported Killed.*
	~~21800~~	,,	~~J.Milligan,~~ *Now reported Killed.*
	~~13005~~	,,	~~R.M.Gash,~~ *Delete.*
	13396	,,	T.S.Stewart,
	29xx		

The following Other Ranks were wounded slightly "AT DUTY".

No. 8850 Sgt. C.H.Chisholm, 26/4/17. "A" Company.
    9735 Pte. J.D.MacNaughton, ,,   "G"

14th (S)Bn. Argyll and Sutherland Highlanders.

Nominal Roll of Other Ranks wounded on 24/4/17 Raid.

"B"Company.

```
       40802 Pte. R.McCullum,
No.     242  Pte. D.McWilliams,
       40809  ..  F.McTaggart,
      270047  ..  D.Mathieson,
       14975  ..  W.H.C.Matthew,
        8683  ..  W.A.Patterson,
       11881  ..  J.Patterson,
       20676  ..  D.M.Robertson,
        8054  ..  B.G.Smith,
       14977  ..  J.Sutherland,
        9988  ..  W.Smith,
         365  ..  J.R.Thomson,
       13400  ..  G.White,
        9104  ..  J.H. Purvis
```

"C"Company.

```
No.   9918 Sgt.   A.Telfer,
         (Died of wounds 24/4/17)
      8853 Sgt.   R.Fleming,
     12808 Cpl.   D.Harris,
      9047 L/Cpl. W.Ballingall,
       855  ..    A.Hogg,
     13032  ..    H.McGuffin,
     12545  Rtd.  J.W.Boyd,
     15169  ..    S.Bickley,
     13285  ..    G.Buchanan,
     12433  ..    G.Clark,
     13315  ..    A.Craig,
     16802  ..    R.Cameron,
     40756  ..    W.Creelman,
     40757  ..    A.G.Crystal,
     11827  ..    C.Coyle,
      5855  ..    F.Grimshaw,
     15395  ..    D.Grant, (slight)
     14375  ..    L.Hutt,
     14722  ..    E.Hedges,(slight)
     11941  ..    J.McAlpine,
     40514  ..    R.Montague,
     40515  ..    J.Morrison,
     40610  ..    J.Nelson,
      7575  ..    F.Newman,
     40619  ..    F.Onyet,
     13354  ..    W.Pitcher,
     13910  ..    J.Philip,
     15049  ..    W.Patrick,
     15970  ..    C.Smith,
     12958  ..    J.Simpson,
     40704  ..    P.Travers,
     40780  ..    W.Taig,
     16355  ..    H.Taylor   deponied 28.4.17.
      9530  ..    J.Welsh,
     12790  ..    S.F.Wright,
```

"D"Company.

```
No. 43107 Pte. Fyfe, T.
         (Died of wounds 25/4/17)
     1184 Sgt.  A.James,
     8849  ,,   J.Kidd,
    13885  ..   A.McDougall,
     9917  ..   R.Clarkson,
     8563  ..   C.Campbell,
     9864 Cpl.  F.C.Ross,
    10579 L/Cpl. W.J.Pendrich,
    12397  ..   A.Whyte,
    12110  ..   R.Porter,
    14860  ..   A.L.Swinton,
                R.H.Allan,
```

14th (S.Bn. Argyll and Sutherland Highlanders.

Other Ranks killed in action on 24/4/17. Contd.

"D"Company,
No. 12375 Pte. J.M.Menzies,
    18253 ,, J.C.Nash,
    14281 ,, J.Patterson,
    13490 ,, J.F.Robertson,
    9902 ,, E.A.Smith,
    15865 ,, T.Stoddart,
    40768 ,, R.Thomson,
    9422 ,, R.C.Thomson,

    14359 ,, J. R. Grant.
    9106 ,, D. Angus.
    8040 ,, J. BROWN.
    12832 ,, J. MILLIGAN.
    40604 ,, M. McInnes.   Coy. "B"

Artillery Table of Tasks for 24th April, (To accompany 40th Div. Order No.5.).

XVth Corps Heavy Artillery.

Time.	Units.	Targets.		Rate of fire.	Notes.
Zero to +12.	6" Hows.	(1)	LA VACQUERIE.	Slow.	
Zero to +36.	-do-	(2)	Trench in R.14.a.90.00 R.14.b.15.20. R.14.b.20.15	Medium.	
Zero to +66.	-do-	(3)	Ravine R.8.c & R.14.d.	Medium.	
Zero to +36.	-do-	(4)	North end of VILLERS PLOUICH in R.7.	Medium.	
+36 to +66.	-do-	(5)	R.7.central.	Medium.	
+36 to +120	-do-	(6)	Road R.7.b.10.70 to R.1.d.10.70.	Slow.	
+36 to +120	-do-	(7)	BOAR COPSE.	Slow.	
Zero to +120.	60 Pdrs.	(1)	Trench R.21.b to R.15.c.	Slow.	
-do-	-do-	(2)	GOOD MAN FARM.	Slow.	
-do-	-do-	(3)	Search Valley R.8.central to R.2.b.	Slow.	
-do-	-do-	(4)	Road R.7.b.10.70 to R.1.d.10.70.	Slow.	
-do-	-do-	(5)	Valley Q.11.b.90.80. to Q.6.a.10/ -	Slow.	

At +120 all batteries stop firing or as situation necessitates.

Artillery Table of Tasks for 24th April.(To accompany 40th D.A.Order No.56.).

181st Brigade, R.F.A.

Time.	Batteries.	Targets.	Rate of Fire.	Ammunition.	Notes.
Zero to +6.	3 - 18-pdr Batteries.	Trench (reported) R.13.d.30.35 to R.13.c.05.70.	Rapid.	"A"	
+6 to +26.	-do-	Creep at rate of 50 yards lifts every 2 minutes to line:- R.14.a.10.00. to R.13.a.70.85. where Barrage remains stationary.	Medium.	"A"	
+26 to +36.	-do-	-do-	-do-	"A.X."	
+36 to +56.	-do-	Again creep at same rate to line R.14.a.95.65 - R.7.d.20.62. where Barrag remains stationary.	3 rounds per gun per minute.	"A"	
+56 to +66.	-do-		Medium.	"A"	
+66 to +90.	-do-	Again cr p at sam: rat. to lin. R.8.d.70.30 - R.8.a.95.15 -R.7.b.70.50 wh.re Barrag remains stationary.	Medium.	"A"	
+90 to +120.	-do-		Slow.	"A.X."	
	1 4.5" How.Bty.				※ These points are as given in captured enemy map.
Zero to +66.	{ 1 Section. 1 Section.	M.G. at ※ R.8.c.55.20. M.G. at R.14.a.50.90.	Medium.	"B.X."	
+66 to +120 both ab.v. s.ctions.		Lift to GOOD MAN FARM (R.9.a.)	Slow.	"B.X."	
Zero to +36.	1 section.	M.G. at ※ R.13.b.95.50.	Medium.	"B.X."	
+36 to +66.	-do-	Lift to ravin. R.14.b.20.70-R.8.c.75.20.	Slow.	"B.X."	
+66 to +120.	-do-	lift to GOOD MAN FARM(R.9.a.).	Slow.	"B.X.".	
		At +120 all batt.ri.s stop firing or as situation necessitates.			

Artillery Table of Tasks for 24th April (To accompany 40th D.A. Order No.50).

278th Bde. R.F.A. (Continued)

Time.	Battery.	Target.	Rate of fire.	Ammunition. & Notes.
	1 4.5" How.Battery.			
Zero to +12.	1 section.	Post at Q.12.d.40.10.	Rapid.	"E.X."
+12 to +66.	-do-	Lifts to R.7.central.	Medium.	"E.X."
+66 to +120.	-do-	Lifts to line R.7.b.20.60 to R.7.b.00.60.	Slow.	"B.X."
Zero to +36.	1 section.	M.G's. { R.7.c.55.15. / R.7.c.35.25.	Medium.	"E.X."
+36 to +66	-do-	Lifts to R.7. central.	Medium.	"B.X."
+66 to +120.	-do-	Lifts to line R.7.b.20.60 to R.7.b.00.60.	Medium.	"B.X."
Zero to +66	1 section.	R.7.central. line	Medium.	"B.X."
+66 to +120.	-do-	Lifts to/R.7.b.20.60.-to R.7.b.00.60.	Slow.	"E.X."

At +120 all batteries stop firing or as situation necessitates.

Artillery Table of Tasks for 24th April.(To accompany 40th D.A.Order No.50).

178th Brigade., R.F.A.

Time.	Batteries.	Targets.	Rate of fire.	Ammunition.	Notes.
Zero to + 6.	1 18-pdr Bty.	Line R.13.c.05.70 to Q.18.b.90.00.	RAPID.	"A"	
+ 6 to + 26.	-do-	Creep at rate of 50 yards lift every 2 minutes to line R.13.a.70.85 to R.7.c.40.00 where.	Medium.	"A"	
+ 26 to + 36.	-do-	Barrage remains stationary.	Medium.	"A.X."	
+ 36 to + 56.	-do-	Again creep to at same rate to line R.7.d.10.65 - R.7.c.20.85 where.	3 rds per gun per minute.	"A"	
+ 56 to + 66.	-do-	Barrage remains stationary.	Medium.	"A"	
+ 66 to + 90.	-do-	Again creep at same rate. to line R.7.b.60.50 - R.7.c.65./.60 where.	Medium.	"A"	
+ 90 to + 120.	-do-	Barrage remains stationary.	Slow.	"A.X."	
Zero to + 6.	2 18-pdr Batteries.	Barrage trench(reported) Q.18.b.90.00.- Q.18.b.00.60.	RAPID.	"A"	
+ 6 to + 26.	-do-	Creep at rate of 50 yards lift every 2 minutes to line.- R.7.c.40.00 - Q.12.d.00.60 where.	Medium.	"A"	
+ 26 to + 36.	-do-	Barrage remains stationary.	Medium.	"A.X."	
+ 36 to + 56.	-do-	Again creep at same rate to line - R.7.c.80.85.- Q.12.b.00.60 where.	3 rds per gun per minute.	"A"	
+ 56 to + 66.	-do-	Barrage remains stationary.	Medium.	"A"	
+ 66 to + 78	-do-	Again creep at same rate to line - R.7.a.65.60 - Q.11.b.00.60 where.	Medium.	"A"	
+ 78 to + 120.	-do-	Barrage remains stationary.	Slow fire.	"A.X".	

Artillery Table of Tasks for 24th April. (To accompany 4th D.A. Order No.5).

91st Brigade, R.F.A.

Times.	Batteries.	Targets.	Rate of Fire.	Ammunition.	Notes.
Zero to +5.	3 – 18-pdr Batteries.	Barrage trench (reported) Q.18.b.00.65 to Q.17.b.9.75.	Rapid.	"A."	
+5 to +25.	–do–	Creep at rate of 50 yards lifts every 2 minutes to line Q.12.d.00.60 to Q.11.d.90.60. where	Medium.	"A."	
+25 to +35.	–do–	Barrage remains stationary.	Medium.	"A.X."	
+35 to +55	–do–	Again creeps at same rate to line Q.12.b.00.60 to Q.11.b.90.60 where	3 rounds per gun per minute.	"A."	
+55 to +120	–do–	Barrage remains stationary.	Slow.	"A.X."	
1. 4.5"How.Battery.					
+0 to +44	1 Section.	Q.12.central.	Medium.	"B.X."	
+44 to +120.	1 section	Lifts to trench Q.6.a.75.15 to Q.6.a.30.10.	Slow.	"B.X."	
0 to +20.	2 sections.	Headquarters in Q.12.c.	Medium.	"B.X."	
+44 to +120	–do–	Lifts to trench Q.6.a.75.15 to Q.6.a.30.10.	Slow.	"B.X."	

At +120 all batteries stop firing or as situation necessitates.

Artillery Table of Tasks for 24th April, To accompany 40th D.A. Order No.50.

33rd Brigade, R.F.A.

Time.	Batteries.	Target.	Rate of fire.	Ammunition.	Notes.
Zero to + 6.	3 18-pdr Batteries.	R.20.a.75.52 - R.13.d.30.35.	RAPID	"A"	One of these batteries to be detailed to the zone covering the strong point in R.14.c.
+ 6 to + 26.	-do-	Creep at rate of 50 yards lift every 2 minutes to line:-- R.14.d.32.32-R.14.a.10.00 where	MEDIUM.	"A"	R.20.a.07.90.-- R.13.d.86.09.-- R.14.b.13.10. R.14.b.45.45.) Zone marked blue in attached map.
+ 26 to + 36.	-do-	Barrage becomes stationary.	MEDIUM	"A.X." (zone	
+ 36 to + 56.	-do-	Again creep at same rate to line:-- R.14.b.95.20 - R.14.a.95.70 where	3 rounds per gun per minute.	"A"	
+ 56 to + 66.	-do-	Barrage becomes stationary.	MEDIUM.	"A"	
+ 66 to + 90.	-do-	Again creeps at same rate to line R.14.b.95.20 -R.8.d.70.30 where	MEDIUM.	"A"	
+ 90 to + 120.	-do-	Barrage becomes stationary.	SLOW.	"A.X."	
	1--4,5"(How.)Bty.				
Zero to + 12	1 section	M.G. at R.14.c.40.80 lift to Trench R.21.b.20.40.to R.21.b.20.80.	RAPID	"B.X."	
+ 12 + 60	"	LA VACQUERIE	MEDIUM	"B.X."	
+ 60 + 120	"	"	SLOW.	"B.X."	
Zero to + 36.	2 sections.	Trench R.14.b.15.25 to R.14.c.60.90. lift to Trench R.21.b.20.80.to R.15.d.00.60.	MEDIUM.	"B.X."	
+ 36 to + 60.	"	--do-- LA VACQUERIE	MEDIUM.	"B.X."	
+ 60 to + 120.	"	--do-- LA VACQUERIE	SLOW.	"B.X."	

At + 120 all batteries stop firing or as situation demands.

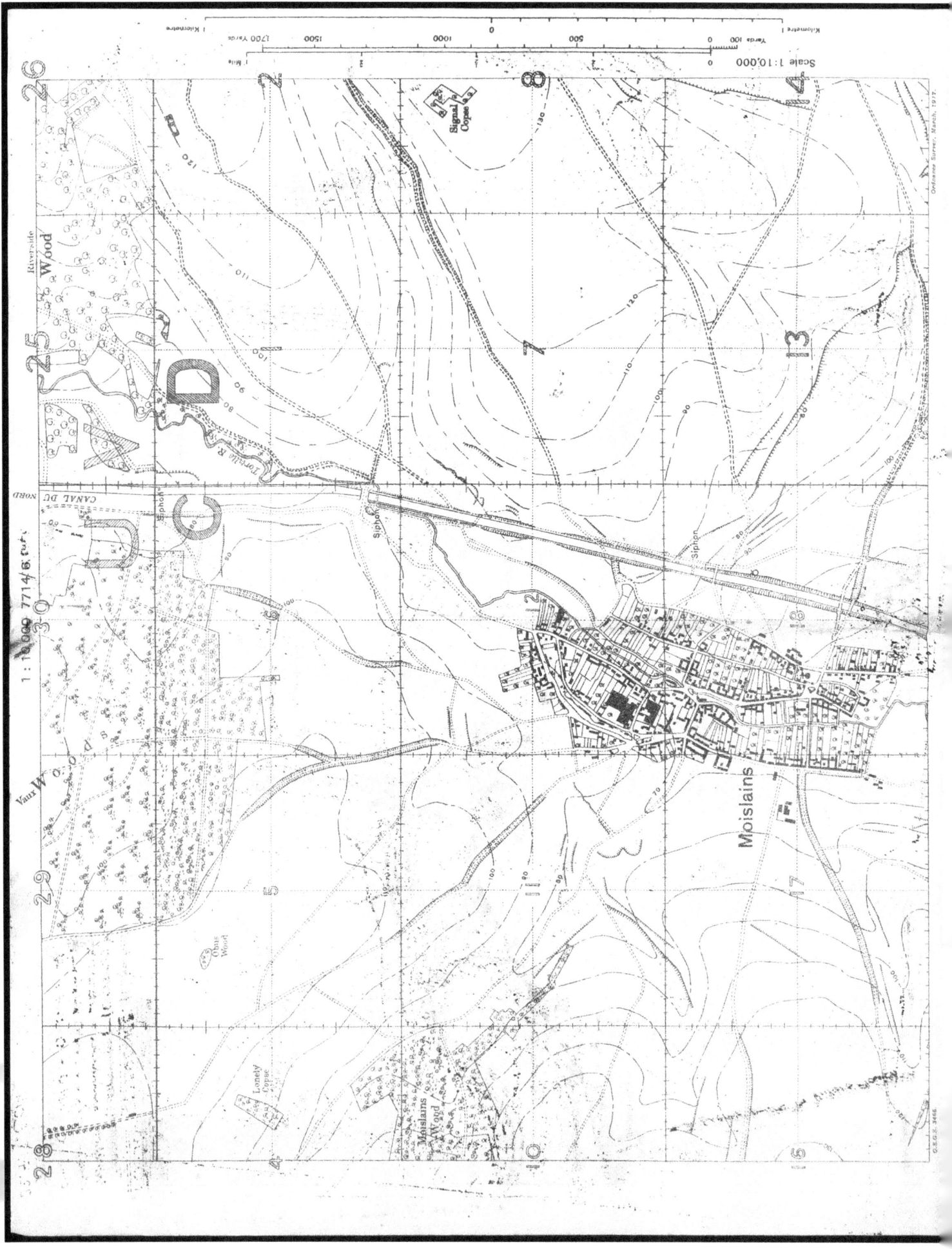

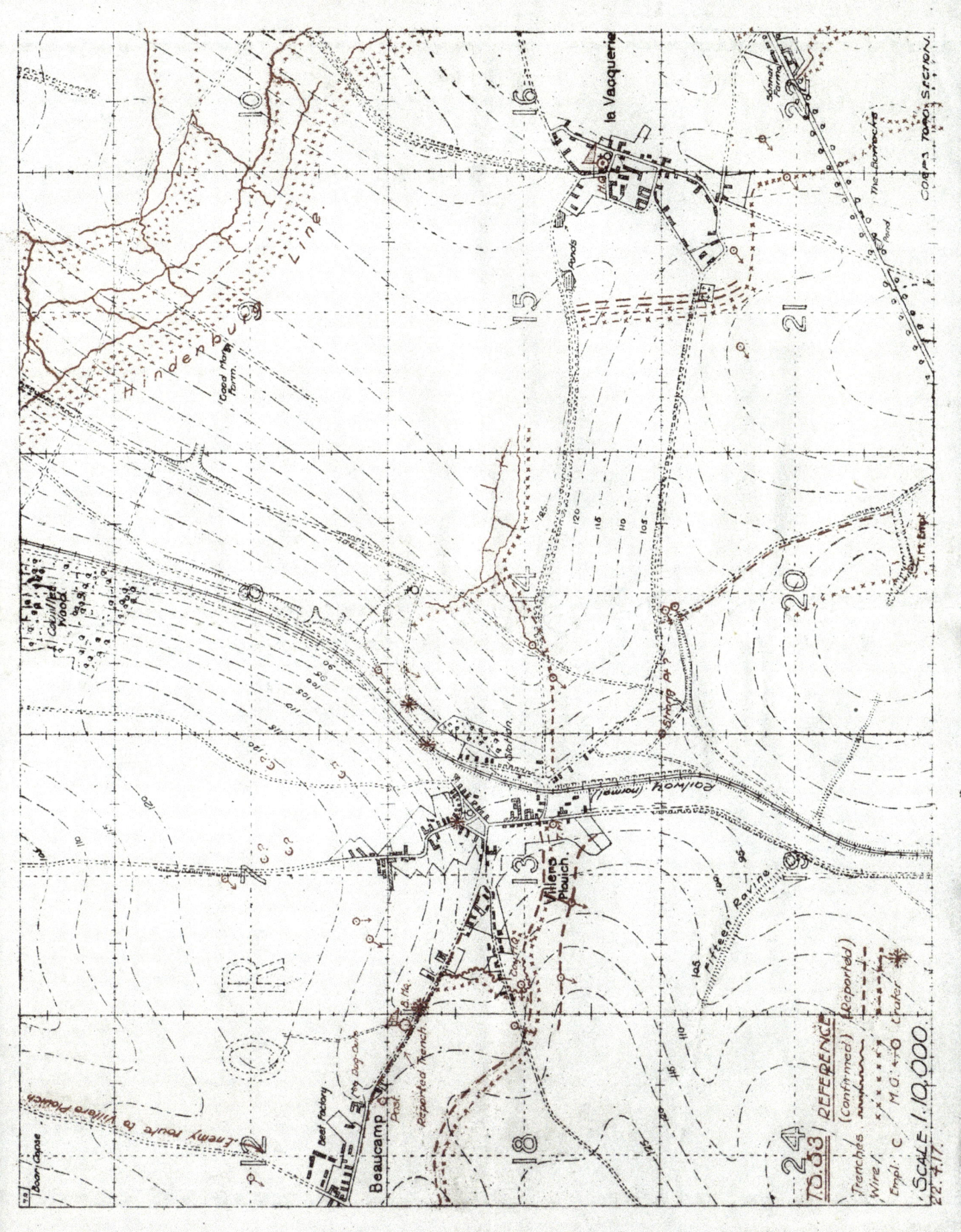

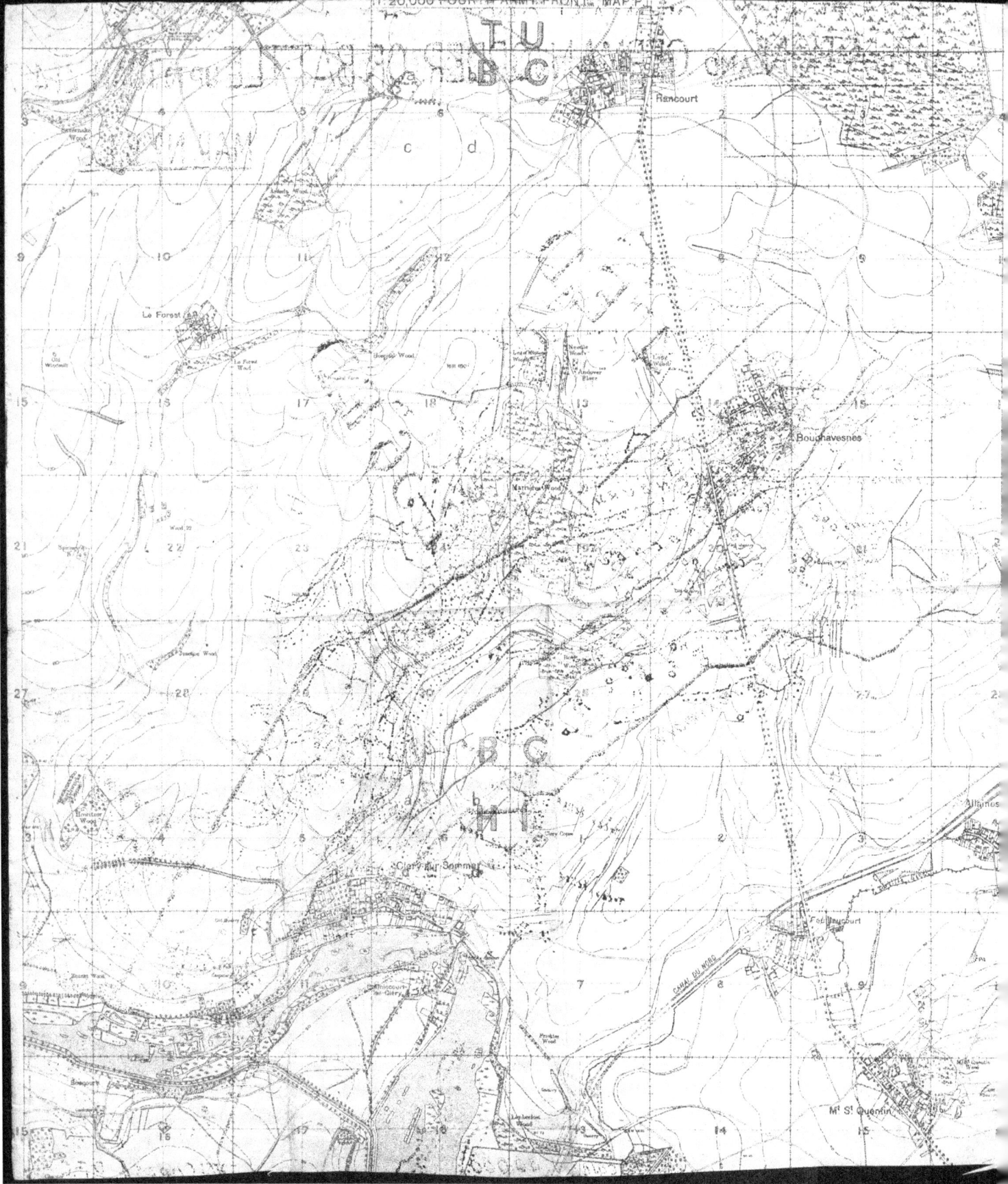

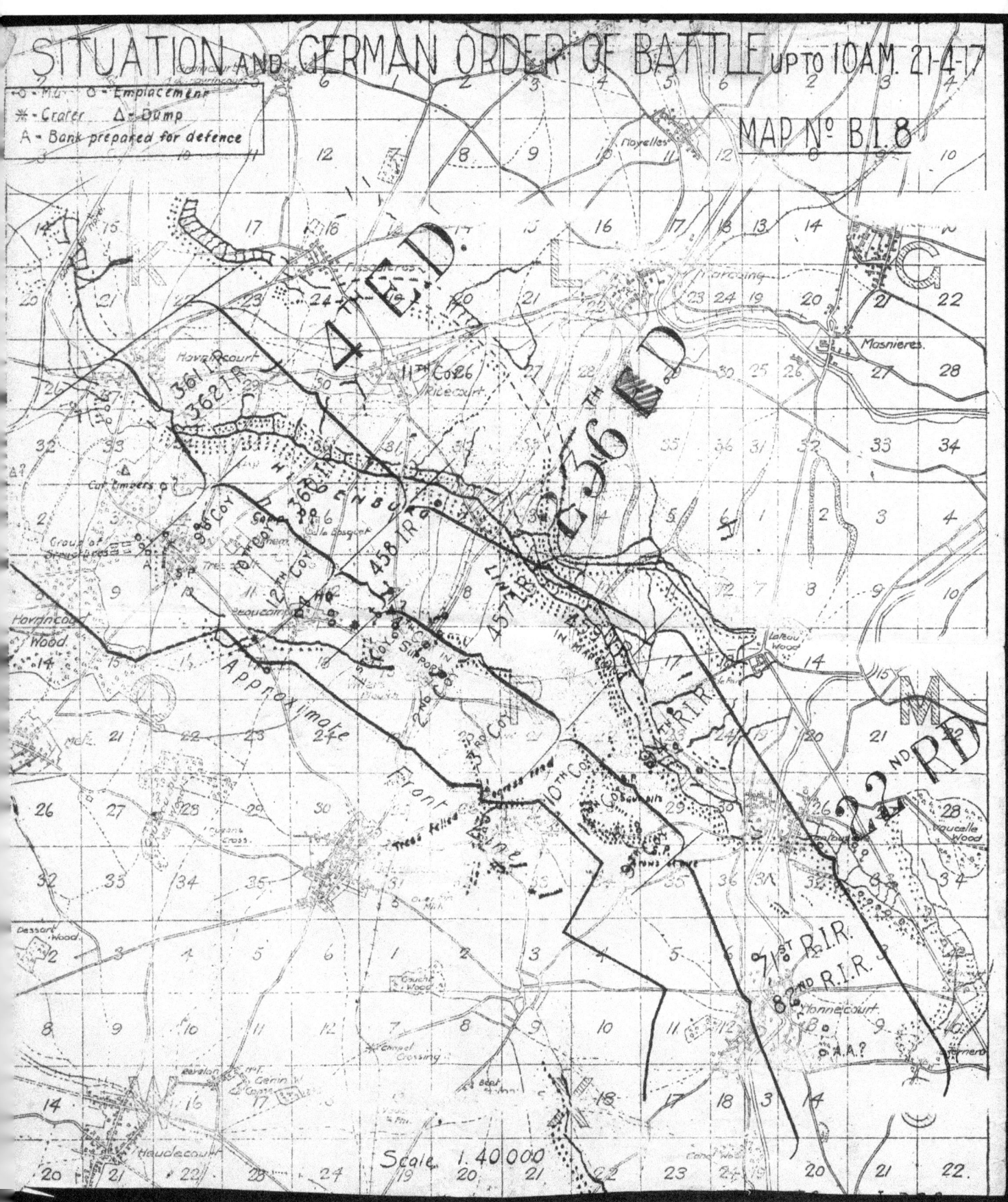

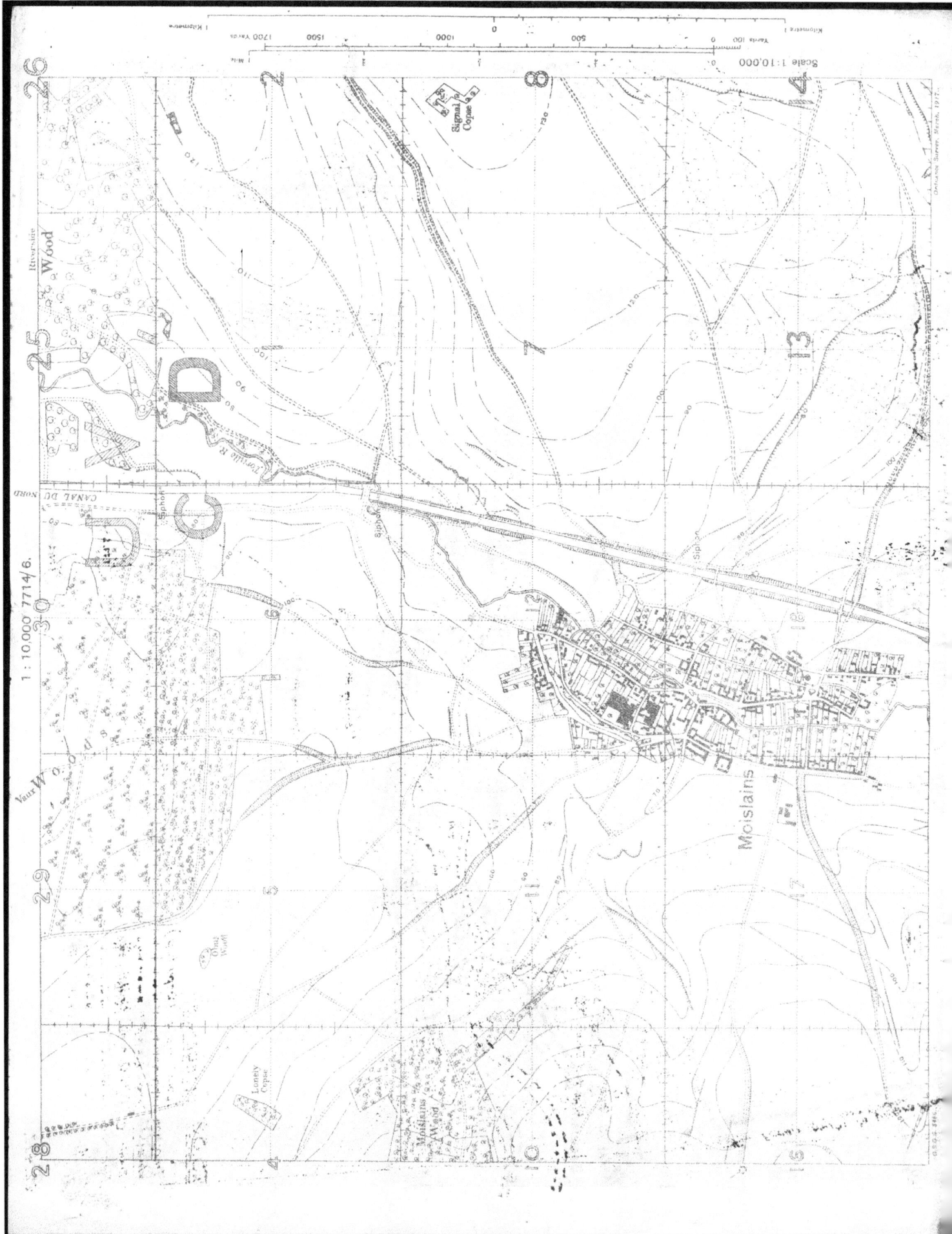

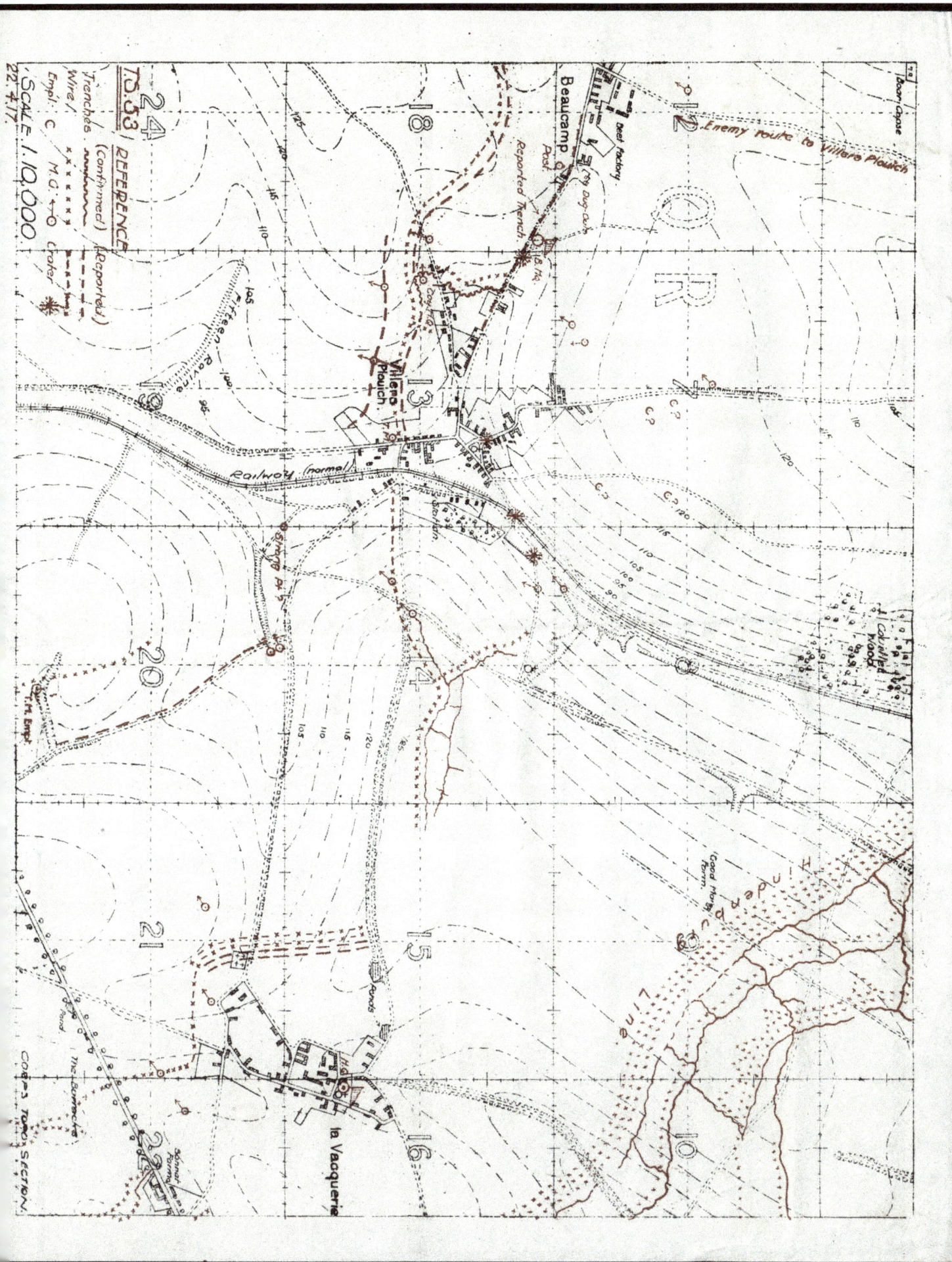

Reference 120th Infantry Brigade Order No.99, dated 25/4/17.

1. Transport Lines.
The 1st Line Transport of Units and Q.M's. Stores will remain in present locations.

2. Water.
The 11th R. Lanc. R. will arrange to hand over 50 tins of water to relieving Unit - 21st Middlesex R.
The Right Line Battalion can draw 48 full tins from Brigade Ammunition Dump, GOUZECOURT WOOD.
Rations and water carts of 11th R.Lanc. R. should be taken to DESART WOOD. Those of H.L.I. and A.& S.H. to GOUZEAUCOURT WOOD.
Rations for East Surreys will remain at EQUANCOURT.

3. Petrol Tins.
As many empty tins as possible should be taken from the line and handed in at Dump, GOUZEAUCOURT WOOD.

4. Ammunition.
Ammunition etc. at both Brigade Dumps will be handed over tomorrow, 26th inst.

5. Brigade Dumps.
The Parties i/c Brigade Dumps will be relieved tomorrow 26th inst. by 121st Brigade and they will then rejoin their Units.

6. Brigade Tools.
Brigade Reserve of Tools at Dump, GOUZEAUCOURT WOOD will be handed over o 121st Brigade who will arrange to leave their tools at their Quartermaster's Stores, ETRICOURT.

"C" Form.
MESSAGES AND SIGNALS.

Army Form C. 2123.
(In books of 100).
No. of Message_____

Prefix SM Code____ Words 24

Received. From FBIR By [sig]

Sent, or sent out. At____m. To____ By____

Office Stamp. F/25/

Charges to collect

Service Instructions. FB1

Handed in at____ Office____m. Received 8.5 m.

TO Y NCORD

Sender's Number: HB17H
Day of Month: 25
In reply to Number:
A A A

Para 6 appendix to brigade order no 99 does not apply to tools on battalion charge aaa

FROM PLACE & TIME UNCLOSE 7.50 pm

MARCH TABLE TO ACCOMPANY 120th Infantry Brigade ORDER NO&99

DATE.	UNIT.	RELIEVED BY	TO WITHDRAW TO
April.			
25.	13th E.Surr.R.	13th Yorkshire R.	EQUANCOURT.
25.	11th R.Lanc.R.	21st Middlesex R.	DESART WOOD.
25.	14th High.L.I.		BRIGADE SUPPORT.
26.	14th High.L.I.	12th Suffolk R.	ETRICOURT.
26.	14th A.& S.H.	20th Middlesex R.	ETRICOURT.
26.	120th M.G.Coy.	121st M.G.Coy.	EQUANCOURT.
26.	120th T.M.Battery.	121st T.M.Battery.	EQUANCOURT.

SECRET.   COPY NO. 9
        120th INFANTRY BRIGADE ORDER NO.99.
                                        25/4/17.

1.   The 121st Infantry Brigade will relieve the 120th Infantry
Brigade in the Left Sector on the nights 25/26th and 26/27th April
in accordance with attached Table.

2.   From the night 25/26th April the left sector will be held on
a two battalion front. Dividing line between battalions : Strong
point R.7.central - R.13.a.0.8., both inclusive, to Right Battalion.

3.   Battalion in Brigade Support will have one Company in old German trench in Q.13.b. Remaining Companies will be in Advanced Line
of Resistance.

4.   Battalion in Brigade Reserve will be in GOUZEACOURT WOOD in Q.
22.d.

5.   All details of relief will be arranged between Commanding Officers
concerned.

6.   O.C. 120th M.G.Company and O.C. 120th T.M.Battery will arrange
relief direct with O.C. 121st M.G.Coy. and O.C. 121st T.M.Battery
respectively.

7.   G.O.C., 121st Infantry Brigade will assume command of the Left
Sector at 6 p.m. 26th inst.

8.   Brigade Headquarters will close at Q.27.c. at 6 p.m. 26th inst.
and will reopen at ETRICOURT at the same hour.

9.   ACKNOWLEDGE.

                                                    Captain,
                                                    Brigade Major,
Issued through Signals   120th Infantry Brigade.
at   4-50   p.m.

Copy No.1. G.O.C.   16. 121st Inf. Bde.
       2. Brigade Major.   17. 40th Div. "G"
       3. Staff Captain.   18. 40th Div. Art.
       4. File.   19. Brigade Signals.
       5. War Diary.   20. 60th Inf. Bde.
       6. 11th R. Lanc. R.   21. 40th Div. Train.
       7. 13th E. Surr. R.   22. Bde. Supply Officer.
       8. 14th High. L. I.
       9. 14th A.& S. H.
      10. 120th M.G.Coy.
      11. 120th T.M.B.
      12. 229th F.Coy.R.E.
      13. 178th Bde. R.F.A.
      14. 181st Bde. R.F.A.
      15. 000th Inf. Bde.

SECRET.   COPY NO. 2

120TH INFANTRY BRIGADE ORDER NO. 100.

25-4-17.

1. (a)   The line Q.11.b.9.1. inclusive Q.12 central - R.7.
         central R.8. will be consolidated as a first line of
         Defence.
   (b)   Strong post will be established about Q.11.b.9.1. -
         Q.12 central - R.7.central and R.8.c.2.2.
   (c)   A second line of defence for the front system is pro-
         vided by the old German trench Q.17.a.3.8. to R.13.d.1.9.
         Strong post with V. G. Defence being consolidated at
         Q.17.a.3.8. - Q.18.b.4.5. - R.13.c.5.9.

2. (a)   The front line system will be held by a garrison of one
         battalion each.
            Inter-battalion boundary:-
         R.7.central - R.13.a.0.8. both inclusive to Right Battn.
   (b)   Support Battalion trenches in Q.26 a. and c. and one
         Company Old German Trench West of VILLERS PLOUICH
   (c)   Reserve battalion GOUZEAUCOURT WOOD.
   (d)   Brigade Headquarters Q.27.c.5.5.
   (e)   There will be two Vickers Guns in each of the Strong
         Posts named in 1 (c).
            Two Vickers Guns at Q.17.d.4.8.   Two Guns at Q.17.b.4.1.
         and six Guns in the Main Line of Resistance. ?Where is this?

3.   The first requirement is to construct the Strong Posts
         named in 1 (b), and establish connecting posts to each with
         wire obstacles.
            O.C. 229th Field Coy. R.E. will provide working parties
         to assist the garrison in the construction of the posts at
         Q.11.b.9.1. R.7.central and R.8.c.2.2.

4.   An R.E.Dump. has been established at R.13.a.2.2.

5.   All tools, S.A.A. less 120 rounds per man, and bombs
         will be handed over in relief to-night to in-coming units in
         the front system.

6.   Movement by daylight over the forward slopes to the front
         system should be reduced to the smallest necessity, only Staff
         Officers on duty and Signallers should be permitted to pass
         over them without an order from Brigade Headquarters or O.C.
         Units.
            O.C. Battalions in the front line and Support Battalion
         will mount a guard in suitable position on roads to prevent
         straggling.

Issued through Signals   Captain,
at   9-30   p.m.   Brigade Major,
                                                       120th Infantry Brigade.

Copy No. 1. 14th High. L. I.
         2. 14th A. & S. Hrs.
         3. 13th Yorks Regt.
         4. 20th Middlesex Regt.

SECRET   COPY No. 9

120th Infantry Brigade Order No. 98.

1. The 60th Infantry Brigade on our left will attack and capture BILHEM tonight, 24/25th April, and the line of the road running from BILHEM Q.5.c.7.2. South Eastwards to road junction at Q.11.b.9.1. inclusive.

2. At the same hour 11th R. Lanc. R. will attack and capture the village of BEAUCAMP and consolidate the line Q.12.d.8.7. - Q.12. central - road junction Q.11.b.9.1. exclusive

3. The two assaulting Companies 11th R. Lanc. R., after relieving Arg.& Suth'd.Hrs. will get into position in new trench immediately South of BEAUCAMP. Supporting Companies will be in old German trench Q.18.a., Q.18.b.

4. Artillery Programme.

	Rate of Fire.
ZERO to ZERO plus 5	
18 prs. Barrage Line Q.12.d.4.4. to Q.12.c.0.4.	RAPID.
ZERO plus 5 to ZERO plus 15 Lift to Line Q.12.c.3.6. to Q.11.d.9.6.	MEDIUM.
ZERO plus 15 to ZERO plus 30 Lift to Line Q.12.a.7.5. to R.7.a.5.5.	SLOW.
ZERO plus 30 to ZERO plus 60 Q.12.a.7.5. to R.7.a.5.5.	1 Round per Gun every 2 min.

During 2 last barrages Batteries will search back 500 yards.

ZERO to ZERO plus 30	
4.5 HOWS 2 Hows on Q.6.a.25.10.	1 Round per
2 Hows on Q.6.d.20.00.	How per
1 How on Q.7.b.05.80.	Minute.
ZERO plus 30 to ZERO plus 60	
2 Hows on Q.6.a.25.10.	1 Round per
2 Hows on Q.6.d.20.00.	How every
1 How on Q.7.b.05.80.	3 Minutes.

5. O.C., 120th T.M.Battery will place two Mortars at the disposal of the O.C., 11th R. Lanc. R.

6. Tools will be taken over from the Arg.& Suth'd.Hrs. and will be carried by Supporting Companies.

7. Assaulting troops will light red flares when called upon to do so by contact aeroplanes.

8. Prisoners will be sent back to Brigade Headquarters.

9. Headquarters 11th R. Lanc. R. will be in strong point Q.17.a.

10. ZERO hour will be 4.15 a.m.

11. ACKNOWLEDGE.

Captain,
Brigade Major,
120th Infantry Brigade.

Issued through signals at 9.20 p.m.

1. G.O.C.	7. 13th E.Surr.R.	13. 178th Bde.R.F.A.
2. Brigade Major,	8. 14th High.L.I.	14. 181st Bde.R.F.A.
3. Staff Captain.	9. 14th A.& S.H.	15. QQC Inf.Bde.
4. File.	10. 120th M.G.Coy.	16. 121 Inf.Bde.
5. War Diary.	11. 120th T.M.B.	17. 40th Div."G"
6. 11th R. Lanc R.	12. 229th F.Coy.R.E.	18. 40th Div.Art.
		19. Brigade Signals.
		20. 60th Inf.Bde.

SECRET.　　　　　　　　　　　　　　　　　　　　　　　　COPY No. 9

120th Infantry Brigade Order No.97.

24/4/17.

1.   11th R. Lanc. R. will relieve the 14th Arg.& Suth'd. Highrs. in the trenches South of BEAUCAMP on the night 24/25th April, as follows :-

2.   2 Companies 11th R. Lanc. R., at present in the Line of Resistance, to relieve the 14th Arg.& Suth'd. Hrs. by 12 midnight.
  The 2 Companies of 11th R. Lanc. R. at and about strong point 17.a. will be relieved by 1 Company Arg.& Suth'd. Hrs., strength at least 2 Officers and 60 O.Ranks, as soon after midnight as possible.

3.   Headquarters 14th Arg. & Suth'd. Hrs., less one Company, will withdraw to Brigade Reserve at GOUZEAUCOURT WOOD, on completion of relief.

4.   All details to be arranged between Commanding Officers concerned.

5.   ACKNOWLEDGE.

　　　　　　　　　　　　　　　　　　　　　　　　　　Captain,
　　　　　　　　　　　　　　　　　　　　　　　　Brigade Major,
　　　　　　　　　　　　　　　　　　　　　120th Infantry Brigade.

Issued through signals
at　　　　9　　p.m.

Copy No. 1. G.O.C.
　　　　2. Brigade Major.
　　　　3. Staff Captain.
　　　　4. File.　　　　　　　　　　　12. 229th Field Coy. R.E.
　　　　5. War Diary.　　　　　　　　13. 178th Brigade R.F.A.
　　　　6. 11th R. Lanc. R.　　　　　14. 181 Brigade R.F.A.
　　　　7. 15th H. Surr. R.　　　　　15. 119th Infantry Brigade.
　　　　8. 14th High. L. I.　　　　　16. 121st Infantry Brigade.
　　　　9. 14th Arg.& Suth'd.Hrs.　　17. 40th Division "G"
　　　10. 120th M.G.Cby.　　　　　　18. 40th Division Art.
　　　11. 120th T.M.B.　　　　　　　19. 60　Inf Bde

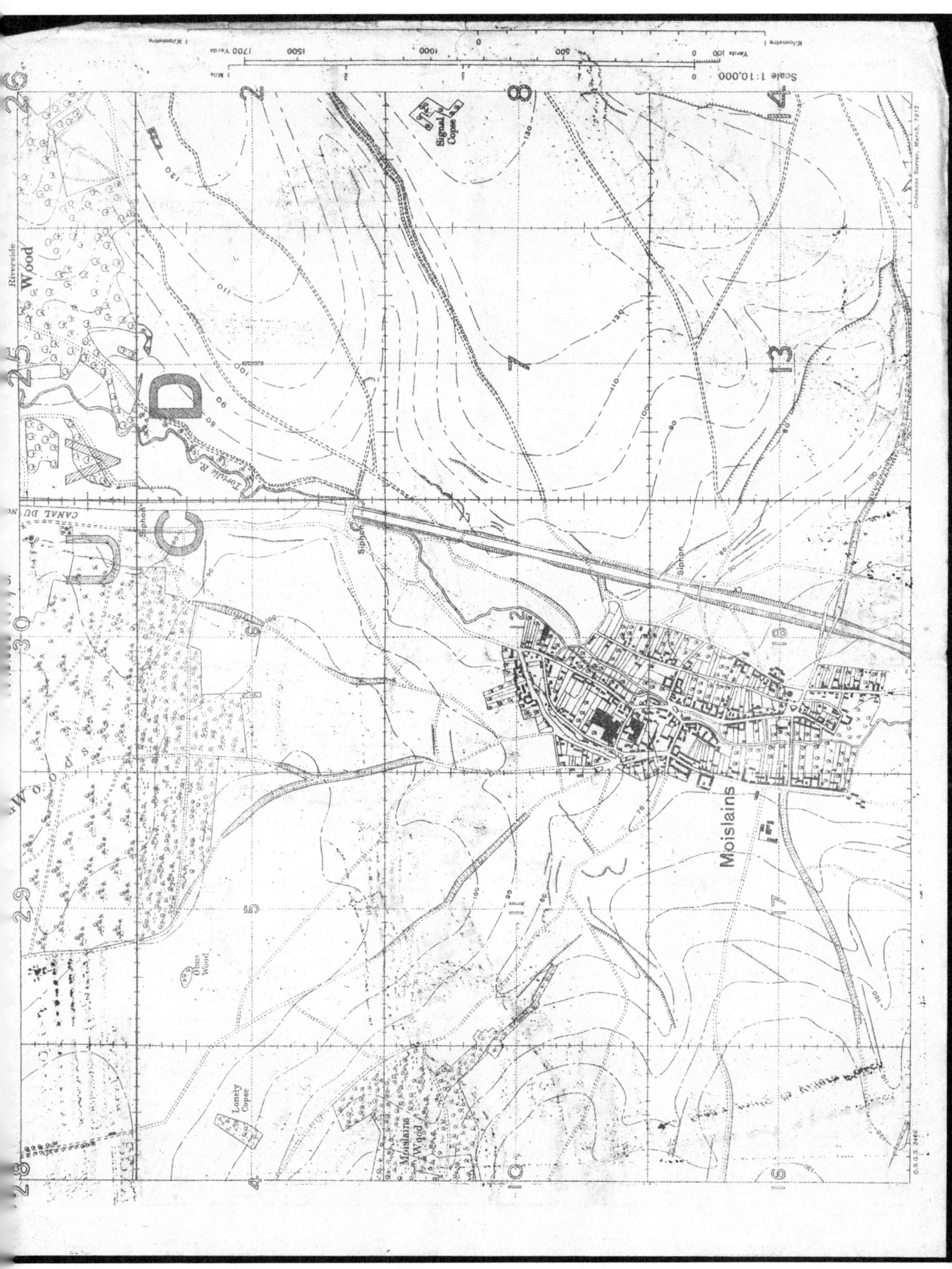

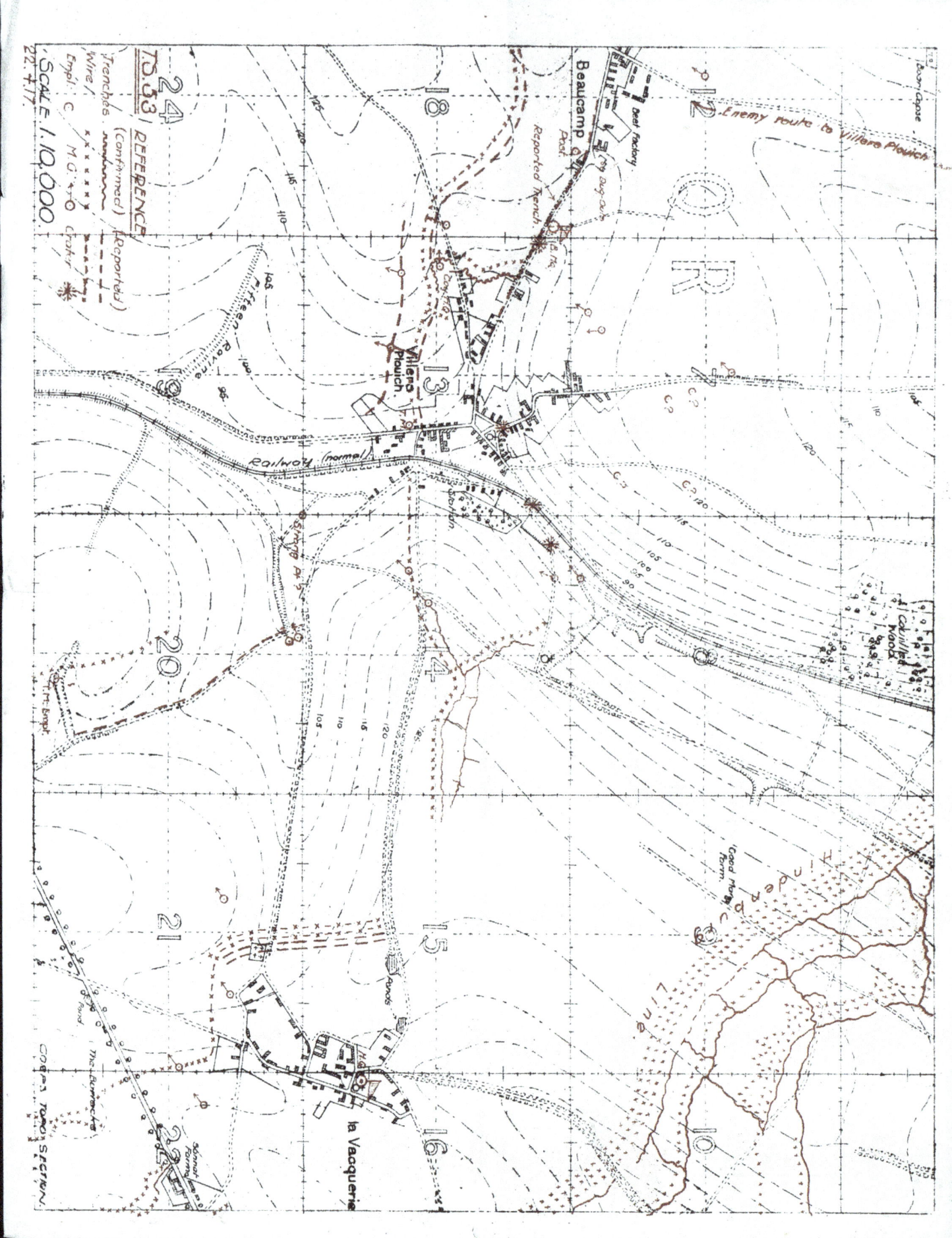

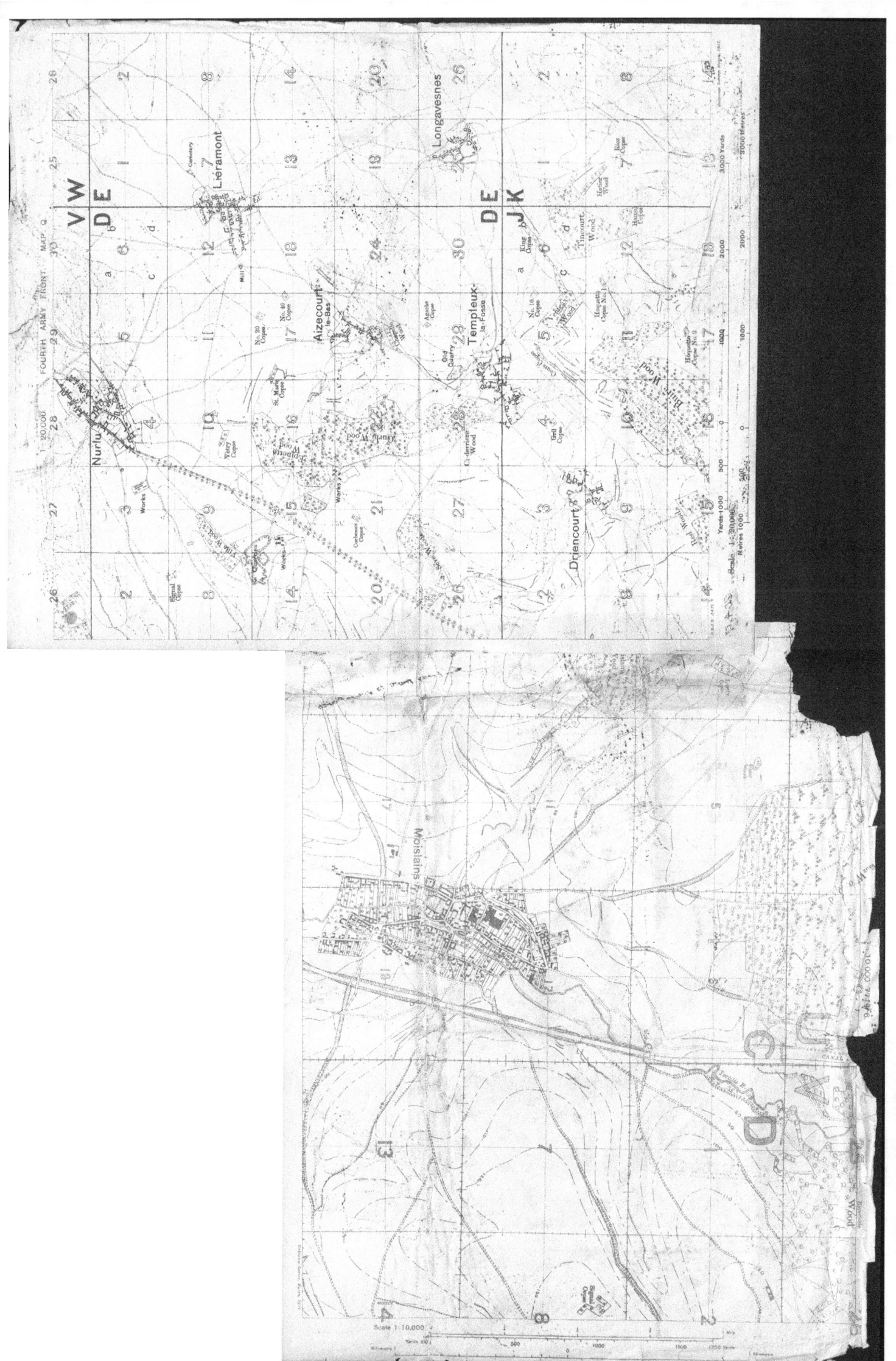

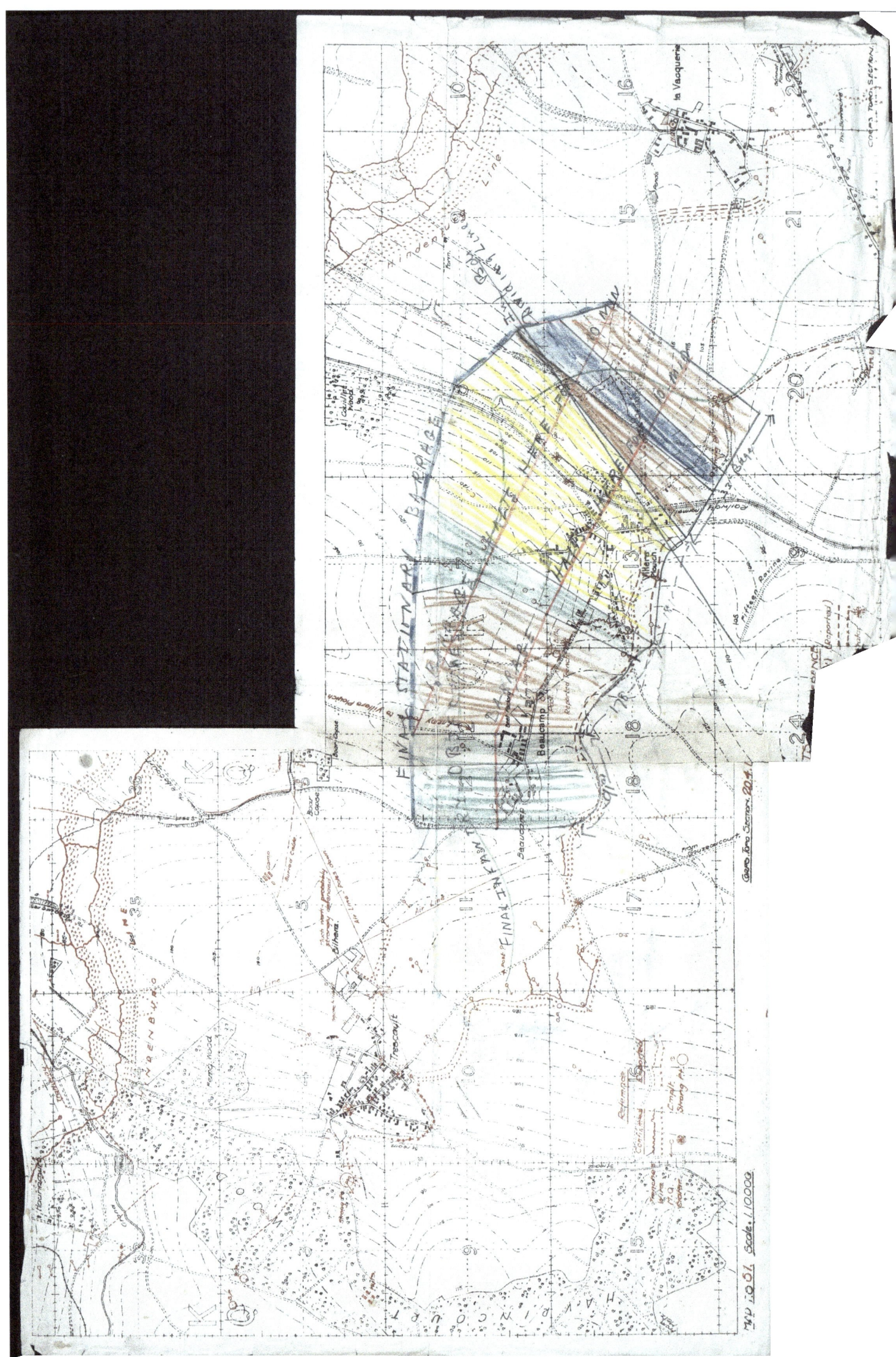

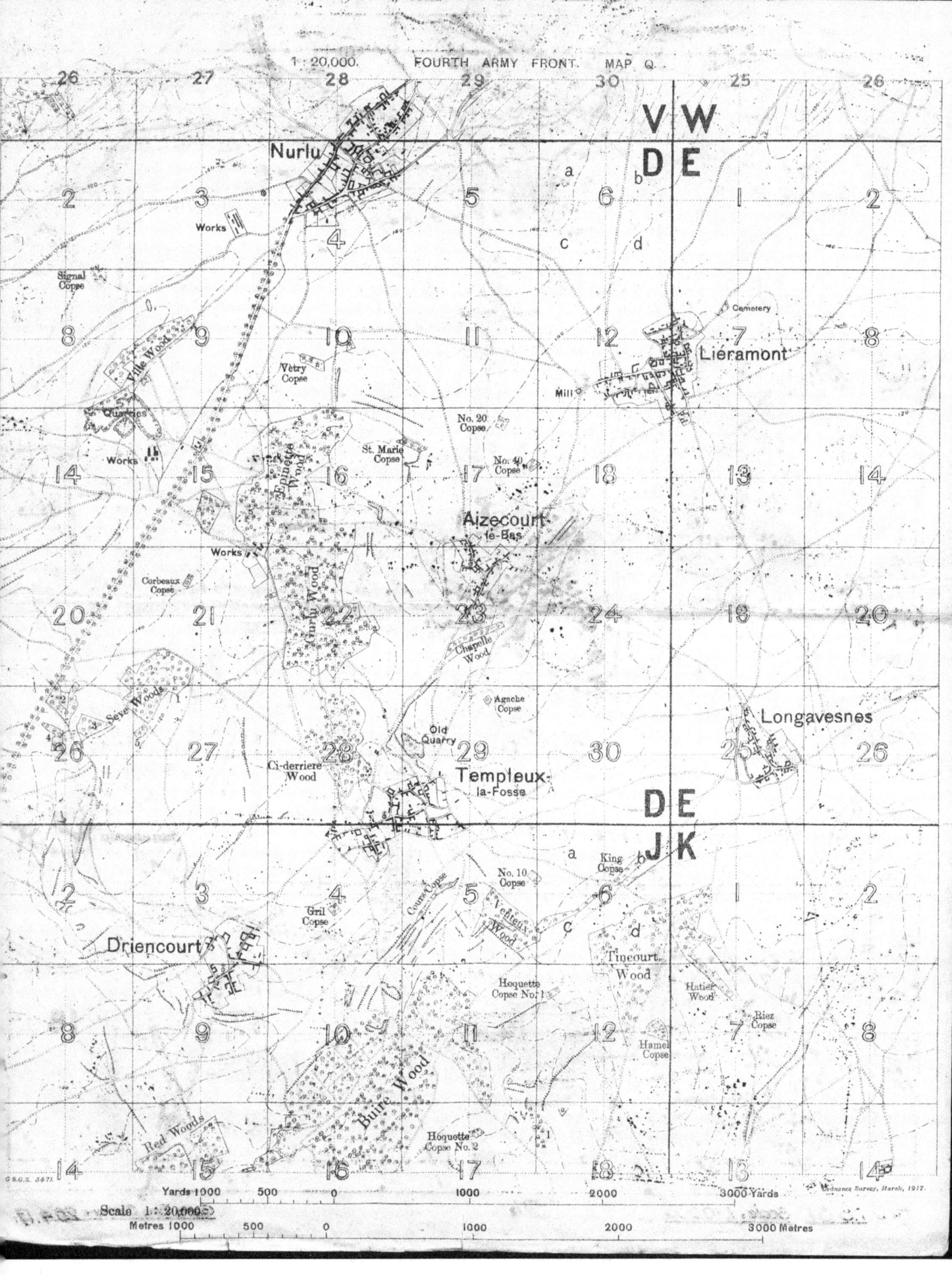

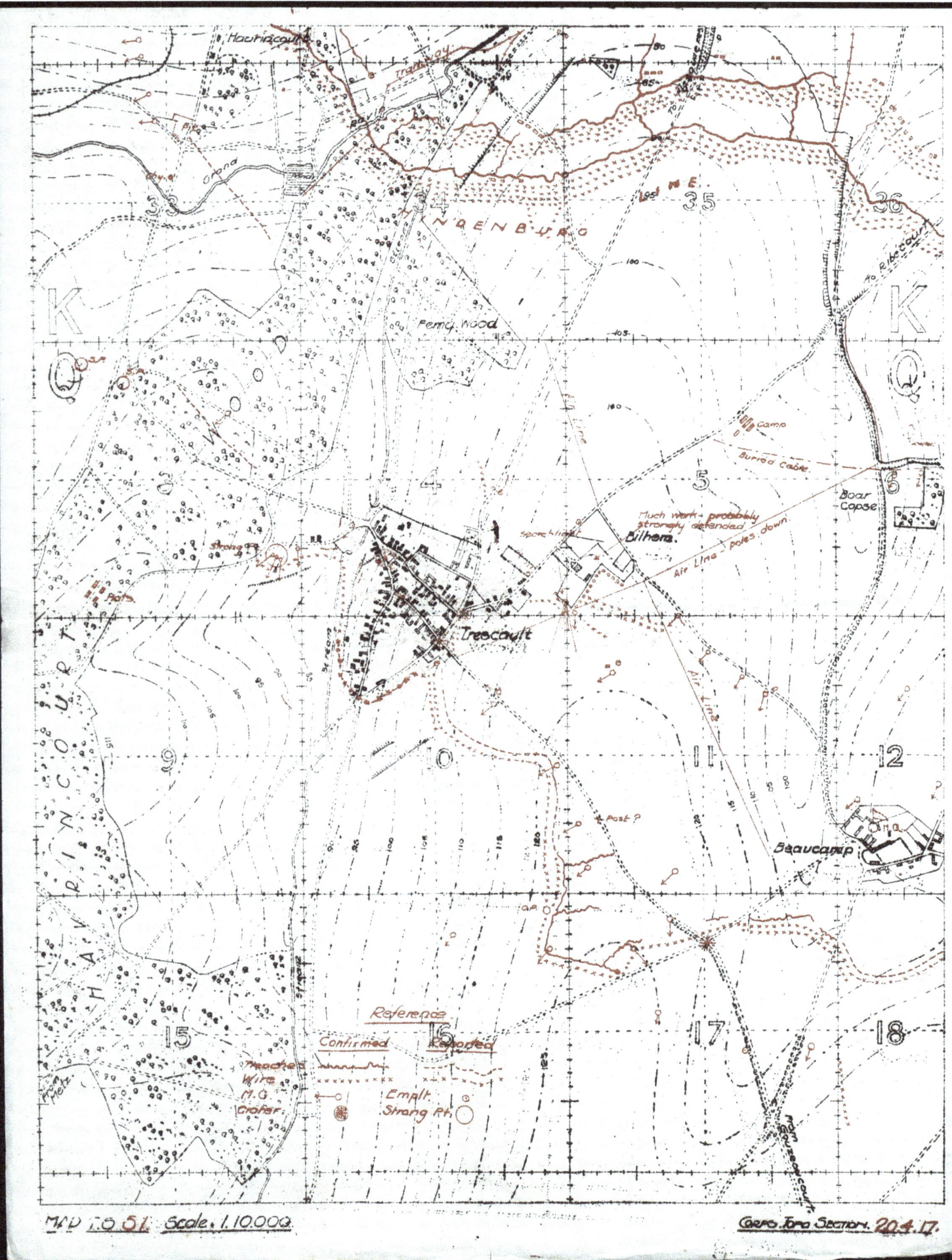

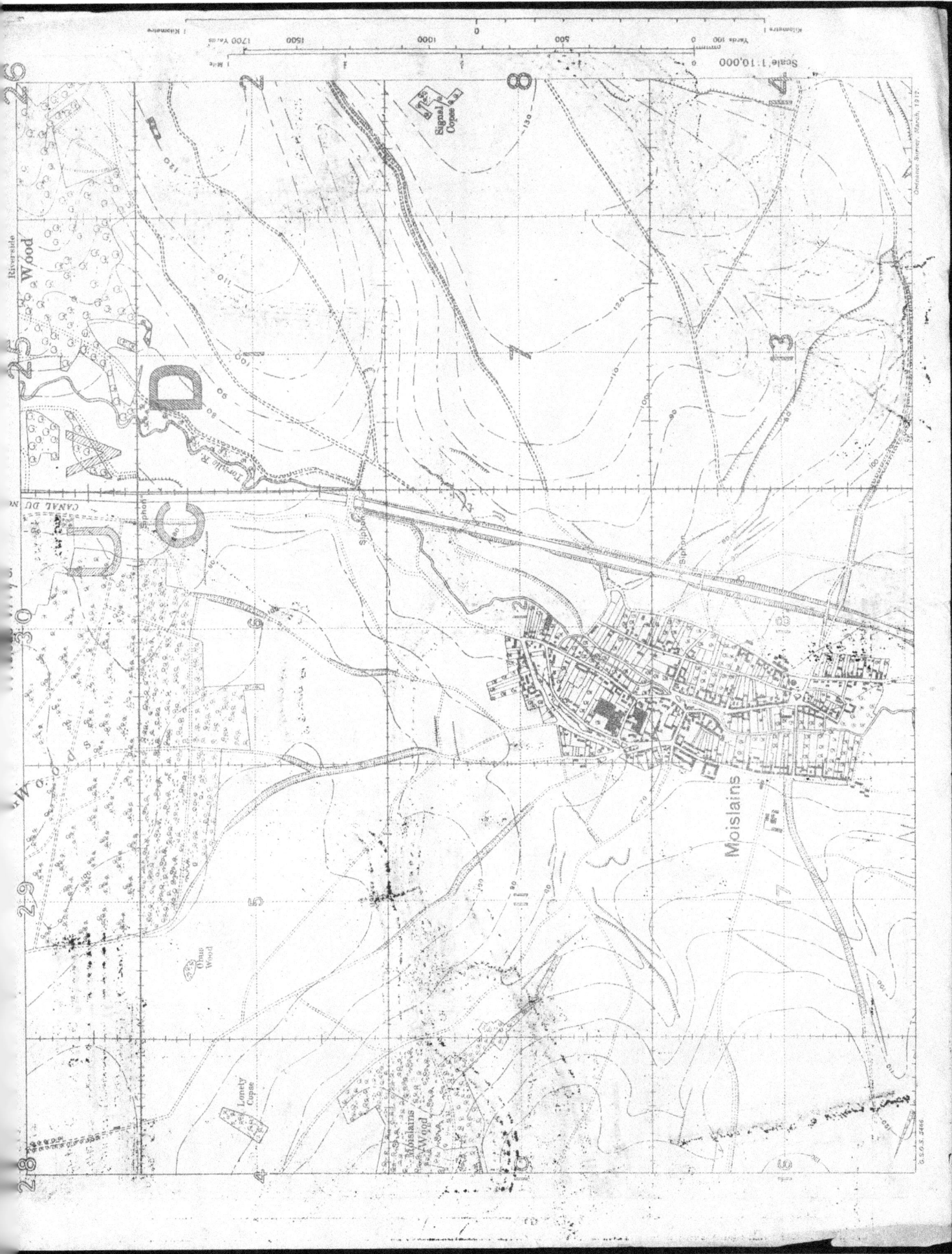

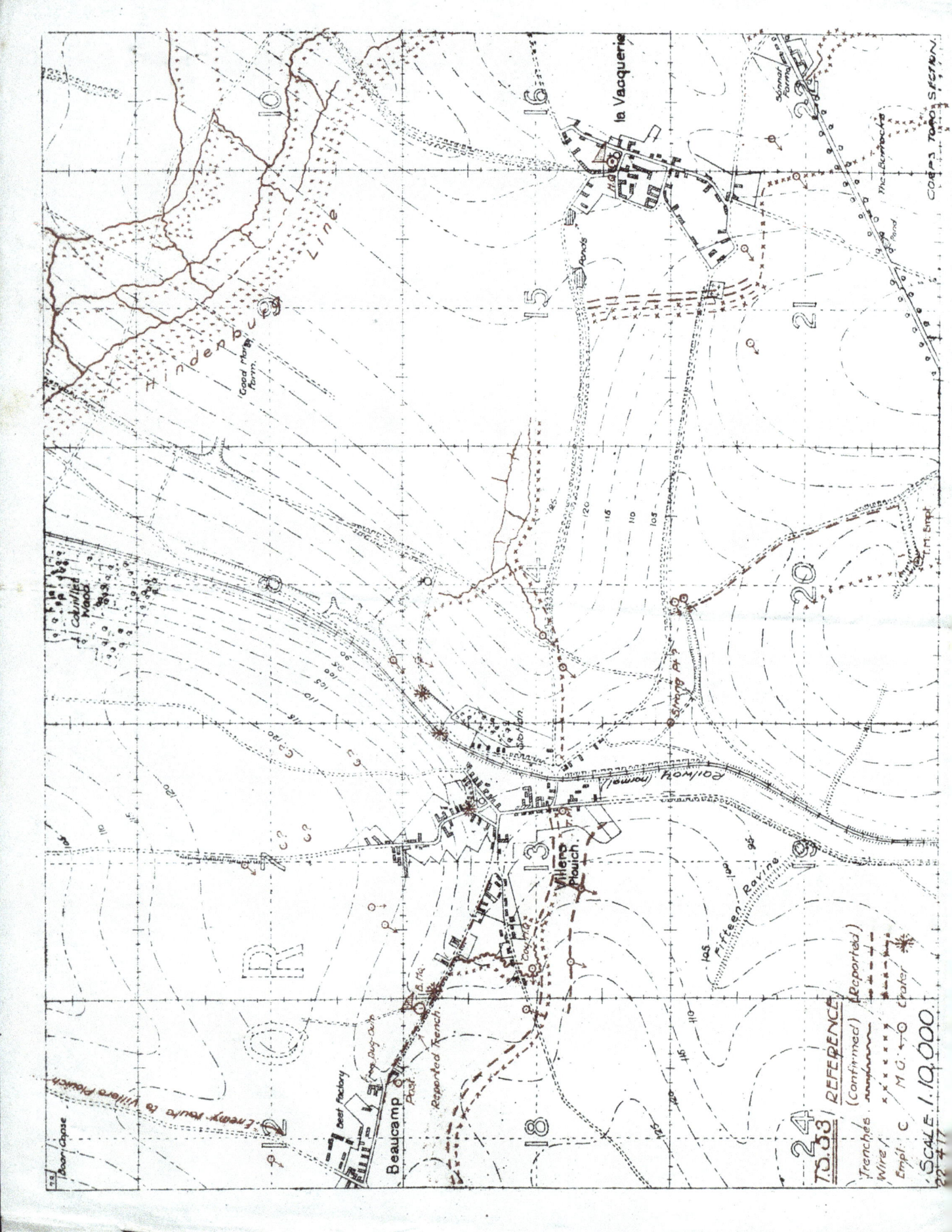

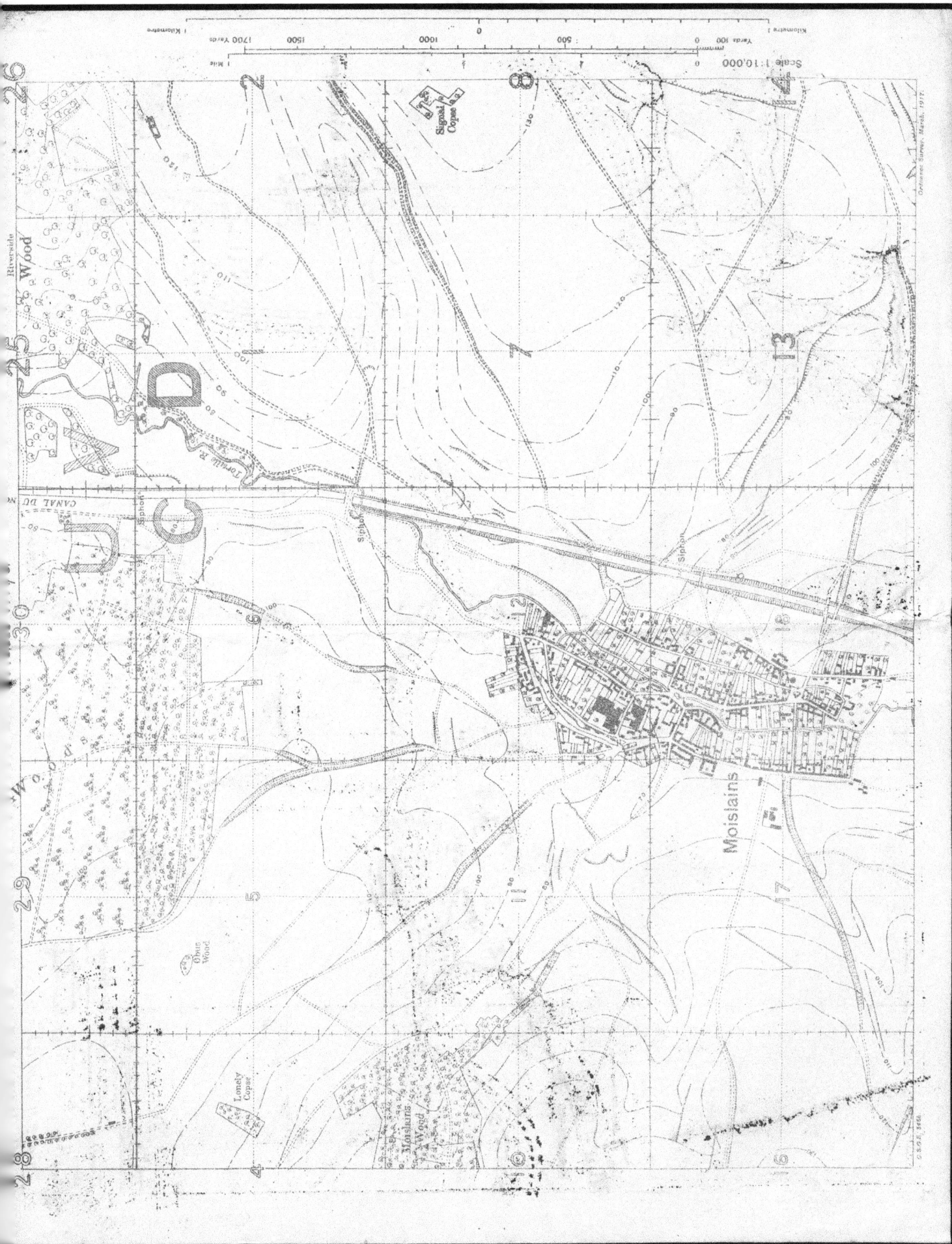

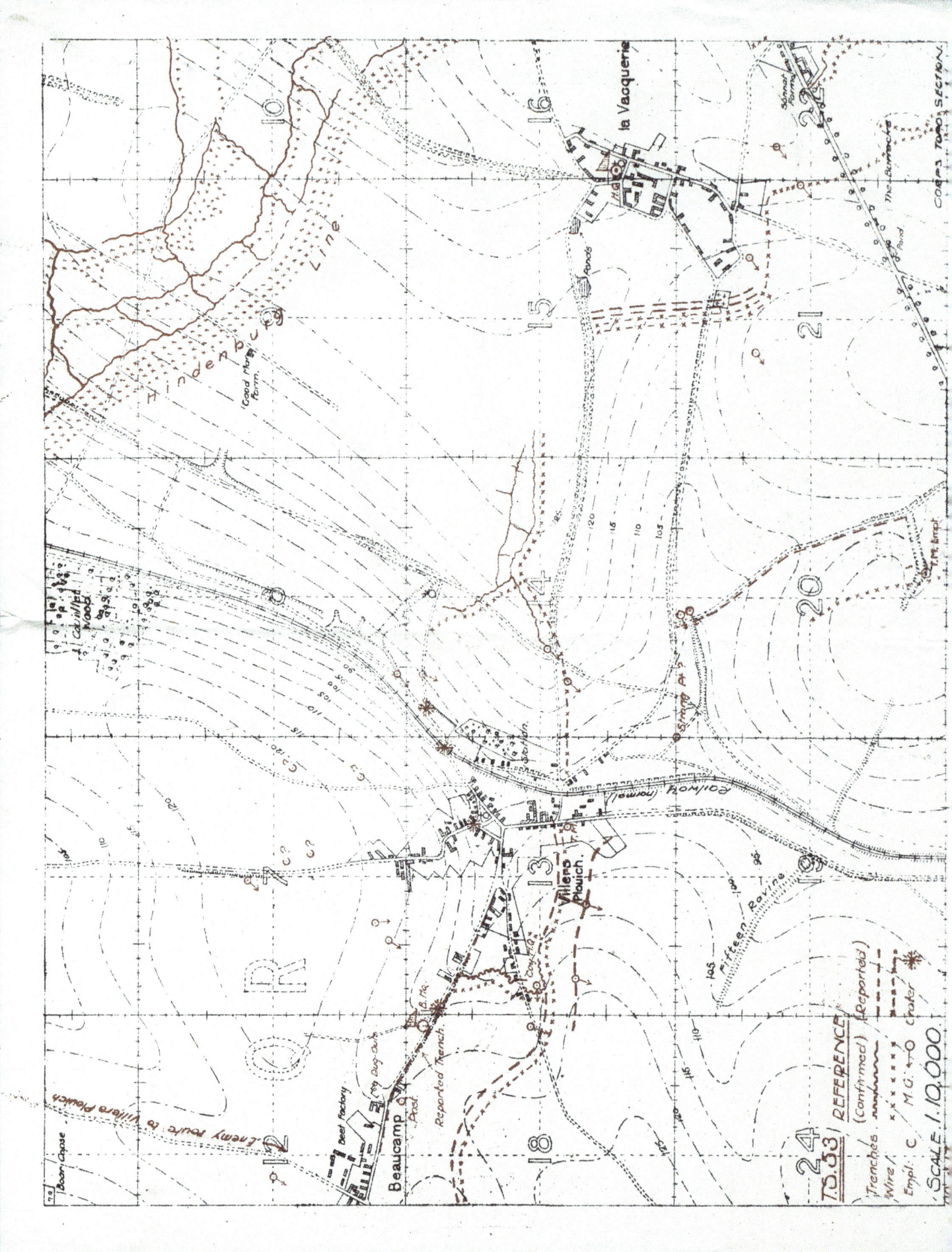

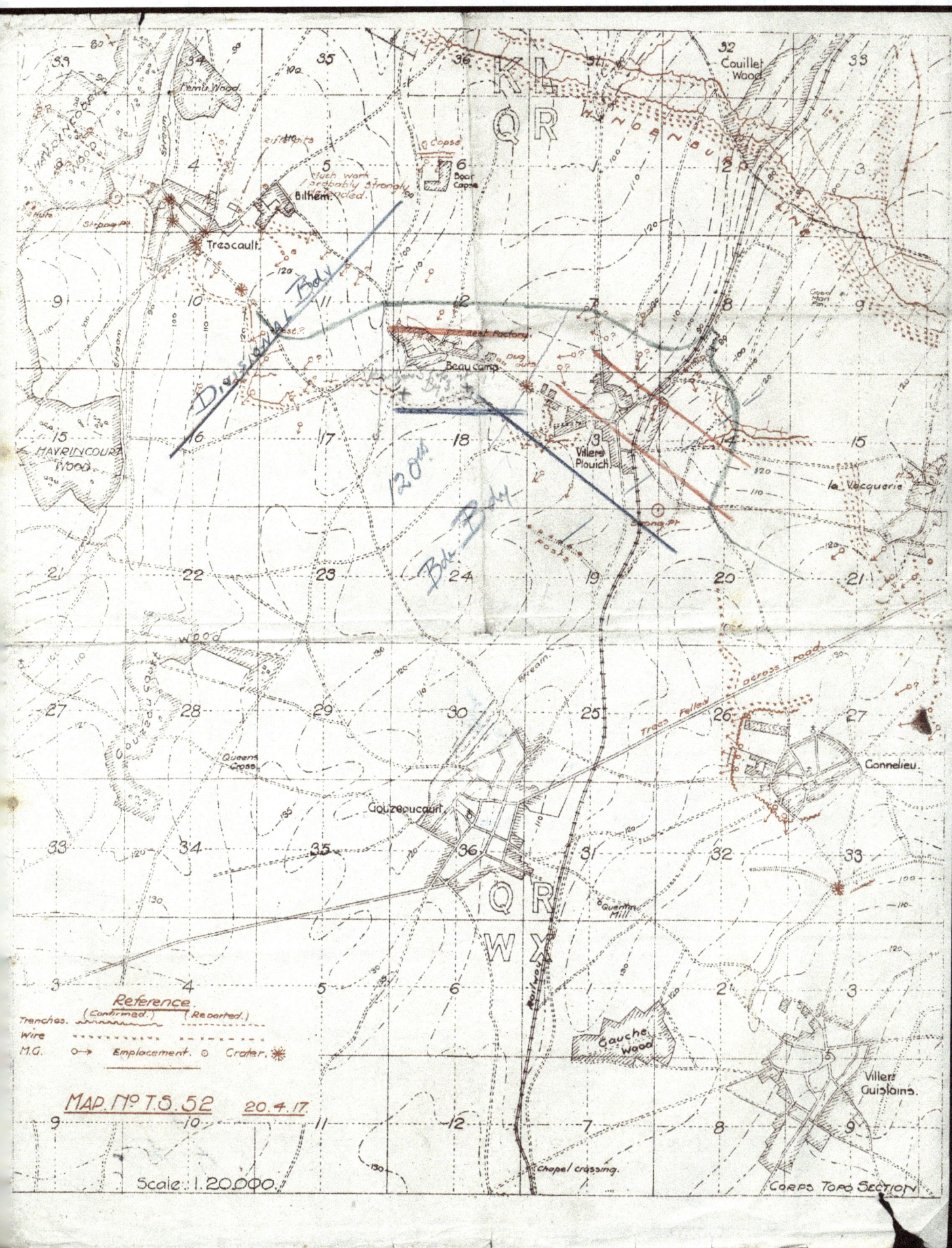

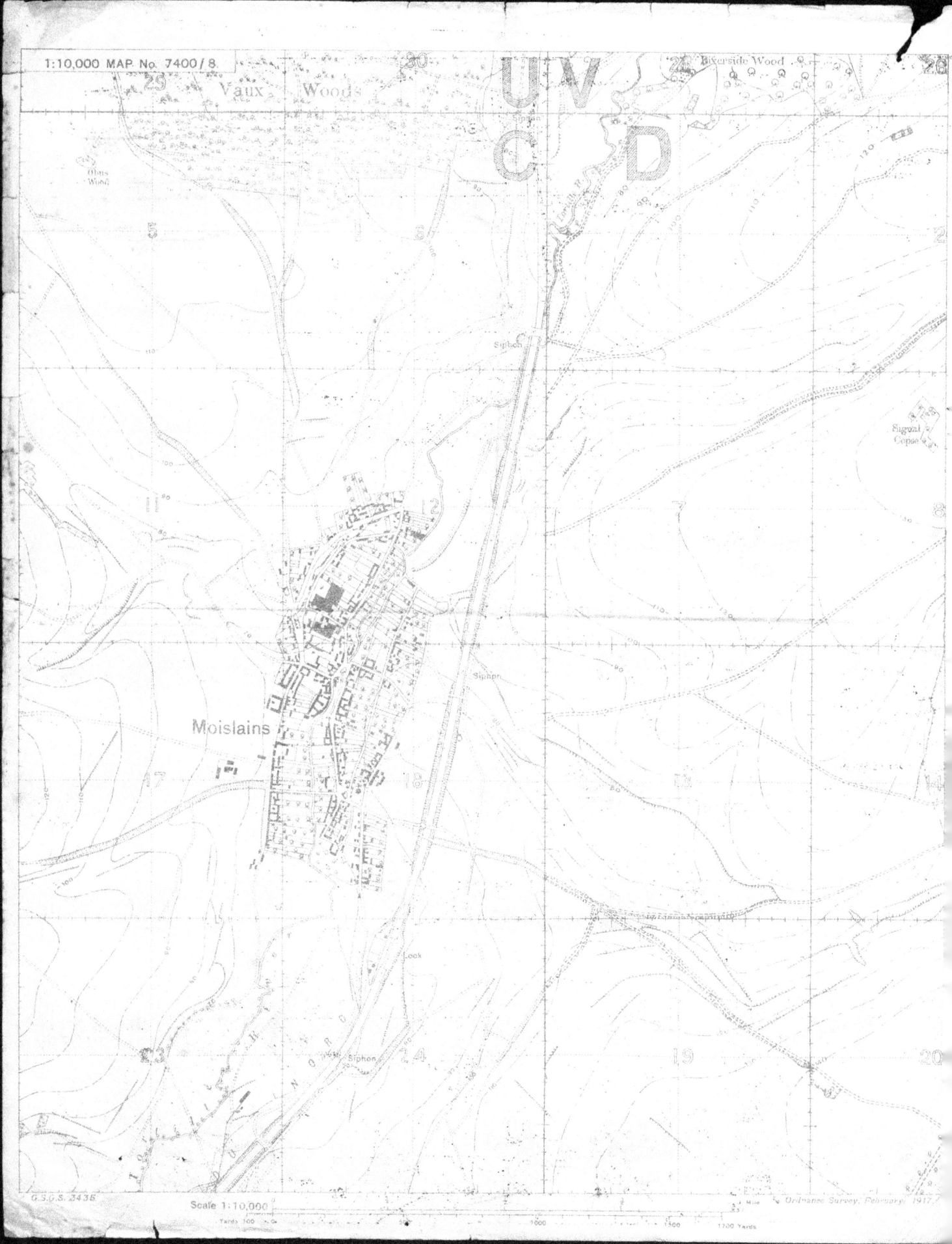

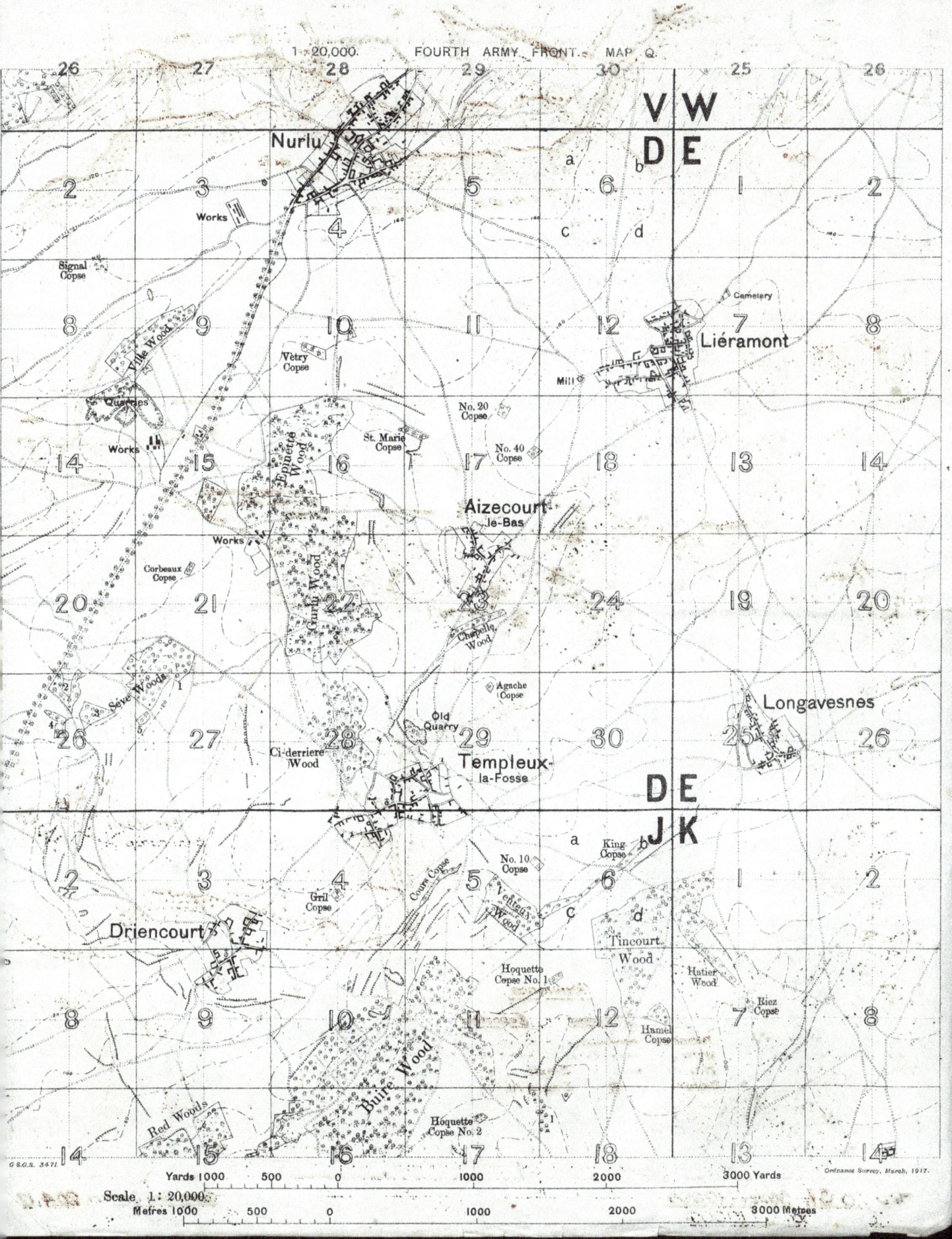

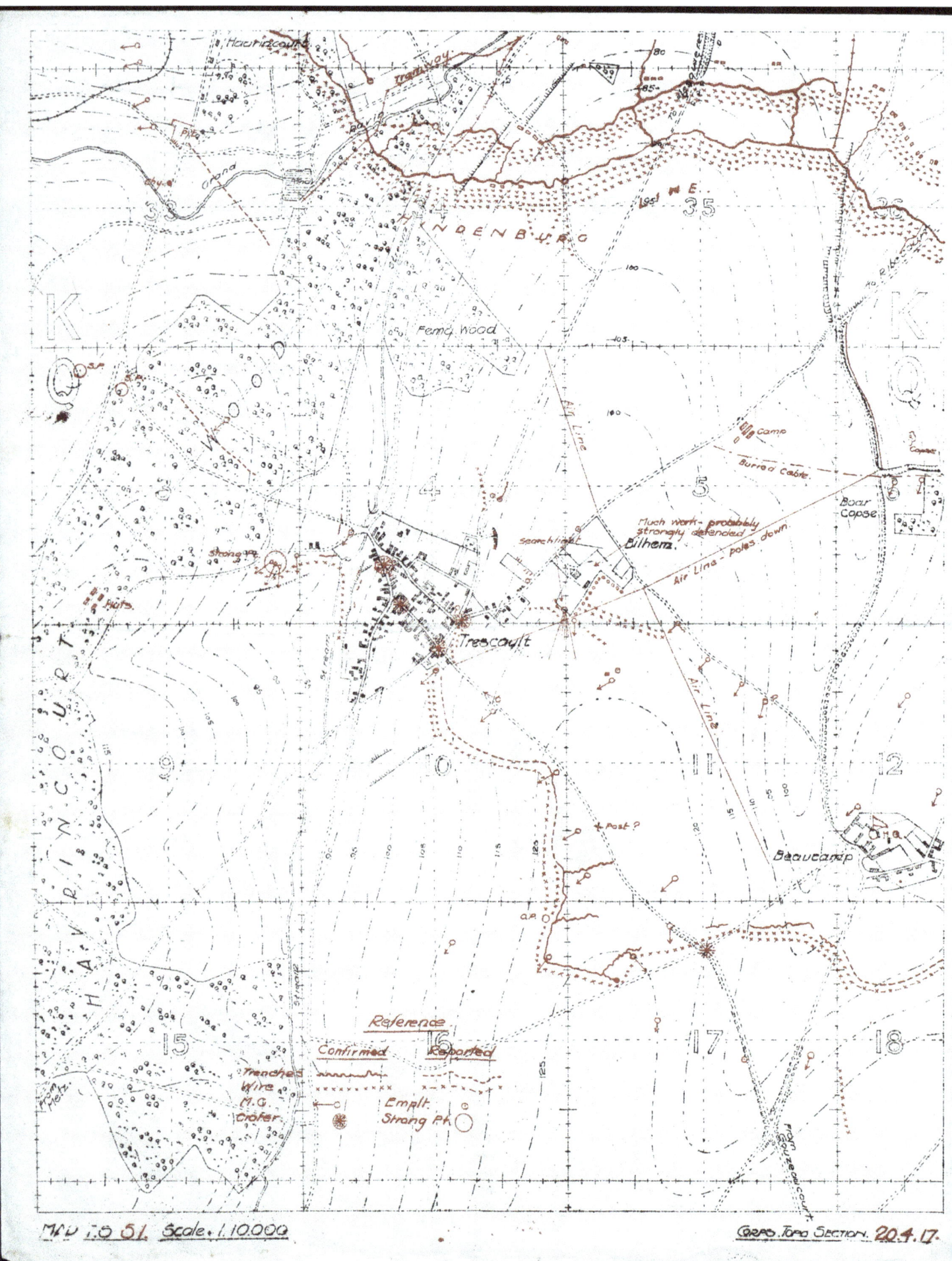

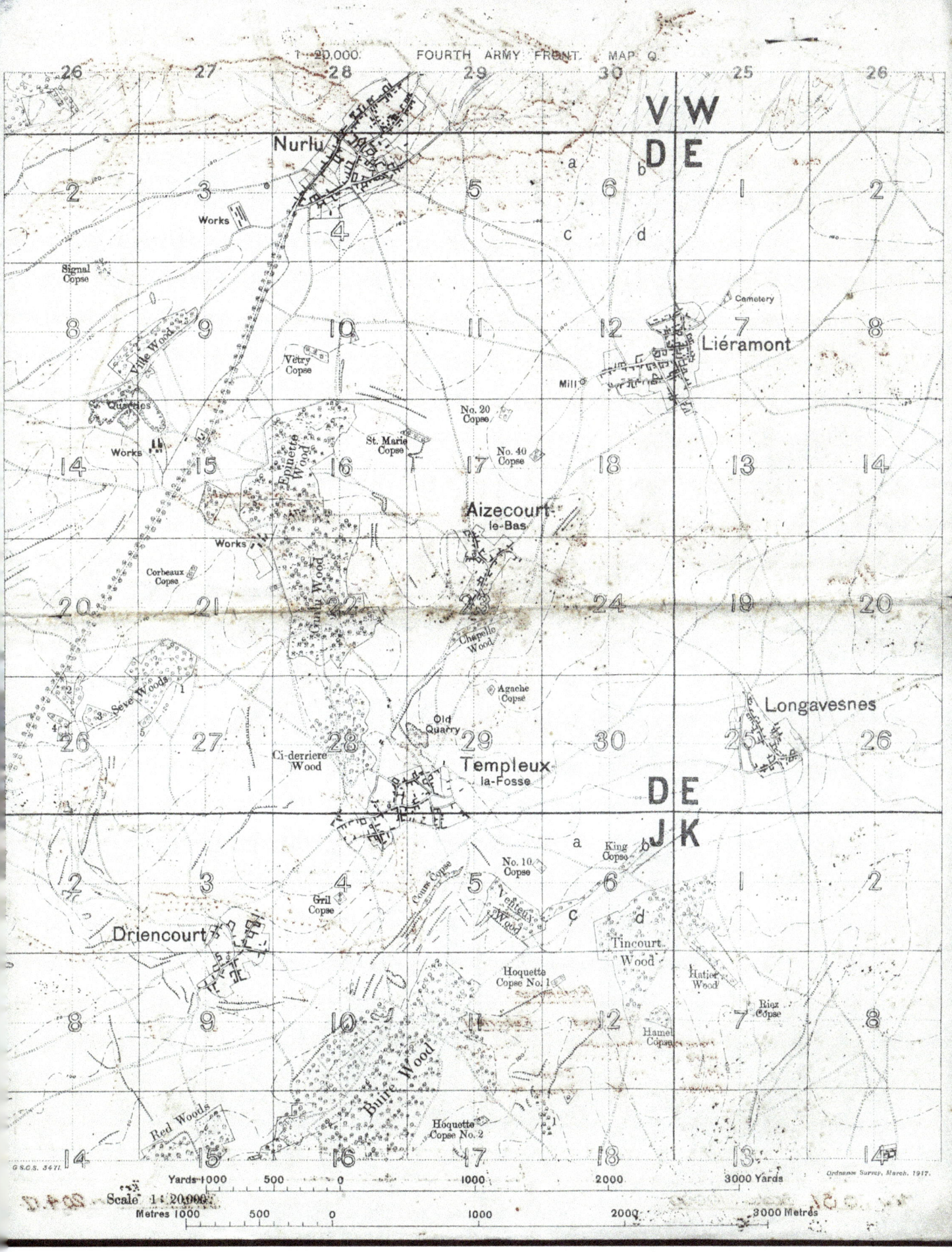

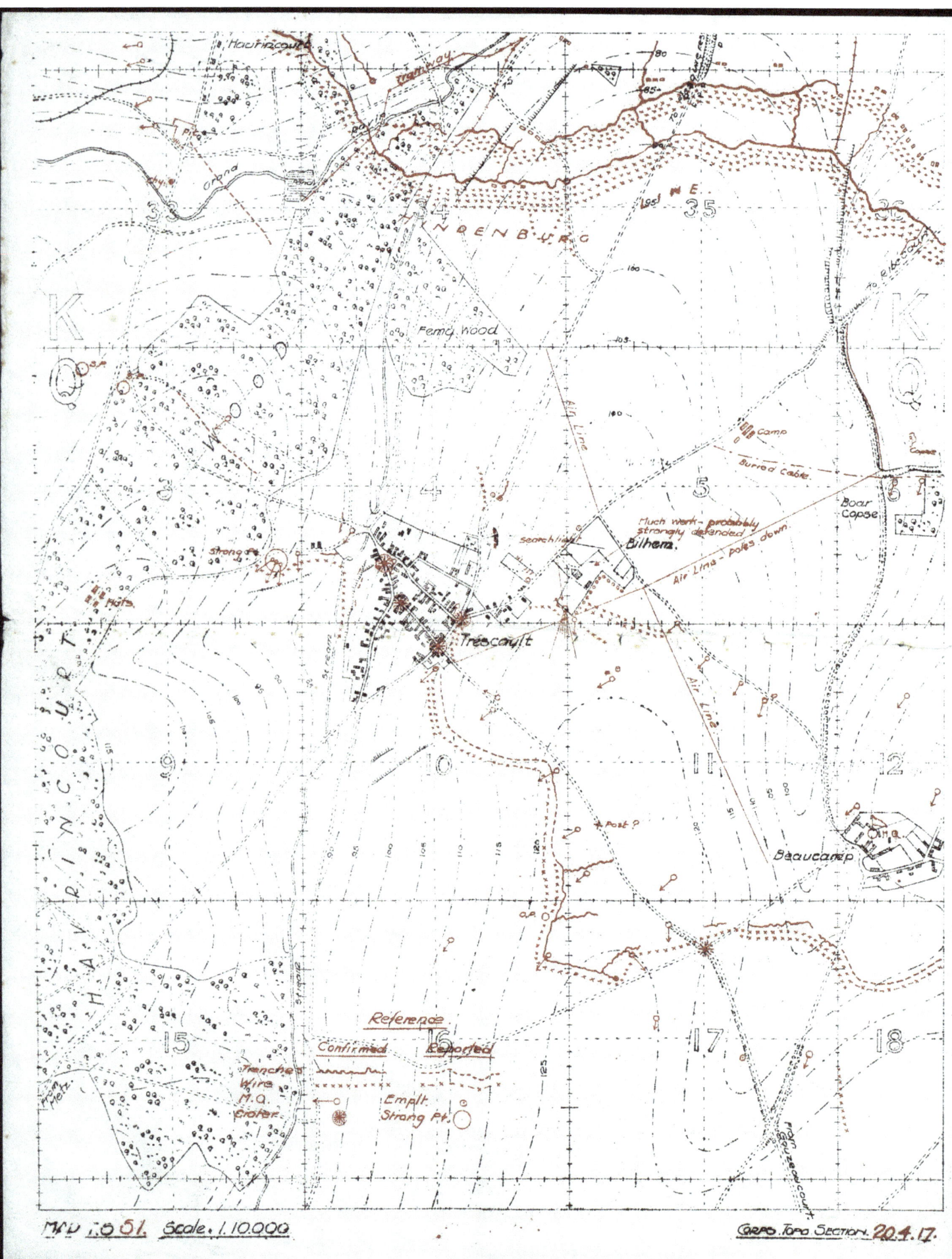

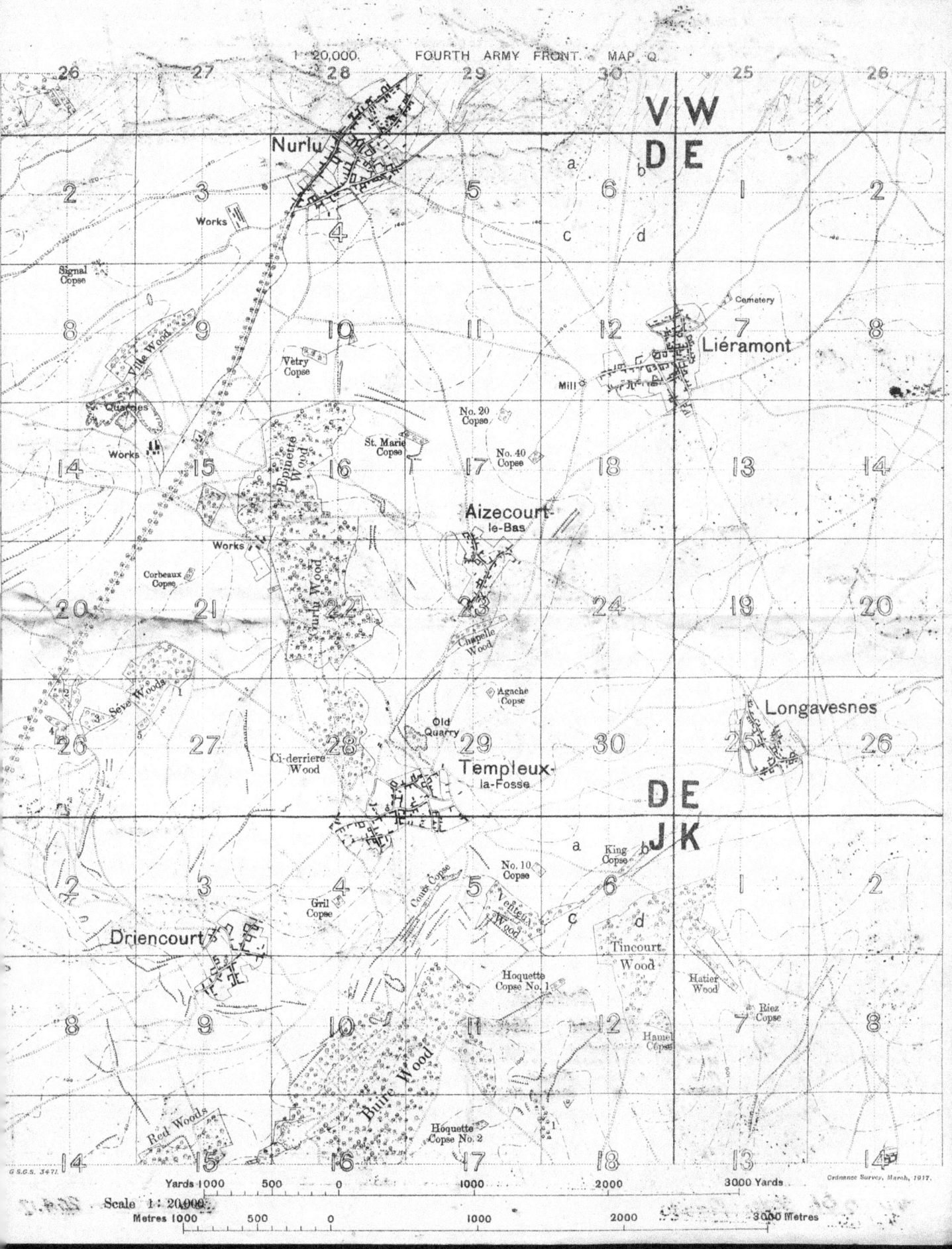

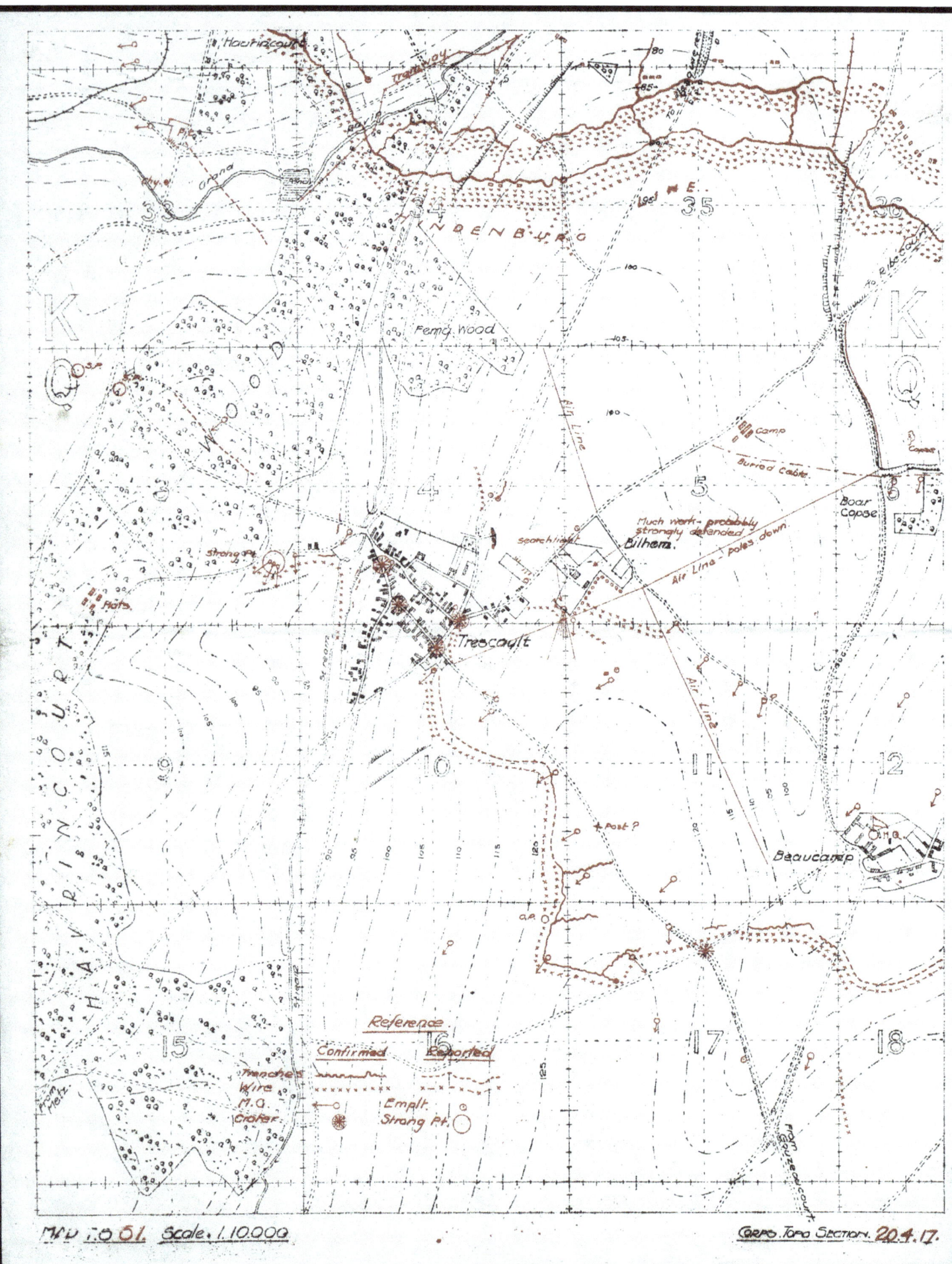

R. Lanc Regt.
E. Surr Regt.
High. L. I.
A. & S. H.
M. G. Coy.
T. M. Battery.

With reference to 120th Infantry Brigade Order No. 96 dated 22.4.1917, the following are the arrangements regarding ammunition etc.

1. Brigade Ammunition Dump will be in GOUZEAUCOURT WOOD at Q.29.c.2.9. O.C., R. Lanc Regt. will detail an officer to take over temporarily charge of this Dump. He should report as soon as possible and will be responsible for sending ammunition etc. to Forward Dump.

2. The Forward Dump from which units should draw is situated at Q.23.b.8.4. O.C., R. Lanc Regt. will detail a party of 1 Officer and 50 Other Ranks to report at Dump, GOUZEAUCOURT WOOD at 9 p.m. to-night to carry forward S.A.A. and Grenades to Forward Dump.
L/Cpl. McArthur and 2 Other Ranks of 13th East Surrey Regiment will to-night move to Forward Dump to take charge.

3. <u>Water.</u> In addition to full water bottles and full petrol tins as arranged by units, there will be available a supply of 50 tins to be sent forward by O.C., R.Lanc Regiment to A. & S. H. and 120 tins at Brigade Dump, GOUZEAUCOURT WOOD.

4. <u>Flares.</u> A. & S. H. and E. Surrey Regt. will arrange to draw an additional 50 Flares from Brigade Dump, GOUZEAUCOURT WOOD.

5. <u>White Tape.</u> 36 Coils of white tape will be available at Dump, GOUZEAUCOURT WOOD. A. & S. H. and E. Surrey Regiment may each draw to the extent of 18 coils.

6. <u>Advanced Dressing Station.</u> The Advanced Dressing Station will be at GOUZEAUCOURT.

An advanced Bearer Post will be situated at METZ Q.20.d.5.2. Bearer companies will be sent forward from there places.

H.B. Kew
Captain,
Staff Captain,
120th Infantry Brigade.

23/4/1917.

WAR DIARY or INTELLIGENCE SUMMARY

Army Form C. 2118.

14 A & 8 H
May 1917

Place	Date	Hour	Summary of Events and Information	Remarks and references to Appendices
EPRICOURT	1		Bn preparing to move into Brigade Reserve. The Bn marched off from EPRICOURT after being relieved by the 2nd Irish Guards at 7pm and arrived in GOUZEAUCOURT WOOD in Brigade Reserve about 12 midnight. The companies were billeted and situated as follows. HQ & "B" Coy. Sunken Rd. in GOUZEAUCOURT WOOD. "A" in huts on N.W. edge of the wood. "C" Coy on the edge of wood on the BROWN LINE. "D" were behind in the Sunken Rd leading to HEUDICOURT Rd.	
GOUZEAUCOURT WOOD	2		The Bn started work in various places. "D" Coy made new shelters in the Sunken Road - also latrines. "A" Coy started work on the Brown Line working at night on deepening the Trench and during the day, owing to the edge of the wood, two companies supplied working parties for the front line. Bn working on the Trench being consolidated in front of BEAUCAMP and VILLERS PLOUICH. RAP.	
"	3		The same scheme of work as the previous day was carried on — the work was good and good progress was made by "D" Coy with the new accommodation. HQ Coy built a new Guard Shelter in the road beside BnHQ. RAP.	
"	4		The companies carried on the same as before. The company which had previously been working on the Brown Line instead of deepening and making a triangle of fire on the NW side — supplying it deep and making a triangle of line on the outside of the existing line this company worked shores during the night and returned billets quarters at 11pm. 2/Lt Black was admitted to hospital. RAP.	
"	5		The day was spent in the same way as previously. At night our neighbours on the right were making a raid on the hostile defences of LA VACQUERIE. As the war times for 11pm there was no work for the Bn on the front line. All available men were therefore turned on to the BROWN LINE — the work was carried on till 1am when the day was all of ours & the required depth and width obtained. 2/Lt. H.K. Mansfield admitted to hospital. RAP.	

WAR DIARY
or
INTELLIGENCE SUMMARY.

(Erase heading not required.)

Army Form C. 2118.

May 1917.

Place	Date	Hour	Summary of Events and Information	Remarks and references to Appendices
GOUZEAUCOURT WOOD	6.		Orders received to relieve 1/2 11th KORLR in the left sector BEAUCAMP. The L.O. and Adjutant went up to the head quarters of the 1/KORLRs and arrangements for the relief that night were made by Battalions necessary arrangements for the relief that night were made by Battalions. Arrived at the nunthap and the Bn moved up to the line by platoons. Intervals of 100 yards at the Quarry (Bn. H.Q.) at 9pm. B Company moved up to front and took over the left company front from BIRCH RIDGE to the N.W. Corner of BEAUCAMP. "C" Company took up the left company front including half South side of the village. "A" Company were in Support position in the line trench near the CRATER while "D" Company were in Support at the QUADRILATERAL TRENCH. Bn.H.Q. was in the QUARRY. Reported Best to Hospital Back.	
BEAUCAMP	7		The Companies all settled down and the usual routine of holding the line was resumed by all. Special A.A. Lewis gun mounting what was taken over by "A" Company in the hall was manned by a L.G. team and was in action against enemy aircraft on several occasions. This was an answer but for some intermittent shelling of BEAUCAMP. The day was quiet but for some intermittent shelling of BEAUCAMP. The rations no casualties. A light patrols were sent out by both companies. The rations were brought to Bn. H.Q. on pack ponies and carried both com- panies in the line by carrying parties. RSM.	
"	8		The same routine was gone through as the previous day. The line was again quiet. At about 4pm one of our airplanes was brought down just below HEIZ. The total machine flew very low and all our LGs opened but with no satisfactory result. Patrols were sent out at night – no signs of the enemy. P.O.R.	

Army Form C. 2118.

WAR DIARY
or
INTELLIGENCE SUMMARY.

(Erase heading not required.)

May 1917.

Instructions regarding War Diaries and Intelligence Summaries are contained in F. S. Regs., Part II. and the Staff Manual respectively. Title pages will be prepared in manuscript.

Place	Date	Hour	Summary of Events and Information	Remarks and references to Appendices
BEAUCAMP.	9.		The day was again quiet but for the intermittent shelling of BEAUCAMP and the usual activity. There was nothing to report except a staff on the enemy balloons opposite our front. There was nothing of interest. 2/Lt. G.W. Wetton & Sgt. Bradford to FLIX ECOURT. R.M.	
	10.		During the day everything was quiet and the weather excellent. An inter-Company relief took place. "A" Company relieved "C" Coy on the right and "D" Company relieved "B" Company on the left. "A" & "B" Companies moved after relief into Support and Reserve positions respectively. A new ration dump was made at the trali. This allowed the companies to be all nearer the dump and so fresh bread came right up to the front. The carrying was not so great. R.M.	
	11.		The day was quiet — weather good. "D" Company sent out two observers who stayed out in front of our lines all day in a shell hole from which they commanded a good view of HAVRINCOURT & its roads towards behind it. Little movement was seen. Patrols were again sent out. R.M.	
	12.		The Bn. was relieved by the 12th R.Bs. and after relief moved back to accommodation in DESSART WOOD – The last company arriving there having finished at 2:30 a.m. Accommodation was very limited, the weather being good many of the men elected to sleep outside; R.M.	
DESSART WOOD.	13.		Rested all day, and in the evening prepared for the move which was to take place. Before moving off the 33rd Div. 100th Bde. MG Coy 1/9th H.L.I. recd. refreshment off.	

WAR DIARY or INTELLIGENCE SUMMARY

Army Form C. 2118.

May 1917

Place	Date	Hour	Summary of Events and Information	Remarks and references to Appendices
DESSART WOOD	13.		The Bn. moved off from the wood at 8.45 p.m. proceeding by the FINS - BOUZEAUCOURT Rd. to BOUZEAUCOURT. The Bn. had this journey across the railway embankment, thence after the village and on to the Quarry on the BOUZEAUCOURT - LEATHER Rd. It relieved the 2/4th Bn. Leather Rifles. H.Q. was in the Quarry. Companies were all in a trench about 150 yds in advance of the Quarry. Companies HQ were on the far side of Quarries, while the other 3 companies had their HQs on the trench. The relief was carried out early, and after the transport etc, had been very difficult in reaching the front, had been off loaded things settled down. The Bn. was then in Brigade Support in the BOUZEAUCOURT SECTOR. The companies had each sent an officer to find out the way to the front line during the day. Maj. Bunn murdoch to Hospital. 2/Lt Doughty to same at EARL.	
QUARRY R. 31. c.	14.		During the night there was very heavy thunder rain and all the shelter and trenches were awash. Much damage was done and in the night work was started digging drains and trench holes. Work parties were also supplied to the LEFT FRONT Bn. EACH.	
" "	15.		Work carried on. The same as usual - new shelters has to be erected and drainage carried on. Working companies working with the front line Bn. again.	
" "	16.		The day was spent in work. Came that the train immortality ingress after line. Called the GREEN LINE. Elaborations were made and the work of improving the trench started EARL.	

Army Form C. 2118.

WAR DIARY
or
INTELLIGENCE SUMMARY.
(Erase heading not required.)

May 1917

Place	Date	Hour	Summary of Events and Information	Remarks and references to Appendices
BONNELIEU	20.		The line was quiet but the usual shelling on BOUZEAUCOURT Ave the only thing of importance. Enemy patrols were very active and a discreet one was taken by Lt Joseph Tyson. Enemy planes over the snowlands of the enemy at the BUNDO HOUSE. Shells on our night company front. Half O.R. found dead. 2nd Lt Simpson - 2nd O.S. Walker. 2nd Lt Watkins turned. to Hos. 2nd. Lt Ruddin admitted hospital. RNA.	
"	21.		The day was quiet - work which had been started on half pressing night has in full swing - Things of ROR.E.R. working on front line - R.E.'s laying out patrols. Our own front line responses carrying & waking in hill of war. The German bombers working on lented trench behind left company front. Enemy aerial activity very marked. RNA. Batt. company relief carried out. "D" day took over left front from "B" Coy. "A" day took over right front from "C" Coy. Work and Battalion carried on as usual. Lt Shawn granted leave. RNA.	
"	22.		Line was quiet. Quiet. An artillery action brought a rain harass left of BOUZEAUCOURT-CAMBRAI Rd. Our enemy T.M. was always from BONNES STONE Rd &c. Aircraft activity abated the late day work being on in enemy wire. The artillery were dead on the path, was dispersed. RNA.	
"	23.			
"	24.		The day was quiet - in the evening the enemy had numerous aeroplanes on the front. These flew over our lines and were unmolested except by M.G. fire from our own men - Patrols sent out a few feet out little BARRACKS + BUNDO HOUSE. No enemy seen. RNA.	

WAR DIARY
INTELLIGENCE SUMMARY

Army Form C. 2118.

May 1917

Place	Date	Hour	Summary of Events and Information	Remarks and references to Appendices
QUARRY R.31.C.	17		Orders received for relief of 11th KORRS on following night. 60 ord Ranks went up to make all arrangements - took was carried on the lines as usual both with the front line & in the BREEN LINE. Lt Murison & Lt Petty-Campbell 2nd Lieut Jones, the Bn Lr things and 2nd Lt Butler & 2nd Lt Petty-Campbell 2nd Lt Bag & 2nd Lt RSM Campbell "A" & "B" Companies were platoon (temp) H.Q.s. Lt Robt Scott SOR the R.E.F. SOR Scott from the 11th KORRS.	
QUARRY - BONNELIEU	18		The Bn moved up to take over the front line Posts at Companies moved up by platoon writing guides at various known points. "B" Bn took over the Left Front from GOUZEAUCOURT - CORDORAL RD - to the first switch Rd taking out at BONNELIEU. "C" Company took over the right front from that point to attack the S.W. point of BONNELIEU. "D" companies in the trench beside Bn HQ.. at R26 d.7.6. The relief was a difficult one owing to the enemy artillery retaliating on our lines for a short which our artillery had given him in the early part of the evening. The relief was carried out without casualties however. The artillery strafe went on through out the night but by morning all things were normal again. R.O.D.	
BONNELIEU	19		The line was quiet the greater part of the day - a little shelling went on during the day, mostly centred on BONNELIEU and the right Coy HQ. At night Patrols were sent out and information about the enemy activity arge work obtained. Lt MacMillan returned from hospital. Lt J.C. Rudman proceeded to the Balloon Observation section. Lt Blake & Lt Johnston evacuated W.O.K. Sick.	

Army Form C. 2118.

WAR DIARY
or
INTELLIGENCE SUMMARY.
(Erase heading not required.)

1 Aug 1917.

Instructions regarding War Diaries and Intelligence Summaries are contained in F. S. Regs., Part II. and the Staff Manual respectively. Title pages will be prepared in manuscript.

Place	Date	Hour	Summary of Events and Information	Remarks and references to Appendices
BONNELIEU	25		A.Coy. relieved company into front and out. B-D & left front and C-A in right front. Before being relieved both A & B companies sent out strong patrols for the purpose of supplying any left parties and gaining identification.	
			(1) "D" Coy. 2/Lt. W.E.G. Butler and 19 O.R. with a Lewis Gun went out from our left company front and proceeded along the GOUZEAUCOURT-CAMBRAI RR and took up his position above the cistern there. He fixed his position and fired and waited. During the night he saw no movement — he returned about 2.30 am.	
			(2) "A" Coy. 2/Lt. Lt. W.H. Lurison and 24 O.R. with 2 Lewis Guns, left our right company front and took up a position with his party, two Lewis Guns about 120 yds from the enemy wire. An enemy Lewis German came out by the front and proceeded in the open towards his gun, hoping the MacDonald took for were forward both were hit no identification cover helped — on reaching the wire Lt MacDonalds our party were finished at by 3 Germans and then by rifle to wire — the party was dispersed by a front rifle which rifle fire was opened from the German trench. The party then withdrew & returned to lines without casualties.	

Lt. Bartholomew H-in Gazelin Sussex Rgt. M.O.d.

WAR DIARY
or
INTELLIGENCE SUMMARY.
(Erase heading not required.)

Army Form C. 2118.

May 1917.

Place	Date	Hour	Summary of Events and Information	Remarks and references to Appendices
GONNELIEU	26.		The line was quiet all during the day except for the usual spasmodic shelling of GONNELIEU and the usual activity about 2 a.m. in the afternoon one of our snipers got up on the Mont St Bois who was wounded by a rifle bullet through the left thigh. The nature of the ground was a piece of wood. Before leaving the acts as usual. The relief was a quiet one. The Battalion relieved the United Sword in relief. Company sent north and occupied Brigade Reserve — 2 Companies (B & C) being the sunken road to C.A. while the remaining two Companies (A & D) moved to Brigade Headquarters Bois.	
H.Q. W.b.d.	27.		with H.Q. in the Sunken road. The Coys were to rest for the day. 'A' Company & 'D' Company has paths on fires. All companies worked on shelter, which were very few in number. The accommodation for the men was started. A new H.Q. was and dugouts accommodation was started by the 183 Pioneers under the direction of 2nd Lieut [?]. 'B' Company went back to the Res by Brigade H.Q.	R.M.
"	28		During the day we were on. 'C' Company went back and took over from 'D' Company. A Company then took over one companies accommodation from the Support Bn (13 E.S.R.B) in R.31.c — the Hd Qrs of the Coy being in the sunken road here QUENTIN MILL. M.G.A.	R.M.

WAR DIARY
or
INTELLIGENCE SUMMARY

Army Form C. 2118.

(Erase heading not required.)

Place	Date	Hour	Summary of Events and Information	Remarks and references to Appendices
HQ K.6.d.	29.		Improvement and extension of accommodation carried on. Strong points on X.16.d.&.a's & trellis cleared. Very little sniping and very little fatigues on day. The RE's supplied material for the trellis fence during the night. Tho' RE's supplied material for the trellis fence was but following the night. Red.	
"	30.		Improvements still being carried on. Small parties working on the strong points front and rear. "A" Coy one outside company worked on it during the night. There was food down - see trip chutle being possible and Co Latrine. Red.	
"	31.		During the day the same programme of work was carried on. In the evening the HQ and was finished, "C" Company relieved "A" Company in the Support Bn Trench at R.31.a. The relief was carried out without incident and was by Company reaching "C" Bay leaving their "A" bay on relief/accommodate and took over "A" bay at 11.15pm. - "C" bay's old accommodation. Red.	

HONOURS & REWARDS - - - - - - - - - - - - - - - - See Appendix 'A'

O.D.Carmichael Lt. Col.
Comm.g. 1/6 A&S H.

Appendix "A".

WAR DIARY
INTELLIGENCE SUMMARY.

May 1917.

Capt. W. G. L. Keddie M.C. was awarded the Military Cross for gallantry in action on the 24th April 1917 when the Battalion took the village of BEAUREP??D in an attack.

No. 13364 Pte. H. J. Auld. was awarded the Distinguished Conduct Medal for gallantry in action on the 24th April 1917.

No. 13226 Sgt. J. W. Crawford was awarded the "Médaille Militaire" for gallantry in action on the 24th April 1917.

Lt. Col. G. Gunn –
Capt. R. Dickie –   were mentioned in Despatches of 9th April 1917.
No. 12344 Sgt. L. McMillan was mentioned in Despatches of 9th April 1917.

R. Carmichael Lt. Col.
Comm. O.C. 14th Bn. A+S.H.

14 A.I.S.H.
June 1917
Vol / 13

WAR DIARY or INTELLIGENCE SUMMARY.

Army Form C. 2118.

Place	Date	Hour	Summary of Events and Information	Remarks and references to Appendices
Wbd.	1		Bn in Brigade Reserve - 3Kd. and 1 Company at W6d - 2 Bays in support Battalion and 1 Coy beside Bde Hq. The day was quiet except for shelling with support Battery behind GOUZEAUCOURT and on the Western front leading to the village. Looked fratilly at night. The left Bn left advanced trench on the front line Rd GOMMIECOURT Rd.	
" "	2		The day was quiet. No hostile shelling of Battalion. Arrangements were made for the relief on the following night. R.A.H.	
" "	3		Bn preparing for move up to the line - Aftn abandoned. A great deal of the KRR, R.P. moved off at 6. The Lift under CONNELIEO Coloniae the KRB KRPL R.P. The relief was carried out successfully. "B" Coy going into left front and "C" Coy to alley were covered in support. The gas alarm was raised during the relief Right front - DVA being on our front was not effective. The rest of the night OCU continued Refrg. The left but our right were all not from there was quiet - nothing unusual happened. The several arms patrols were pushed out from the line. This section is always busy in the air. At night patrols met some of the enemy. Except both Bn fronts - this was cut all right. The night was quiet. R.A.H.	
GONNELIEU	4		A great deal of enemy was seen. The enught was very windy and exceptionally quiet day - except that snip and recently in R26d7.7 was shelled about 4pm. A heavy thunder storm came on and the trenches were very muddy. Patrols out the same as previous night. An enemy working party was discovered and dispersed with artillery fire. R.A.H.	
" "	5			
" "	6		Quiet front - work and patrol at night the same as before. Considerable artillery activity on the left of our sector - for side of GOUZEAUCOURT - CAMBRAI Rd - our sector was quiet. R.A.H.	

Army Form C. 2118.

WAR DIARY
or
INTELLIGENCE SUMMARY.
(Erase heading not required.)

June 1917

Instructions regarding War Diaries and Intelligence Summaries are contained in F.S. Regs., Part II. and the Staff Manual respectively. Title pages will be prepared in manuscript.

Place	Date	Hour	Summary of Events and Information	Remarks and references to Appendices
GONNELIEU	7.		The day was quiet. No intercompany relief. D relieving B on the left – A relieving C on the right. Patrols were sent out after the relief – while covering parties had been posted during the relief. The front was quiet. Enq.	
	8.		Situation on the front normal. Patrols out as usual. Enemy carried on about the whole front. Enq.	
	9.		The situation quiet. Right Coy. T.M. active against right bay H.Q. which were by the establishing in a deep dugout. Lt. T.M. was active against Kyte Bay H.Q. as on the previous day. 2/Lt. Bartholomew & 2/Lt. Nicol exposed. Enq.	
	10.		Today was again quiet. Lt. T.M. was active again the previous day by 2/Lt. Bartholomew. Enq.	
	11.		The Battalion was relieved in the evening by the 12th Suffolk Regt. on completion of the relief the Bn marched by companies to NW. corner of SOREL LE GRAND. The last company arrived camp at 4.20 am (12th Inst.). Enq.	
SOREL LE GRAND	12.		2/Lt. R.T.F. N'thola granted 7 days leave. General cleaning up was carried on. The Battalion paraded for Baths. 2/Lt. G.J. Macdonald was absorbed in the No. X Corps School Establishment and about 96 the OR strength. Enq.	
	13.		The Battalion paraded after cleaning up in the morning for Drill. 2/Lt. W. Hamilton was transferred to England (Sick) and was struck off the strength accordingly. 2/Lt. W.M. Hill admitted to hospital. Enq.	
	14.		General improvement of camp. Platoon & Company drill under Company & up. Enq.	
	15.		Lieut. McEwen rejoined from 4th Army School and took over command of draft of D'104. from 2/Lt. Hamilton. Officers football match against E. Surrey Regt. resulted in a draw. Enq.	

WAR DIARY or INTELLIGENCE SUMMARY

Army Form C. 2118.

June 1917

Place	Date	Hour	Summary of Events and Information	Remarks and references to Appendices
SOREL-LE-GRAND	16		All available men working under R.E.s on road & track repair. Brigadier General e.g. Drummond Willoughby CB. CMG. presented the military cross to Capt. W.G. T. Kellie. The Belgian Minister honoured Medal to No. 13364 Pte. W.J. Cole. H.E. the French Minister presented the Medaille Militaire to No. 13226 C/Sgt. W. Crawford.	
"	17.		All available men working under R.E.s on the day before. 2/Lt T. Shearer appointed assistant Adjutant from this date (Authority P.R.O. 1242). 2/Lt W. Kilgour was granted leave. Regimental Football Match with 14th M.I. resulted in a draw. R.E.F.	
"	18.		Church parade in morning at 10.30 a.m. Battalion sports in afternoon and evening won by "C" Company with H.Q. Coy second. R.E.F.	
"	19.		Battalion bathed in morning, marched off from SOREL-LE-GRAND at 9.30 p.m. through GOUZEAUCOURT and relieved the 18th WELSH R.G.T. as Support Battalion VILLERS-PLOUICH Sector Dispositions - Bn. HQ. and "C" Company in Sunken Rd. at Q.30.c.7.1. at N. end of GOUZEAUCOURT - 3 companies in FIFTEEN RAVINE.	
SUNKEN RD at N end of GOUZEAUCOURT	20		Bn. carried Lewis Gun during last hour of relief. R.E.S. Work during day on improvement of shelters in FIFTEEN RAVINE and in Sunken Road. Bn. Headquarters - Coy HQ. Signal station and first aid post connected. R.E.B.	
"	21.		GOUZEAUCOURT village persistently shelled between 10 a.m. and 3.0 p.m. with 4.2s and 77mm shells. There were no casualties. Work on general cleaning up of company areas carried on. Lieut./Lt. G. R.F. Bartholomew granted permission to wear the badge of Captain. R.E.B.	

WAR DIARY
or
INTELLIGENCE SUMMARY.

Army Form C. 2118.

June 1917

Place	Date	Hour	Summary of Events and Information	Remarks and references to Appendices
SUNKEN Rd. West of GOUZEAUCOURT.	22.		Took on the previous days working & patrol supplies to left Bn. VILLERS- PLOUICH sector. Lept. Rev. R. Bates & 2/Lt. Randall granted leave. Maj. Fred. arch. Lt-Col A.D. Barnshaw joined to details prior to going on leave. Maj. R.E. Hames assumed command of the Bn. 2/Lt. O.J.P. Elliott struck duty from leave. R.O.B.	
	23.		Nav. H.Q. completed on Sunken Road. Work as on day before. Working parties at Bn. 2/Lt. O.J.P. Elliott struck duty from leave. R.O.B.	
	24.		The day was quiet. Work carried on the same as previous day. 2/Lt & O.M. Patterson joined the Battalion right to left sector. The weather was fine.	
	25.		Rain chills during morning & cricket lie. Pioneers took work on new front line Bn. H.Q. in R.O.B. ready from VILLERS- PLOUICH accommodation for front line Bn. H.Q. 2/Lt. Hennings joined the Battalion at 15 RAVINE Remainder of the day was quiet. R.O.B.	
	26.		B.SA.vCAMP. Remainder of the day was quiet. Work was carried on both at 15 RAVINE Day quiet. rather showery weather. Arrangements were made for the relief under 17th H.L.I. and I.K.C at VILLERS-PLOUICH on the following night.	
	27.		The day was quiet. The Bn. marched off from Support position – Bay from Ravine moved into Right Support. "C" Coy from Sunken Rd. at GOUZEAUCOURT. "D" Coy. took over Left Front position: Bn. H.Q. were established at R.13a 6.5. Left Support. A Coy took over Right Front position H.Q. and "D" Coy. the Left Front position. Relief was completed successfully at about 2.15 a.m. The relief was very slow but "C" was carried out our own Coys. during the night enemy was very ready and shortly there was not lowering parties of the H.L.I. were not during the relief R.O.B.	

Army Form C. 2118.

WAR DIARY
or
INTELLIGENCE SUMMARY.
(Erase heading not required.)

Instructions regarding War Diaries and Intelligence Summaries are contained in F.S. Regs., Part II. and the Staff Manual respectively. Title pages will be prepared in manuscript.

Place	Date	Hour	Summary of Events and Information	Remarks and references to Appendices
LEFT BK VILLERS PLOUICH aulin	28		The day was Quiet. The usual movement was seen on HINDENBURG LINE - At night our patrols were out - one on the extreme left and one on the extreme right - both patrols brought good reports and were uneventful. RWR.	
	29		The day was Quiet but for the usual sniping along the whole front. A few shells dropped near left Coy HQ. At night Patrols again went out from both Company fronts & were successful in making 505 reconnaissance without encountering any of the enemy outside his trench. Rain had fallen heavily during the day & the trenches were very wet. The road & paths in the Ravines were practically impassable. At midnight the enemy put a heavy barrage fire down on our right (off the relief) followed by a raid as reported. The raid however repulsed. The remainder of the night was Quiet but for a slight M.G. activity against our Right day. RWR. Rains heavily all day. Elsewhere had one the front very Quiet. Rain stopped at night and Patrols out the Sausses a light before. Left bay patrol from Rifle Grenade nets a snoked post in FRITH TRENCH which appeared to be quite successful. The again bombers the front line during the night our artillery replied on PINE COPSE. Left of 15 OR Issued Bt- 29/6/17. Capt Hamilton took over command of "C" Coy from 27/-. RWR.	
	30.			

Maxwell Rees, Major,
Commdg. 14th A.I.H.
1 July, 1917.

WAR DIARY
~~INTELLIGENCE SUMMARY~~

(Erase heading not required.)

Army Form C. 2118.

14 A&SH July 1917

Place	Date	Hour	Summary of Events and Information	Remarks and references to Appendices
VILLERS-PLOUICH	1.		The Bn was in the front line. The day was quiet. "B" relieved "A" on relief who carried out. "B" relieved "D" on the left. The left post was shelled with 7mm. during the relief + 3 of "D" Coys covering parties became casualties. Patrols during the night the same as usual. 1914.	
	2.		The day was quiet. Weather fine. Hand patrols at night. B's working parties on both fronts. The Bn working party, which had been particular on the right by front, both Company fronts the same as usual. We wire on right bay from. Patrols on both Company fronts the same as usual. Very numerous MC in no-man's-land and front walking unusual to report. Sgt Lockhart and Lefle Niven proceeded to the U.K. to take up their commissions. R.H.	
	3.		The day was quiet except for intermittent shelling of front line system. Alright working and patrolling carried on the same as before. R.H.A.	
	4.		During the day a steady shelling was maintained by the enemy on our left bay front. He came out in two places, one big gap in the centre of bay front, and another smaller gap near the railway on the right. This was kept up till evening. As a hostile raid was practically certain steps were immediately taken to counter out an attempt. Lewis Lena Guns were posted in the line and RE approach gaps were watched. At 11.30pm 2 Ptes of the enemy were seen to approach the centre gap this was a whole storm valence of bombs. One at least short - on RGs out rifle opened on them and they fled. Immediate search was made for identification but non could be found. The rest of the night passed off quietly. Lieut Hamilton took over "C" bay from 2/Lt/17 R.S.P.	
	5.		The day was quiet and during the afternoon advance parties were sent down to take over from the 71st B/HQRs. in Brigade Reserve. On the night 5/6 7/C	

WAR DIARY
or
INTELLIGENCE SUMMARY.

Army Form C. 2118.

July 1917.

Place	Date	Hour	Summary of Events and Information	Remarks and references to Appendices
VILLERS-FAUCON	5.		Battalion was relieved by the 14th Bn. H.L.I. During the relief covering parties were still retained after completion of relief. The Bn. was relieved by platoons to Brigade. Left at Sunken Road N.W. of GOUZEAUCOURT, while "D" Company went right front to DESSART WOOD. Bn. H.Q. was established at Q29central. (57SE.) The Bn. was in Bivouac by 2.45 am.	
Bn. RESERVE NEAR GOUZEAUCOURT	6.		There were no parades - men rested & cleaned up during the day. Two companies worked under R.E. on front line Left Bn. VILLERS-PLOUICH Sector. "D" Coy. had rifle by arrangement at FINS. "D" Coy. carried out Musketry Range practice during the day at DESSART WOOD. P.9.A.	
	7.		Bn. working on shelters during the day. Improvement of accommodation in all Company areas was carried on. During the afternoon a heavy bombardment took place on our right sector. The Brigade H.Q., in case of an attempt at attack from the enemy & moved then Btn. H.Q. in Q29. "A" Company A.B. stood to in the Brown Line for the night and moved down to DESSART WOOD in the morning. The night was quiet on the front and working parties as before carried on. R.9.d.	
	8.		Work carried on as usual, making shelters, improving platoon accommodation and cleaning up lines generally. Bn. H.Q. moved to Sunken Rd. running from GOUZEAUCOURT - TRESCAULT owing Bde. H.Q. taking over our old place. "C" Company had bath & canteen out musketry as per return. P.9.d.	
	9.		Work the same as before. "B" Coy. was to DESSART WOOD. "C" Coy. came up. 2/Lt. W.A. Kilgour 74 Seaforths proceeds to Course at 59 Reserve R.F.C. R.9.d.	

(A.7092.) Wt. W12559/M1093. 75,0.0. 1/17. D. D. & L., Ltd. Forms/C.2118/14.

Army Form C. 2118.

WAR DIARY
or
INTELLIGENCE SUMMARY.
(Erase heading not required.)

July 1917

Place	Date	Hour	Summary of Events and Information	Remarks and references to Appendices
Bde RESERVE near BOUZEAUCOURT	10.		Programme of work the same as usual. Two companies working under the R.E. with left Bn. in the line. "B" Company had baths and are then uncertain to work at DESSART WOOD. 2/Lt R. Miller (Scottish Rifles) attached 14th A.S.H. Joined 6th 120th T.M. Battery with effect from 4.6.17. R&A	
	11.		Was attached to the 120th T.M. Battery with effect from 4.6.17. R&A. Work the same as on previous days. "A" Company went to DESSART WOOD and "B" Coy came up to BOUZEAUCOURT - TRESCAULT Rd. R&A	
	12.		Work during the day on shelters carried on the same as before. No working parties were required at night owing to minor subsidiary being attempted on the front. "A" Coy bathed & fired the musketry course at DESSART WOOD. R&A	
	13.		Work during the day carried on the same as usual. In the evening advance parties were sent up to left Bn. to take over. The Bn. moved off by platoons to relieve the 14th Bn. H.L.I. on the left sub. sect. VILLERS - PLOUICH. The relief was carried out successfully - the night was quiet. Capt R. Duke took over the duties of 2nd in Command from 10/7/17. R&A	
VILLERS-PLOUICH	14.		The day was fine - "A" Coy on the right - "D" on the left - "B" supporting "A" & "C" supporting "D". The right Coys were Stella's during the day - especially DICK AVENUE and SURREY RAVINE. The observation over the site of SURREY RAVINE were successful and the trench blocked. This was shelled at night time. Patrols were out from both coys fronts but saw nothing and were unable to report. Much aerial activity during the day, increasing as usual towards night. R&A	

Army Form C. 2118.

WAR DIARY
or
INTELLIGENCE SUMMARY.
(Erase heading not required.)

July 1917.

Place	Date	Hour	Summary of Events and Information	Remarks and references to Appendices
VILLERS PLOUICH	15		The day was quiet, but for the usual intermittent shelling on Front & Support Trenches with field guns. SURREY RAVINE again receiving much attention. Patrols at night were out and both patrols reached the enemy wire. On the night nothing unusual to report. The police from "D" Coy on the left fired some rifle grenades from No-man-land into a hopeful enemy post - this drew M.G. fire from the post - this established the fact of this being a post then. The village snipers were still intermittently during the evening on artillery fired a concentration on DIVE COPSE at 5.15 p.m. Enemy artillery replies (this about 6.20 - firing on 15 Ravine, RH9, the usual intermittent shelling during the day) both our patrols at night the same as before. Lt A. Maclellan rejoined their home leave. Pvts (Corps) (1st Bn), R.S.R.	
	16.		The day was quiet. A day light relief was carried out. our platoon at a time being relieved. It is interesting to note that this is the first "day light" relief carried out by this Bn. since October 1916. B Coy relieved A Coy, and "C" Coy relieved "D" Coy. At night the patrols were taken over by the two front coys. Nothing unusual happened. R.S.R.	
	17.			
	18.		The day was quiet. Work and patrolling carried on the same as usual. R.S.R.	

Army Form C. 2118.

WAR DIARY
or
INTELLIGENCE SUMMARY.

(Erase heading not required.)

July 1917.

Place	Date	Hour	Summary of Events and Information	Remarks and references to Appendices
VILLERS-PLOUICH	19.		The day passed quietly. The weather continued fine. At night the work on trenches and wire was carried on. The issue as usual. Patrols were out in front Company fronts RAS.	
	20.		Today was again quiet - hostile artillery showed increased activity in front Line system - no great damage done. At night a patrol was sent out by the right company back to a flank spark between our wire & our taking place on our immediate right. The patrol withdrew after the stretcher bearers had got safely back with our own dead. Our stretcher bearers patrols were out and helped to carry in a wounded man from No-Man's-Land 130⁰A during the morning. SORRY RAVINE was heavily shelled with 7mm - one casualty only was sustained. Capt MACKINNON B Coy. The rest of the day was quiet till about 8pm. It was then reported that some enemy snipers were clear up to Advanced trench. Lieut Smith ordered a lance corporal and two men to try and locate these men and to fire rifle grenades at them & was found that a party of the enemy (about 10) had entered our outfield piece of MOUNTAIN ASH TR. Lt LANDELL who was on duty, at once proceeded, with 9Corpl SNOWDON and a bombing party to clear out the enemy. They were met on the C.T. leading up to the advanced trench. A bombing fight took place in which LT LANDELL was mortally wounded. 9Corpl SNOWDON was also wounded. The enemy was forced to retire. 9Corpl SNOWDON guarded the head of ST LANDELL until Capt SMITH took a party past them and (Claud) MOUNTAIN ASH TR of the enemy. Posts were successfully established in the advance trench and a platoon of the Sherwoods brought up.	
	21.			

Army Form C. 2118.

WAR DIARY
or
INTELLIGENCE SUMMARY.
(Erase heading not required.)

July (9)

Place	Date	Hour	Summary of Events and Information	Remarks and references to Appendices
VILLERS-PLOUICH	21.		Bttn. was relieved by the 11th K.O.R. Lancs. during the night. There were enemy patrols out in front whilst the forward trench was held. After the relief the Bttn. withdrew to Brigade support. Headquarters and 3 Companies (A.B.D.) while "C" Company were in shelters in the BOOZEAUCOURT–TRESCAULT RD. R.A.A.	
BRIGADE SUPPORT	22.		Bttn. rested during the morning. Shoved equipment, clothed the alarm in the afternoon. R.E. working parties supplied to right Bn. VILLERS PLOUICH (2 companies). R.A.A.	
	23.		Shelters and accommodation in all company areas improved – new shelters were put in construction. Work at night same as before. R.A.A.	
	24.		Work the same as before. 15 RAVINE slightly shelled. R.A.A.	
	25.		Work the same as before. Capt. Johnstone joined the Battalion at Josel 24/7/17 ?	
	26.		Work as before. Col. Bryant – the acting Brigadier presented the military medal to L/Cpl PATERSON – "C" Company for work done on the night of 4/5. Pt. Stewart	
	27.		"C" Company went to VILLERS-PLOUICH on night of the precolation. The attempted enemy M.M. post was not at the precolation. Also received the H.M. hut was not at The precolation. Tn B? was relieved by the 8 Huy Command who went to work. Capt ? said that he was extremely pleased with the Battalion – the clean-liness of the shelters – and discipline and efficient state of the men. He intimated that he would report the above to Lient. General. R.R.H.	
	29.		Work the same as usual during the day. Rain came on heavily in the evening. No working parties at night. R.A.A.	

Army Form C. 2118.

WAR DIARY
or
INTELLIGENCE SUMMARY.
(Erase heading not required.)

July 1917

Place	Date	Hour	Summary of Events and Information	Remarks and references to Appendices
15 Ravine	29.		We took on Shelter during the day. Also carried on the same as normal. Advance parties were sent to A.L.L. in Right sector VILLERS-PLOUICH to take over fr. the narrow companies going into the line that night. The Bn moved off by platoons from 15 RAVINE and proceeded by PODS AVENUE to relieve the 11th Br. N.L.I. This was done successfully - the right and left companies went and the relief was complete by 12.5 am. The rest of the night passed quietly. RNCA.	
	30.		The night was quiet - patrols sent out from both companies points and searched all the ground in front - nothing unusual was encountered. RNCA.	
	31.		During the day the left company post (D.Coy) was shelled with Minnen - the rest of the day was quiet. Rain set in about 8.30 pm. RNCA	

Maxwell Rowe Major.
Comdg. 14th PH/Hdrs.

WAR DIARY
INTELLIGENCE SUMMARY

Army Form C. 2118.

14 Aug S H
Vol 15
159

Place	Date	Hour	Summary of Events and Information	Remarks and references to Appendices
Villers-Plouich	Aug 1 1917		Battalion in Villers-Plouich sector. The day was quiet. Rain clearing. Garrison in night to 19th Bn. who detailed off. Relief was established. Advance parties sent off to 19th Welsh HQ. Trench clear. Activity in afternoon. West weather. Relief completed about 12.45 pm. HQ went to front in Q29d. 2 Coys in Gouzeaucourt Wood. 1 Coy Q24C and 1 in Desart Wood.	
	" 2		Day wet. Rested in morning. HQ shifted to Gouzeaucourt Wood. Coys Bgm. wet. Companies entered in shelters. Men allowed into catz for stuff. Ration up by 7.30 pm.	
Gouzeaucourt Wood	" 3		Day wet. clear, rested. Church parade and Reber in coys, also concert.	
	" 4		Fine weather. Preparations for going up the line. Advance parties sent off. Relieved East Lancs Regt in afternoon. Regt. strength B Coy H. Front (relief 10.15 am) C Coy left pt C 9 D support Bn HQ at R.13 a 8.4. Night quiet. Patrols as usual.	
Villers-Plouich	" 5		Dull, warm, quiet. Patrols at night. 2/Lt Shisholm proceeds on leave.	
	" 6		Fine weather. Lad slipped to left, took over from 14/L HL 1 ...	
	" 7		C Coy moved over usual. D Coy took up position in C. left at 6.30 pm. ...	R.Wasters A (evacuated)
	" 8		with two platoons in close support, Thunderstorm. Patrol out on all company fronts. 2/Lt Wood appointed Bn L.G.O.	2/Lt William (killed) C
	" 9		Day quiet. Trench Coy HQ shelled at noon. Thunderstorm 4 pm.	2/Lt Archibold ...

WAR DIARY
or
INTELLIGENCE SUMMARY.
(Erase heading not required.)

Army Form C. 2118.

Place	Date	Hour	Summary of Events and Information	Remarks and references to Appendices
Villers- Bocage	Aug 9		Trenches in a very muddy state. Evening quiet with exception of our own activity at night especially about picketing L.C. Coys. very busy raiding party driven off when they got within 30 yds. our tombs and three three wounded. Capt. Younger joined Bn as O.M. Patman to come off orderly after.	2/Lt M. MacDonald wounded
	10		Day quiet. Telephone activity in evening. Took over a Portable R/g & S.I. (Rabbit) arrived at 9.30 P.M. Were cut off until relief Bn Rd No 217. Taken to refil possible road. 2 Platoon L.G. sent to Plough	
	11		Support entering all night. Quiet. Patrols out. Slight shelling at night by day and other fronts.	Lt J Farewell (wounded) Lt Decans (wounded) 2/Lt R J Lowan (wounded)
	12		Afternoon Patrols enter on all fronts. A coy relieved B in night front in the evening B coy moved to Pouton near Villers Plouich station.	3
	13		Quieter than usual. About in trench shelling round Keanly at intervals.	
Gonnecourt Wood	14		Relief in afternoon by 14th H.L.I. Battalion moved down to Brigade support. Bn H.Q. A & D Coys in Gonnecourt Wood B coy in sunken road at Q 29 central (About 700 x N E of Queen +) C coy in Dessart Wood.	
Dessart Wood	15		Rest. Cleaning up etc. Heavy showers.	
	16		Company training. Showers. Generally work carried out. Range Machine Gun at Dessart Wood. Bombing	

Army Form C. 2118.

WAR DIARY
or
INTELLIGENCE SUMMARY.
(Erase heading not required.)

Instructions regarding War Diaries and Intelligence Summaries are contained in F. S. Regs., Part II. and the Staff Manual respectively. Title pages will be prepared in manuscript.

Place	Date	Hour	Summary of Events and Information	Remarks and references to Appendices
Gouzeaucourt / Dessart Woods.	Aug 17		Company training at Dessart Wood. B coy moved down to Dessart Woods.	
	18.		Company training.	
	19.		Company training. Church parade in Company areas. Congregated in Gouzeaucourt Wood. Bombing Sound finished. Sermon ad Dubf. Competition completed. Judged by B.O.C.	
Villers-Beaumont	20.		Coy inspection. Relieved 14th H.L.I. in Villers Beaucourt sector. 3.30 B. Coy right ½ C. centre, "D" left, "A" in support. Relief quiet.	21.8.17
	21.		Left company shelled in early morning. Enemy barrage commenced 7 p.m. active on Ref. offence. and others cannot sleep. Day quiet. Patrols out with special orders of locating hostile M.G. posts. Right Coy patrol had 2 hrs, killed 1 wounded and one man also. On artillery stopped shelling 7 p.m. which was firing at 6 a.m.	
	22.		Day quiet. Hostile 7 p.m. again on right Coy front about 5.30. a.m. Very Lt. carelessly erected to detail, and hence to 3½ Coys. Bombing school: Instructor. 3 men slightly wounded. Lts. Cummings, Gallagher + Bell. Very few craters. Special patrolling cancelled by Brigade	Ref. offence. 22.8.17
	23.		A. Coy reliever B. Coy on the right front.	Ref. offence. 23.8.17

Army Form C. 2118.

WAR DIARY
or
INTELLIGENCE SUMMARY.
(Erase heading not required.)

Instructions regarding War Diaries and Intelligence Summaries are contained in F. S. Regs., Part II. and the Staff Manual respectively. Title pages will be prepared in manuscript.

Place	Date	Hour	Summary of Events and Information	Remarks and references to Appendices
Villers–Beaucamp	Aug 24		2 men wounded in "A" Coy front whilst on patrol. Day pretty quiet, a few scattered T.M. active on right Bn front.	
	25		At 6.30 p.m. enemy attempted to raid D coy. On toving party of that company ejected the enemy from the trench, and drove off identification. At had two casualties. The prisoner was got the 12th Coy, 3rd Bn, 31st I.R. 18th Div. Patrols went out all night to see if there was any trace of dead a wounded, none were found. Still looks T.M. on the right company front.	25 I.S.
	26		Relieved during afternoon by H.L.I. and proceeded to Brigade support. B.H.Q. & C. Coy. in Fighters Ravine. D Coy Ellens– Plouch – Beaucamp Road. A & B coy to the Intermediate line.	
	27		Cleaning up under Company arrangements. Work as per programme for support Battalion. Rain, very cold.	
	28		Weather still very bad. Company training and working parties.	
	29.		Weather fair. Training and working parties as usual.	
	30.		Training and working parties. 2 Coy's accommodation found. (C. Coy)	
	31.		Weather fair. Usual company work. Lieut A. Duchee reported to HQ 120th Inf. Bgde	

(A7093.) Wt. W12859/M1093. 75 m.p. 4/17. D. D. & L., Ltd. Forms/C–2118/14.

WAR DIARY or INTELLIGENCE SUMMARY

Army Form C. 2118.

14th (S) Bn. A & S H'rs
September 1917 VOL. XVI

Place	Date	Hour	Summary of Events and Information	Remarks and references to Appendices
VILLERS-PLOUICH	1st		Relieves 14th Bn. H.L.I. in Right Front. Coys as usual. ABCD Support Right Centre Left respectively. Day fine and fairly quiet. Capt. R. Dickie attaches to 120 Bde for course of instruction. 2/Lt. Shearer takes over the duties of Adjutant vice Capt. Dickie.	
	2nd		Major (A/Lieut Col) Maccreadie. C. Rowe proceeds to U.K. as is struck off strength. Capt (a/Major) C.G. Johnstone took over command of the Battalion. 2/Lieut Forrester, 4th Army Musketry School Pont Remy. Day very fine – Bright Moonlight – Quiet – Enemy Front trenches with Around dark & H.T.Ms.	Casualties 2/9/17 — 325604 Pte R. Pattison accidentally wounded Rifles
	3rd		"B" Coy – Right Front – 3mm Relief in "B" Posns. 13881 A/Cpl Pattison J.: 7757 Pte Marshall D. 9082 Pte Shuttle, A.G. Bty Trench. [Casualties] A Coy Relieved B Coy in Right Front – Enemy fairly active during relief – Quiet.	302240 Pte Sinclair wounded
	4th		Day Quiet. Nothing unusual to Report. Quiet.	
	5th			
	6th		Enemy Enterprise. 2/Lieut A.C. Chisholm and 34 O.R. ("A" Coy). When Bangalore party went out a party of 15-20 of the enemy were discovered lying outside his own wire. The "Laying" party with Bangalore withdrew and a fighting patrol went out. This patrol withdrew discovered that Enemy has had considerable casualties – Some shots were fired by the enemy who returned to his trench and kept his men under close observation. It is considered that the Element of Surprise was ready for the patrol entering the Enemies line W.IK	6/9/17 27823 Pte F. Olive
GOUZEAUCOURT WOOD	7th		Relieved by 14th Bn H.L.I. and withdrew to Bde Reserve in GOUZEAUCOURT WOOD. B.H.Q. C & B Coy GOUZEAUCOURT WOOD. A & D Coys DESSART WOOD. Day fine. Quiet.	
	8th		Major A.D. Carmichael reported from hospital and took over Command of the Batt. Leaving area Coy avoided fire. Capt. G.W. McGown relieved from leave. Day fine. Quiet	

WAR DIARY
or
INTELLIGENCE SUMMARY.

SEPTEMBER 1917. Army Form C. 2118.

VOL. XVI

Place	Date	Hour	Summary of Events and Information	Remarks and references to Appendices
GOUZEAU- COURT WOOD.	9th		Training under Coy arrangements. Football. D Coy baths. Day fine – Wind	
	10th		" " " " " " " B Coy " Musketry GOUZEAUCOURT Rd	
Bde. Reserve.	11th		DESSART WOOD – Day fine – Wind	
			C Coy baths – Sports under Coy arrangements – D & C Coy Concerts. Wind	
	12th		Training as usual. Wind	
VILLERS-PLOUICH	13th		Relieved 14th Bn. H.L.I. – Coys as before – ABCD, Support, Right, Centre, Eff. respectively. Very clear day. Normal rifle & repeat. Wind	
	14th		Good day – Very clear. Enemy shelling concentrates on Right. No material damage. No casualties. Wind	
	15th		During the night Pamphlets (facsimile of letter written by German Prisoners in our hands June, in some case being in enemy wire, others thrown over in Rifle grenades and stokes shells – Very calm day. Wind	
	16th		A Coy relieved B Coy in Right front. Everything quiet during relief. 2/Lt. A.H.P. Campbell allowed wear bars of Rank. Lieut. Leaving gazetted Wind	
	17th		Notice L.M. Activity on Right front. Coys in SURREY Ravine. Rotation. Satisfactory Wind	
	18th		Very fine day. Observation of back areas very clear.	
XV RAVINE	19th		Relieved by 10th Bn. A.S.I. withdrew to Bde Support. AHQ & D Coy XV Ravine "C" Coy (Letters) BEAUCAMP Rd. "B" Coy Claring Coy. H Coy Intermediate Line – Heavy working parties on night of Mbr. working on Regt Coy Front. Digging and carrying Heavily of clearer progress to "40" Divisional Wind	

WAR DIARY or INTELLIGENCE SUMMARY

Army Form C. 2118.

VOL XVI

Place	Date	Hour	Summary of Events and Information	Remarks and references to Appendices
3/ XV RAVINE	20th		Cleaning up. Parade under Coy Commanders. Coy looking very lost.	
	21st		H officers arrived 2Lieuts Alison (A Coy) Hamilton (A) Moffat (B) Morgan (C). Working parties on roads during night. Wnk.	
	22nd		Battalion bathed at GOUZEAUCOURT. Took during the night on road - leads fine & warm. Wnk.	
	23rd		Sunk as usual. Weather fine & warm. Wnk.	
	24th		Lieut R.H. Air proceeds on leave to U.K. Weather fine. Drafts of 30 ORs joined the Bn. Wnk.	
VILLERS PLOUICH	25th		Relieves 14th Bn H.Q.I. on Right front - Bn as usual. A B C D support Right Coy respectively. Bn front Coy H/Qrs. Considerable damage to trenches - to Canadian. Weather fine. Wnk.	
	26th		Enemy more active - Bn Casualties 'Kelts.' 3 wounded by 5.9 shell in TAFF VALE above Bn H.Q. Casualties - 12661 Pte McFagan 8857 Sgt Murdoch W; 8005 L/Cpl Wright J; 13682 Pte McFarlane J; 40516 Pte Allen G; died of wounds W. (Rifles)	
	27th		Enemy more active. Shelled LINCOLN AVENUE & VILLERS PLOUICH. Rather dull during morning. Wnk.	
	28th		Enemy still active with T.Ms on whole Battalion front. Chiefly AVOID + JERSEY RAVINE. Wnk.	

Army Form C. 2118.

WAR DIARY
or
INTELLIGENCE SUMMARY.
(Erase heading not required.)

September 1917.

VOL XVI

Place	Date	Hour	Summary of Events and Information	Remarks and references to Appendices
VILLERS- PLOUICH	29		Enemy aircraft very active both TM & Artillery - Centre Coy Slopes during the day - Situation quiet.	
	30		Enemy unusually active with TM & Shells - TMs on Br. Posts during the afternoon and evening. At 9.15 pm Artillery opens fire on HIGHLAND RIDGE - Majority of shots falling round ASHBY & the PULPIT - Right of MOUNTAIN ASH Tr Shelled. CAPT BARTHOLOMEW wounded in the head by a shell. Enemy succeeded during the evening with TMs/MGs over the whole front. Our Retaliation good but unsatisfactory - Enemy Batteries untouched. After midnight till 4.15 am 1/10/17 - Considerable damage done to the trenches - Quiet.	1/10/17

A.D. Carmichael
Lt Col
Comdg. 14 (S/B) Argyll Suth Hds

WAR DIARY or INTELLIGENCE SUMMARY

Army Form C. 2118.

OCTOBER 1917

14th Bn, Suffolk Regt.

Vol. XVII

Place	Date Oct 1917	Hour	Summary of Events and Information	Remarks and references to Appendices
VILLERS-PLOUICH	1st		Relieved by 14th Bn H.L.I. and withdrew to Brigade Reserve at Bn HQ A & D Coys at GOUZEAUCOURT WOOD, B & C Coys at DESSART WOOD. Day fine.	
Bde Reserve	2nd		General cleaning up. Football for all Coys during the afternoon	
	3rd		Officers v Parties rendezvous to SOREL for taken football.	
	4th		Battn parties to SOREL football. Sports - wet	
SOREL (LE GRAND)	5th		Bn relieved by 6th K.S.L.I. and withdrew to SOREL. Camp very dirty. Weather wet. Spent the night in huts.	
PERONNE	6th		Brigade or Relief. Battalion proceeded in busses to PERONNE (arrived 2.30pm.) Breeks very bad. Weather very wet. Capt R. Cooper joins the Battalion and is posted as second in Command. Capt W.G. Johnstone relinquishes acting rank of Major and took over Command of 'A' Coy. Capt W.H. Hamilton took over Command of 'C' Coy. Capt W.G.T. Keddie is attached to 13th Bn East Surrey Regt. as Second in Command.	
	7th		Church Parade - Weather very wet	
	8th		Route March by Companies - weather fine	
	9th		Battalion entrained at PERONNE and proceeded by BOIRE & BOISLEUX au MONT. Battalion marched from there to STHENCOURT and was billeted in huts. Accommodation good, huts in bad condition. Wet	
STHEN-COURT	10th		Cleaning up. Weather wet.	

WAR DIARY or INTELLIGENCE SUMMARY

OCTOBER 1917 — Army Form C. 2118

Vol. XVII

Place	Date	Hour	Summary of Events and Information	Remarks and references to Appendices
SIMENCOURT	11th		First day of training. Parades under Coy. Arrangements during morning - Inspection & Ceremonial. Afternoon football - weather cold & wet.	
	12th		Heavy rain - Kit inspection in huts. 2/Lieuts. Brown, Mackay & Paxton join the Bn. 2/Lieut. Lawn returns from L.G. Course at Etaploes. L. Kilgour proceeds on leave. Commanding Officers lecture to Officers in evening. wet	
	13th		Home training by Companies - Shot in the afternoon for Chief Paterson proceed to U.K. wet	
	14th		Church parade in morning. Weather fine - 2/Lieut w/L. Lunn appointed Bn. I.G. Officer. wet	
	15th		Weather fine. Bn. training at BERNEVILLE. Bly/Saths henown C by afternoon wet	
	16th		Bn. training as usual - Baths. wet	
	17th		Coast training in morning. Afternoon football. Av.C. (sermon A) B.x D (sermon B) Hougt	
	18th		Home training. Football in afternoon - Picking Britons. 10th/Wales left.	
	19th		Bn. stes day. Weather fine. Lt. Col. Baldwin returns from leave. wet	
	20th		Battalion training in morning & afternoon put of Divisional Football League - Bn. B. Fred/surveys loss to both W.2. wet	
	21st		Church Parade - Bn. plays HCL. won 1-0. wet	

WAR DIARY / INTELLIGENCE SUMMARY

OCTOBER 1917 — Vol XVII

Army Form C. 2118

Place	Date	Hour	Summary of Events and Information	Remarks and references to Appendices
SIMEN- COURT	22ᵈ		Demonstration by fighting Platoon in forenoon. All Officers & Platoon Seargeants present. Coy training in afternoon. 2 men slightly wounded reported for duty. Letters to A.G. — 1 lost	
	23ᵈ		Heavy rain all morning. Companies worked in huts. Battalion Players M.G.C at BERNEVILLE — Run 8-0. Lost	
	24ᵈ		Bn. training at WARLUS — Football in afternoon Bn. Players vs Div. Signals won 3-1. Lost	
	25ᵗʰ		Musketry at BERNEVILLE —	
	26"		Company training at BERNEVILLE — Lost Helgon reliance from leave. Lost	
	27ᵗʰ		Bn. trained. Aldurjson won lees in the evening. Lost	
	28ᵗʰ		Bn. plays final of Divisional Football League — Beat the Middlesex (Pr. B.Se) 3-0. Huava failed. left G, Lovies for LOCHEUX. Men taken	
			Bn marches to HALLOY via ARRAS — DOULLENS Rd. Men in huts.	
HALLOY	29ᵗʰ		Gleck Huts in very bad state. — Lost	
	30ᵗʰ		Coy training. 25% of men allowed passes to DOULLENS. Weather wet rough	
	31ˢᵗ		Coy training. Weather fair. 2/Lt. Lowilton (A.C/Light) arrives by boat while draft came today from G.C.C depot. — Lost Ref'd course at the Major	

1st Nov 17

A.W. Carmichael
Lt Q M & B A T Staffs

WAR DIARY
INTELLIGENCE SUMMARY

VOLUME XVIII November 1917.

Army Form C.2118.

Place	Date	Hour	Summary of Events and Information	Remarks and references to Appendices
HALLOY	Nov. 1		Weather fair. Coy. training in vicinity of Tillet. 25% of the men allowed on leave to DOULLENS. Lieuts. Miller & Allison, W. proceed on leave. 2/Col. Carmichael went to No. 7 C.C.D. Major Cope takes over command of Bn. Capt. Johnston takes over Lieut. duties. Leave to be 14 days instead of 10.	
"	2		Coy. training. Weather fair. Capt. Skeven proceed Bn. training on the ground at Hurtebise Farm.	
"	3		On leave. Lieut. Kilgour takes over duties of Adjutant. 2/Lieut. Beaton taken over Coy. training in vicinity of Tillets.	
"	4		duties of Signal Officer.	
"	5		Bn. training on rural ground. 2/Lieut. Brown is appointed Bn. Lewis Gun Officer, in the absence of 2/Lieut. W.L. Lennon, who proceeds on leave. Bn. night operation.	
"	6		Coy. training in vicinity of Tillets. 2/Lieut. Og. W. Garlak joins Bn. Battalion training on rural ground. "B" Coy. Army Bombing.	
"	7		Coy. training. 2/Lieut. Shisholm reported to duty to the Divisional Depot Bn. Sickly.	
"	8			
"	9		Staff Ride for C.Os. & Signal Officers. Staff holiday in afternoon. Capt. Rutherford proceed on leave. 2/Lieut. Fraser reported & take his place	
"	10			

Army Form C. 2118.

WAR DIARY
~~INTELLIGENCE SUMMARY~~

VOLUME XVIII   November 1917

(Erase heading not required.)

Instructions regarding War Diaries and Intelligence Summaries are contained in F. S. Regs., Part II. and the Staff Manual respectively. Title pages will be prepared in manuscript.

Place	Date	Hour	Summary of Events and Information	Remarks and references to Appendices
HALLOY	Nov. 11		Church parade in forenoon. 2/Lieut. MacMillan proceeded to Fourth Army School at Flexecourt.	
	" 12		Coy. Training. 2/Lt. R.W. Smith joined the Bn, and was posted to "A" Coy.	
	" 13		Bn. Training. Bombing ground at Hurtebise Farm used by B & D Coys.	
	" 14		Coy. Training. 2/Lieut. Knox proceeded to Fourth Army School.	
	" 15		Bayonet competition. G.O.C. presented the football cup. Bn. Training. Officers values to be brought down to 35lbs. Move orders for 16th received. 2/Lieut. E. G. Walker proceeded on leave.	
SIMENCOURT	" 16		Battalion marched to SIMENCOURT and reoccupied the old billets there. Orders received about mid-night to move again on 17th.	
	" 17		The Bn. moved off at 7 p.m. By march to COURCELLES-LE-COMPTE. Roads very bad; arrived about mid-night	
COURCELLES -LE-COMPTE.	" 18		Camp in a very good state; huts very comfortable. Rest & clean up; football, etc.	
	" 19		No parades. Preparations made to move again in the evening. Moved off at 8 p.m.	
BEAULEN- -COURT.	" 20		Arrived about 1 a.m. Accommodated in huts. Weather very wet and stormy. Capt. Shearn returned from leave.	

A.834. Wt. W4973/M687 750,000 8/16 D. D. & L. Ltd. Forms/C.2118/13.

Army Form C. 2118.

WAR DIARY
INTELLIGENCE SUMMARY. November 1917
VOLUME XVIII

(Erase heading not required.)

Place	Date	Hour	Summary of Events and Information	Remarks and references to Appendices
BEAULEN-COURT	Nov 21		Bn. under orders to move at 2 hours notice. Details to be left at Beaulencourt.	
LABUCQUIER	" 22		Bn. marched to Labucquier. 2/Lieut. Allison returned from leave.	
BOURLON WOOD.	" 23		Bn. left at 3.20 a.m. and marched to Hindenburg Support, rested. Ordered to move up to Bourlon Avenue Chapel at 5.30 p.m. placed under orders of 119th Bde. On reaching Avenue Chapel, ordered up to Bourlon Wood A & B Coys. attacked to Welch, C & D Coys. pushed in later. 2/Lieut. Sewers returned from leave to details at BEAULENCOURT.	
	" 24		Attempted to take Bourlon Wood, H.L.I. brought up, K.O.R.L. & East Surrey brought up, attacks & counter-attacks going on all day. Capt. Johnston went up to re-organise.	
TRESCAULT	" 26		Bn. marched to TRESCAULT, accommodation very poor, tents and bivouacs. Details marched in about 8 p.m. Weather very bad, slept most of the night.	
HENDECOURT	" 27		Bn. marched to YTRES and entrained there for BEAUMETZ. Arrived about 7 p.m. and marched to HENDECOURT. Transport proceeded by road.	

Army Form C. 2118.

WAR DIARY

VOLUME XVIII INTELLIGENCE SUMMARY. November 1917.

(Erase heading not required.)

Place	Date	Hour	Summary of Events and Information	Remarks and references to Appendices
HENDECOURT	Nov 28		Rest & clean up. Bn. at disposal of C.C. for reorganisation. Transport marched in about 11 a.m.	
"	29		Bn. Training. Weather fair.	
"	30		Bn. Training. Bn. stores & surplus kit arrived from BEAULENCOURT.	J R Clayton for C.R.

"14th Argyll & Sutherland Highlanders"

Nominal Roll of Officers and Other Ranks killed, Wounded and Missing on 23rd to 26th November 1917.

Officers killed in Action
    Lieut J. ALLISON   23rd Nov. 1917

Died of Wounds
    Captain D. NICOL   Wounded 25/11/17

Wounded
    Lieut H.A.M. TYSON   23rd Nov. 1917
    Capt H.W. HAMILTON   24th Nov. 1917
    " GW McCROW   "   "
    2.Lieut HD McKINNA   "   "
    " JM GARLICK   "   "
    ~~Shell Shock~~ N.Y.D.N.
    2nd Lieut J.Y. FORTUNE   "   "
    J.C. MACLEAN   "   "
    R.H. SMITH   "   25/11/17

Other Ranks killed in Action
    S/9370 Sgt Gregor W.   'A' Coy
    11744 L/Cpl McMorland J.   "
    40566 Pte Docherty W.   "
    40577 " Gilchrist J.   "
    325329 " McMillan D.   "
    21678 " Malloch J.   "
    203323 " Morton A.   "

Other Ranks Wounded

9673	L/Sgt	Young J McG.	(at Duty)	'C' Coy
14437	Pte	Ruthven	S O	
15329	"	Leask	C. Y.	'B' Coy
40736	"	Wilson	J	
325365	L/Cpl	Dennett	J	
16397	Pte	Hunter	A	
1138##	"	Hughes	R.	
13654	"	Bekero	J A	
10573	"	Adamson	J	
10318	Sgt	Logan	C	'A' Coy
40520	Cpl	Jamieson	J	"
11312	"	Hunter	R R.	"
8416	L/C	Harper	J	"
10514	Pte	Bell	J A	"
41554	"	Cassidy	W	"
278060	"	Dunn	W B	"
16480	"	Glass	W	"
40584	"	Houlihan	P	"
19704	"	Welsh	J	"
8970	Cpl	McEntee	J	"
15437	L/C	Adam	A W.	"
275398	Pte	Blair	J	"
4255	"	Lyons	P	"
9143	"	Thompson	G A	"
251441	"	McKinnon	H	"
300768	"	Kerr	M	"
277686	"	McKerracher	M	"
278298	"	Potts	J D	'D' Coy

Other Ranks Wounded (continued)

No	Rank	Name	Coy
43048	pte	Newman G.	'D' Coy
13587	"	Thompson J.	"
17336	"	Mitchell W.H.	"
7701	"	Smith J.	"
301096	"	Bell J.	"
301574	"	McInnes J.	"
9314	"	Davis A.	"
13819	"	Woodcock J.G.H.	"
40799	"	Rankin J.	"
8948	Sgt	Flett J.	'B' Coy
12262	"	Tyndall J.	'C' Coy
303368	pte	Shaw A.	"
40751	"	Muir A. NYDN	"
9036	"	Bell J.	"

Other Ranks ~~Still Sick~~ NYDN

No	Rank	Name	Coy
2293	pte	Coy A.	'A' Coy
325095	"	McGuire J.	"
325830	"	McGrath J.	"
18222	"	Alves J.	"
20626	"	Duncan A.	'B' Coy
8995	L/C	Robb J.R.	"
278027	pte	Milne A.	'D' Coy

Other Ranks Wounded

No	Rank	Name	
16121	pte	Sinclair J.	
300191	"	McIntyre J.	

Other Ranks Wounded (Continued)

277627	Pte	McConway	J	'C' Coy
17709	"	McGonagall	W	"
277772	"	Gemmill	R	"
40749	"	Arthur	J	"
303348	"	Shaw	R	"
278673	"	Collins	G	"
326723	"	Jeffries	C	"
9061	"	McKendrick	P	"
16285	"	Palmer	J	"
277797	"	Smith	J	"
40752	"	Stewart	W	"
17659	"	Strachan	J	"
40781	"	Thomson	J.H	"
15010	"	Young	J	"
19752	"	Garrick	J	"
12109	L/Cpl	Todd	J	"
13649	Sgt	Stockan	J	'D' Coy
3141	L/C	Telfer	J	"
18250	Pte	Young	A	"
321207	"	Michael	J	"
40772	"	Macdonald	A	"
325362	"	Boyce	C	"
10391	"	Martin	J	"
40459	"	Niblo	J.A	"
14067	"	Fraser	F	"
277548	"	Crawford	J	"
277093	"	Austin	J	"
325305	"	Grant	R	'C' Coy

Oth. Ranks Wounded (Continued)

No	Rank	Name		Coy
40746	Pte	Ramsey	G.	"B" Coy
40764	"	Sharpe	J	"
15791	"	Thomson	R.S.	"
9499	"	Thomson	W	"
300347	"	McLachlan	C.C.	"
40741	"	Duff	J.E	"
45096	"	Dalrymple		"
40596	"	Laird	A	"
40605	"	McKellar	J	"
7828	"	Murphy	J	"
10662	"	Buchanan	W	"
19102	"	Gibson	J.M	"
7426	"	Thompson	J	"
10148	"	Wilson	J	"
43217	"	McCartney	W.S.	"
20508	"	Paton	J	"
12472	"	Shipton	W	"
8887	"	Thomson	A	"
3449	"	McDonald	J	"
4068	"	McRae	M	"
300275	"	McGeachy	A	"
40607	"	McLure	J	"
9519	Sgt	Hooks	J	"C" Coy
9442	L/C	Paterson	J	"
12255	"	Paterson	J	"
6562	Sgt	Murrie	J	"
6863	"	Murray	J	"
5082	Pte	Thompson	J	"D" Coy

Other Ranks Missing

No	11107	Sgt	Stewart A	(Believed killed)	'B' Coy
"	9813	Cpl	McCraw G	"	"
"	12149	Pte	Seton E	"	"
	9809	"	Nelson E	"	"
	16335	Cpl	Westaway H.	"	'D' Coy
	277921	Pte	Donaldson	"	"
	~~278298~~		~~Pratt~~		"
	~~275345~~		~~Phelps~~		"
	~~5081~~		~~Thompson~~		"
	8583	"	Cunningham W		"
	350326	"	Clacher		'C' Coy
	~~326305~~		~~Grant~~		"
	9042		Gray		"
	~~9549~~		~~Irvine~~		"
	40618		O'Beirne		"
	~~383318~~		~~Shaw~~		"
	~~40951~~		~~Kennedy~~		"
	275149		Walker W		"
	21737		Scott		"
	~~9036~~		~~Bell~~		"
	~~6101~~		~~Sinclair~~		"
	6083		McCrendie		"
	~~300191~~		~~McIntyre~~		"
	16170		Kerr J.S.		"

Other Ranks Wounded (Continued)

No. 40550	Pte	Cameron M.		'A' Coy
9437	"	Calder E		"
9588	L/Cpl	Nimmo E		"
40556	Pte	Clark W		"
40102	"	Craig J.J.		"
9884	L/C	Millers C.S.		"
300729	Pte	Cofield W		"
40570	"	Ferguson J.W.		"
17362	"	Langston R		"
302645	"	Lithgows S		"
40583	L/C	Henshall E		"
303203	Pte	Galloway A		"
300735	Cpl	Watson J		"
9991	L/Cpl	Clason J		"
12502	Pte	Bannan J.J.		"
40586	"	Hunter R.B.		"
12363	"	Miller R.J.		"
12813	L/Cpl	Morrison W.J.		"
771	"	Anderson J		" (at Duty)
8903	Sgt	Hand A		'B' Coy
944	"	Kestings L		"
9821	"	Ramage L		"
16270	L/Cpl	Matheson H		"
4092	"	McNab J		"
9955	"	Penman J.A.		"
252373	Pte	Cairns J		"
11480	"	Lumsden W		"
276345	"	Phillips A		'D' Coy

Other Ranks Killed (Continued)

No	Rank	Name	Initials	Coy
11890	Pte.	Sutherland	K.J.	'A' Coy
40590	"	Jenkins	J	"
12561	"	Young	R.B	"
325796	"	Barker	J	"
20899	"	Howell	J	"
278079	"	Lawns	J	"
253051	"	Russell	A	"
5738		Purvis	A	'B' Coy
9461	Sgt	Taylor	A	'C' "
7485	"	Shorton	H.E	"
300656	"	McKellar	A	"
8701	L/Sgt	King	T	"
14832	"	Rossie	A	"
12270	Pte	Dron	J	"
300422	"	Connor	J	"
302679	"	McFarlane	R.	"
40754	"	McKay	C	"
10382	"	McRae	J	"
13338	"	Buchanan	J	"
13619	"	Barton	J	"
4719	"	McEwen	P	"
18428	"	Marshall	W	"
6536	"	Campbell	M	"
13224	"	Miller	W	'D' Coy
15063	"	McClure	J.J.	"

WAR DIARY or INTELLIGENCE SUMMARY

Army Form C. 2118.

DECEMBER 1917 VOLUME XIX 14th A & S H'rs.

Place	Date	Hour	Summary of Events and Information	Remarks and references to Appendices
HENDECOURT	1/12/17		Weather fine but very cold. Company training and lectures. Lent. parties took over commands of A Coy.	
			2/Lt. Kilgour " B "	
			" Cowan " C "	
			" Muller " D "	
			" D.F. Prior " H.Q. & Sigs.	
			Lieut. Weir arrived and assumed duties of QM.	
			Major R. Cowan to be Lt-Col. Capt. C.G. Johnston to be Major.	
			Major C.G. Johnston proceeded on leave.	
do	2/12/17		Church parade. Weather cold. 2/Lieut. Walker reported back from leave.	
do	3/12/17		Batt'n marched to ERVILLERS at 7.30am crossing Hun old released the buildings 49 F. Bn. 16th Div'n. Weather fine had frost. C.O. and Coy. Commanders reconnoitered route to trenches. Leave opened.	
ERVILLERS	4/12/17		Weather fine had frost. Company training in the morning. afternoon recreation parade. Snipers on the range. Gaelic officers reconnoitered route to trenches. Dumped mail arrived. 6-8pm concert in the YMCA hut	

Army Form C. 2118.

WAR DIARY
or
INTELLIGENCE SUMMARY.
(Erase heading not required.)

2. 14th A & S. Hrs.

DECEMBER 1917
VOLUME XIX

Instructions regarding War Diaries and Intelligence Summaries are contained in F.S. Regs., Part II. and the Staff Manual respectively. Title pages will be prepared in manuscript.

Place	Date	Hour	Summary of Events and Information	Remarks and references to Appendices
ERVILLERS	5/12/17		Weather. fine hard frost. Morning. Company training 9 firing on range. Afternoon. Recreation. match. Football Etc.	SP
do	6/12/17		Weather fine had frost. Company training and firing on range. Working party of 2 officers & 200 O.R. for work up the line. 2nd Lieut J. Knox returned from Musketry Course Tout. Fenny 2nd Lieut Brown proceeded to be Taught for Lewis gun course. 2nd Lieut Cumming Proceeded on leave.	SP
do	7/12/17		Weather fine but dull. Company training 9 firing on the range. Working party of 1 officer and 50 O.R. Evening Concert and presentation of Bde. football medals by C.O.	SP
do	8/12/17		Weather unsettled. Morning Company training and firing on range. Afternoon Batts. A & S.H. beat R.F.C. 2 goals to 1. The following attended Presdt. 9 members of the regimental canteen president 2Lt. & Lt. Lamon members Lt.Col P.R.Coupar Co. & Sgt. Teller's party of 2 officers & 100 O.R.	SP

WAR DIARY or INTELLIGENCE SUMMARY

Army Form C. 2118.

DECEMBER 1917
VOLUME XIX
14th A & S. H'rs.

Place	Date	Hour	Summary of Events and Information	Remarks and references to Appendices
ERVILLERS	9/12/17		Weather stormy. Church Parade. H.Q. officers and Coy. Commanders reconnoitred the line.	R.I.P.
do	10/12/17		Batt'n moved off in the following order B.C.D.H. HQ. 1 Company H.Q., 14th A&SH. and 1 Coy. K.R.I. relieved the 12 R. Suffolks & 1 Coy. 13th Yorks in right sector, left Coy. Naf. ref. 57BS9d. B.C. coys. front line A 9. 1 Coy H.L.I. in support. Situation quiet.	Fontaine-les-Croisilles
FONTAINE-LES-CROISILLES SECTOR	11/12/17		Weather fine. Own artillery active all day. Occasional shells 9.7m.s from the enemy. Dropt of 90 OR arrived at details	R.I.P.
do	12/12/17		Weather fine. At 6.45am the enemy opened a heavy barrage on our front line S.O.S. lines at 7.15am Suffolk & Communication trenches and artillery sent out barrage. The situation was normal at 7.45am. All communication wires cut. Our casualties 1 man wounded. Very quiet. Our Guns & 7m.s harassed the enemy all day. Aircraft very active. An enemy aeroplane was established game & T.M's were fired on no to right to casualties. A few S.A.P shells were fired on us at night.	R.I.P.

WAR DIARY or INTELLIGENCE SUMMARY.

Army Form C. 2118.

DECEMBER 1917
VOLUME XIX
14th A & S. HRS.

4.

Place	Date	Hour	Summary of Events and Information	Remarks and references to Appendices
FONTAINE-LES-CROISILLES SECTOR	13/12/17		Weather hot misty. Our artillery fired a heavy bombardment on the enemy's lines at dawn, no retaliation from the enemy. A constant fire together with M.G. was kept up throughout the day. Enemy fired gas shells at night no casualties the following officers were wounded 2/Lt Cooper 2/Lt a Maxwell Scott, Capt Baccus, Lieut MacKilligan 2/Lt S.B.M Cooper 2/Lt a Maxwell Scott.	S.P.
do	14/12/17		Weather dull & misty. Artillery quiet on either side, very little rifle & M.G. activity. 14th A.&S.H. were relieved by the 14th H.L.I. in the right sub-section. 14th A.&S.H. withdrew to Bde. right support. (Less 1 Coy)	S.P.
do	15/12/17		Weather very fine. Enemy aeroplanes very active Company's carry on improving accommodation. Four Stretcher bearers of D.Coy. were recommended to carry in some wounded neblot ancestry 2nd Lt Kerr struck off the Strength of the Battn. The following officers joined the Battn. G. Hill. G. Meade, G. Andrews, 2.T. Piffers.	S.P.

WAR DIARY or INTELLIGENCE SUMMARY

Army Form C. 2118.

DECEMBER 1917
VOLUME XIX
14th A & S HRS

5

Place	Date	Hour	Summary of Events and Information	Remarks and references to Appendices
FONTAINE - LEZ - CROISILLES SECTOR	16/12/17		Weather fine very cold. Companies carrying out and improving existing accommodation whilst making good bivies. Day very quiet. The enemy's artillery was very active at night. Major C.C.G. Johnston returned from leave.	J.P.
do	17/12/17		Weather cold. Ground covered with snow. Day Quiet. 2/Lt McKenzie returned from leave. 2/Lt Brown " " " Capt. A. Greenslade returned from Lewis Gun School & Targnet des Fortune P.J. is struck off the Battn strength of the Commando School from 20.11.17.	J.P.
do	18/12/17		Weather frosty & cold. Enemy shelled batteries all morning. Afternoon 14th A&SH were relieved by 7th & 12th Suffolks in the right Subsector and proceeded to Divisional reserve at CLONNEL CAMP HAMELINCOURT. Capt. A. MacMillan took over command Shrapnel of D Coy.	J.P.

A.5834. Wt.W4973/M687 750,000 8/16 D.D. & L. Ltd. Forms/C.2118/13.

Army Form C. 2118.

WAR DIARY
or
INTELLIGENCE SUMMARY.
(Erase heading not required.)

Instructions regarding War Diaries and Intelligence Summaries are contained in F. S. Regs., Part II. and the Staff Manual respectively. Title pages will be prepared in manuscript.

Place	Date	Hour	Summary of Events and Information	Remarks and references to Appendices
HAVRINCOURT	19/12/17		Day opened fresh and cold. Company under Coy Commander. Xmas parcels from Derby issued to the men.	P.P.
do	20/12/17		Weather hard frost. Company training and baths. Working party of 1 officer & 50 O.R.	P.P.
do	21/12/17		Weather hard frost. Company training. Working party of 2 officers & 100 O.R. 2nd Lieut J. Skewer proceeded on leave.	P.P.
do	22/12/17		Weather very fine hard frost. Morning Coys Commander Lectured on enemy methods to meet our bravery during the fighting round BOURLON WOOD. Afternoon Match Officers v. Guard of honour football. Evening Concert in the recreation hut. Working party of 2 officers & 100 O.R.	P.P.

WAR DIARY
or
INTELLIGENCE SUMMARY.

Army Form C. 2118.

DECEMBER 1917

VOLUME XIX

144th A. v S. Hrs.

Place	Date	Hour	Summary of Events and Information	Remarks and references to Appendices
HAMELINCOURT	23.12.17		Weather cold and hoar frost. Normal Church parade. Afternoon - football, officers v. sergeants. Evening - Battalion Xmas dinner. Lt. Forster proceeded on leave.	UK
do.	24.12.17		Battalion moved after the following hours: HQ. A.D. C.B. and 1 Coy. 14th L.I. 14 H.A. & L.A. relieved 13th Yorks in Right Sector - left Bndcott - Fontaine-lez-Crosilles took ref 51 B SWA. A.D. C. Coys in Support line. B. Coy in right support. Coy HQ. Left Support. Situation quiet. What. Bouger proceeded on leave.	
Fontaine lez-Croiselles Sector.	25.12.17		Weather cold: xmas fell during the day. Own artillery fairly active; enemy artillery shelled our lines slightly. 2 Lt. Cummings rejoined Battn from leave.	
do.	26.12.17		Weather cold, dull; ground covered with snow. Day fairly quiet. Own artillery kept up its usual harassing fire. The enemy shelled our lines slightly. 2 Lt. A. J. Grove & 2 Lt Grade joined the Battn.	

WAR DIARY
or
INTELLIGENCE SUMMARY.

(Erase heading not required.)

DECEMBER 1917 Army Form C. 2118.

VOLUME XIX
At S.H.R.S.

Place	Date	Hour	Summary of Events and Information	Remarks and references to Appendices
FONTAINE- lez-CROISILLES SECTOR	27/12/17		Weather cold but clear; ground covered with snow. Enemy artillery rather more active than usual. 14½ A & S.H. were relieved by the 6 Royal Scots and 1 Coy. H.L.I. by 7 Coy. 15 Royal Scots. No casualties. The Batt. proceeded to BOYELLES CAMP I.A.	
BOYELLES	28/12/17		Weather cold and clear; ground covered with snow. 4.2's fell near the camp during the night of 27/28.12.17. Capt Lindeman, Capt Lockhead, 2 Lt Sharp, 2 Lt Monaghan, 2 Lt Walker, 2 Lt Kinnear joined the Batt. Capts Lambieva and Lockhead were attached to H.Q. S. & 2/199 walkers dept for III Army School. wgl.	
BOYELLES	29/12/17		Weather cold and clear; ground covered with snow. 2 Lt Danton left for VI Corps L.G. school. The Batt. moved H.Q in the following order H.Q.A.B.C.D. and relieved the 9th Yorks in BULLECOURT Sector Subsect. wgl.	
BULLECOURT	30.12.17		Weather cold and clear. Still snow on the ground. Day quiet. Working party on New trench line B 3 Macen and Kooner. wgl.	

WAR DIARY
or
INTELLIGENCE SUMMARY.

(Erase heading not required.)

DECEMBER 1917 Army Form C. 2118.

VOLUME XIX

14th A. S. Hrs.

Place	Date	Hour	Summary of Events and Information	Remarks and references to Appendices
BULLECOURT	31.12.17		Weather cold; snow on the ground. Day quiet. Working parts on New trench line. B.3 Officers and women sick.	

C.C. Johnstone Major.
Comdg. 14th Bde Avg South Afs.

Army Form C. 2118.

WAR DIARY
or
INTELLIGENCE SUMMARY.
(Erase heading not required.)

JANUARY 1918 VOL. XX

14th A.J. Bro.

Place	Date	Hour	Summary of Events and Information	Remarks and references to Appendices
BULLECOURT Right Sub Sector	1-1-18		Weather cold and fresh; snow on ground. Our artillery fired several salvos immediately after midnight. Working party of 3 Officers and 100 other ranks found line under R.E.	WK
BULLECOURT Right Sub Sector	2-1-18		Weather cold and fresh; snow still on ground. 14 M.A. & S.H. relieved 14 H.L.I. in front line. Right Batt. Right Brigade in the line using:— "D" Coy. left front; "A" Coy. centre front; "B" Coy. right front; "C" Coy. in close support in RAILWAY RESERVE. Day quiet. 2 O.R.s Radcliffe and McLean joined the Batt.	WK
BULLECOURT Right Sub Sector	3-1-18		Weather cold and fresh with snow on ground. Our artillery rather quieter than usual. Hostile movements. Three casualties in Batt. caused by 4.77mm on RAILWAY RESERVE outside Batt. Coy. H.Qrs. at 11 a.m. 2 O.R.s Com, 1 M.A. Corp. all slight.	WK

C. Hunter Lt Col
Comdg 14th Bn S.H.

209

Army Form C. 2118.

WAR DIARY
or
INTELLIGENCE SUMMARY.
(Erase heading not required.)

JANUARY 1918
VOL. XI
14th A.S.H. Bro.

Instructions regarding War Diaries and Intelligence Summaries are contained in F. S. Regs., Part II. and the Staff Manual respectively. Title pages will be prepared in manuscript.

Place	Date	Hour	Summary of Events and Information	Remarks and references to Appendices
BULLECOURT Right Sub Sector	4.1.18		Weather cold and fresh with snow on ground. Own artillery rather above normal; hostile artillery active especially during afternoon, chiefly on SETEMIS. night and left of Batt. front. Hostile T.M.s active on left of Batt. front during afternoon. Hostile M.Gs. active during left of "B" Coy front. 2 Lt. Kinnear left Batt. for III Army Musketry School course assembling on 5.1.18.	
BULLECOURT	5.1.18		Weather cold and fresh. A few shells fell on our front during hostile raid on left Batt. between 6.15 am — 7 am. Hostile artillery puckie harassing during rest of day, till between 7pm — 9 pm when between 30 and 50 light shells were fired on our front line and on RAILWAY RESERVE, on arrivally on "B" Coy.	

P.C. Hunton Lt Col
Comg 14th A.S.H.

Army Form C. 2118.

WAR DIARY
or
INTELLIGENCE SUMMARY.
(Erase heading not required.)

JANUARY 1918
Vol. XX
14th Arl. Bde.

Instructions regarding War Diaries and Intelligence Summaries are contained in F. S. Regs., Part II. and the Staff Manual respectively. Title pages will be prepared in manuscript.

Place	Date	Hour	Summary of Events and Information	Remarks and references to Appendices
BULLECOURT R/W Sect Sub/y	6.1.18		Weather cold and frost. Carrying rather quieter than usual. 14th A.S.G. were relieved by 14th A.L.I. and 10th Emos Lancers and withdrew to Brigade Reserve at Mory. We counted no lot	
MORY	7.1.18		Weather still cold and frost. Baths at Mory allotted to Batteries. 2.Lt. Shears reported back from leave. Capt. McMillan proceeded on leave.	10R
MORY	8.1.18		Weather cold & frost. Snow fell during the day. E.A.S. bombed vicinity of Camps between 6.30 am and 7pm. Compensation by arrangements	10R
MORY	9.1.18		Weather cold with fog and favour during afternoon. 2.Lt. Shears proceeded to 5 A. Div. for natives school. Coy under Coy arrangements.	

R.J. Blunkerlyn L/Col
Comdg. 14th A.H. Bde.

Army Form C. 2118.

WAR DIARY
or
INTELLIGENCE SUMMARY.
(Erase heading not required.)

JANUARY 1918
VOL. XX
4. 14th A.I.F. Bn.

Place	Date	Hour	Summary of Events and Information	Remarks and references to Appendices
MORY	10.1.18		Weather cold & dull. 2/Lt. Preston returned from leave. 14th A.I.H. relieved the 14th W.I. in right Sub-sector BULLECOURT. Quiet relief. Enemy very quiet during the night. 2/Lt. Knott proceeded on leave.	
BULLECOURT Right Sub-sector	11.1.18		Weather cold, rain in the morning. Trenches in a very bad condition. Situation very quiet. Lt-Col Cooper and 2/Lt Forester returned from leave. 9.15 pm to 9.45 pm and from 2 am to 9 am 12.1.18 our artillery put over a few gas shells. The enemy sent few shells.	
do	12.1.18		Weather cold and damp. Intermittent shelling on both sides throughout the day. One man wounded in D Coy. Capt. Cooper proceeded on leave.	
do	13.1.18		Weather dry, hard frost. Our aircraft very active. Counter battery work on both sides. 1st O.R. joined the battalion. Our man wounded C Coy. 2/Lieut (?) McLean from the battalion on 7.1.18 & is taken on the strength.	

L. A. Johnston Lt Col
Comdg 14th A.I.F. Bn

Army Form C. 2118.

WAR DIARY
or
INTELLIGENCE SUMMARY.
(Erase heading not required.)

JANUARY 1918

VOL. XX
14th A.S.H. Bn.

Place	Date	Hour	Summary of Events and Information	Remarks and references to Appendices
BULLECOURT RIGHT SUB SECTOR	14.1.18		Day opened dry & frosty. Enemy active on front line with whizz bangs. Our artillery fired intermittently. 14th A.S.H. relieved by the 14th H.L.I. 15th A.S.H. withdrawn to Bde Support with the Coys. as under. Quiet relief. 2/Lt Moffat D. Coy. RAILWAY RESERVE C5357 B.Coy. DEWSBURY TRENCH proceeded on B. Coy. PONTEFRACT TRENCH C.Coy. 16TREE CORNER leave. Spirit ration returned from 29 enews 14 O.R. joined the Battn.	
do Bde Support	15.1.18		Weather very wet. Camouflage at the Battn. in MOREUIL. No activity on either side. Trenches very bad and shelters falling in. General were buried in the mud. 6 off & 150 O.R. working party up the line.	
do	16.1.18		Weather very wet. Baths continued. Companies & H.Q. carry on improving accommodation. Situation normal in other Sec. 12 O.R. joined the Battalion.	
do	17.1.18		Dry opened very wet, heavy rain. Companies working at shelters. 2/Lt Cummings proceeded on a 3 days Sanitary Course.	

M. Dunstan Lt Col.
Comm. 14th A.S.H. Bn.

WAR DIARY
or
INTELLIGENCE SUMMARY.
(Erase heading not required.)

Army Form C. 2118.

JANUARY 1918

VOL. XX

14th A.I.F. Bn.

Place	Date	Hour	Summary of Events and Information	Remarks and references to Appendices
BULLECOURT FOE SUPPORT	18.1.18		Day spent a little quieter but dull. Enemy artillery active. 14th A.I.S.H. finished relieving the 14th H.H.I. in the right subsector. Dispositions. B. Coy. left front. A. Coy. right front. D. Coy. left support. C. Coy. right support. Relief conducted over the top, very quiet. The enemy shelled DEWSBURY TRENCH and Batt. H.Q. at frequent intervals during the night. Captain Cast Mullin joined the headquarters of the battalion.	
BULLECOURT RIGHT SUBSECTOR	19.1.18		Weather fine. Enemy artillery on both sides. At 4 am 7 am enemy gun shelled Batt. H.Q. area. R.E's working in H.Q. sector. In the afternoon the enemy shelled RAILWAY RESERVE.	
do	20.1.18		Weather fine. Trenches improved. Aircraft of very active on both sides during the day. Nothing interesting. Two men wounded by shrapnel in "B" Coy. Company relief. D. Coy. left front. C. Coy. right front. B. Coy. left support. A. Coy. right support. Lieut AM Lockhart & 15 other ranks proceeded to support of Brigade. Troops LE TOUQUET 3 O.R's joined the battalion.	

C. J. Sinclair Lt Col
Comdg. 14th Bn A.I.F.

Army Form C. 2118.

WAR DIARY
or
INTELLIGENCE SUMMARY.
(Erase heading not required.)

JANUARY 1918

VOL. XX

14th A.T. S/o.

Place	Date	Hour	Summary of Events and Information	Remarks and references to Appendices
BULLECOURT Right Sub-sector	21.1.18		Day opened fine. Our aeroplanes very active. Enemy showed one two or three at frequent intervals during the day.	
do	22.1.18		Weather fine. Both sides active during the night. Aeroplanes active on both sides. Our guns carried out counter battery work. 14th A.T.H. relieved by the 14th H.L.I. 14th and relieved by Bde Reserve at MORY. F.S. wagons conveyed battalion from the sugar factory to MORY. 3 O.R. joined the battalion.	
MORY Bde RESERVE	23.1.18		Weather fine but dull. Companies carry on cleaning up & improving accommodation. Officers & Coys of the baths.	
do	24.1.18		Weather very fine. Dress and camp fatigues. Working party of 4 officers & 200 O.R. up the line. 2/Lt Allison C.Coy proceeded on leave. Lt D.G. PRESTON returned to unit wearing the badges of Lieutenant.	

C.C. Newberry Lt Col
Comm. 14 A.T. S/o.

WAR DIARY
INTELLIGENCE SUMMARY

Army Form C. 2118.

JANUARY 1918
VOL. XX
14th Aust. Bn.

Place	Date	Hour	Summary of Events and Information	Remarks and references to Appendices
M.D.R.Y. Bde. Reserve	25/1/18		Weather very fine. Trips at Baths for trench foot treatment. Drills, lectures, bayonet and M.G. to Coys. as Coys before work. Capt. MacMillan returned from leave. Capt. Cater entertained by O.C. troops in the evening.	
do	26/1/18		Weather fine but misty. Coys got ready to move up to the line. 14 O.R's relieved at E.3 in rel't intent'y. "A" Coy right front. "B" Coy left front. "C" Coy right support. "D" Coy left support. Quiet relief. Our patrol encountered the enemy in RAILWAY R & S. Reple fire and bombing took place. Enemy retired.	
BULLECOURT Rt. Sub.Sect	27/1/18		Weather damp & foggy. Situation very quiet. Enemy shelled NOREUIL and Bn. H.Q. w'th Gas shell. Wind was'd. Practice S.O.S. was put up. 2.5t Horse returned from leave.	w.r.

C.M.[Scantrell?] Lt Col
Comdg 14 A.I.F. Bn

Army Form C. 2118.

WAR DIARY
or
INTELLIGENCE SUMMARY.
(Erase heading not required.)

JANUARY 1918
VOL. XX
14th Div. S/70

Place	Date	Hour	Summary of Events and Information	Remarks and references to Appendices
BULLECOURT Rt SUB SECT.	28.1.18		Weather fine. Aeroplanes active on both sides. Artillery quiet. Inter-Company relief carried out by 5 pm. E.A. in Longrunkers block & have been heavy in the evening. 2/Lt MELVILL E. returned from hospital. 2/Lt Duncan to transport camp. Rll.	
do.	29.1.18		Weather fine. Aeroplanes active on both sides. Artillery quiet. Numerous E.A. flavours have been brought down within front. R.R.	
do.	30.1.18		Weather fine. Great aerial activity on both sides. Artillery active. Ration and water parties of 14 R.S.L.I. and working parties of R.W.F.S.H. were relieved by 14 R.S.L.I. and ourselves in the support. Dispositions - HqtRs Coys in ECURIE BARRACKS. Bt H.Q. and Coy at IGREE corner. D Coy in DEWSBURY TRENCH. 2nd Rainsborough Trench occupied.	

C.D. Stewart Lt Col
Comdg 14th A.S.H.

WAR DIARY or INTELLIGENCE SUMMARY

Army Form C. 2118.

JANUARY 1918. VOL. XX

14th A.T.Bn.

Place	Date	Hour	Summary of Events and Information	Remarks and references to Appendices
BULLECOURT Bn Hd Qrs.	31/1/18		Weather cold raw and foggy. Men shots fired. N.O.R. V.L. Army Heavy otherwise fired. Lt. Col. Stewart went on 3 days paid award forward R.H.R. to arrange accommodation. w.L.	

C.C. Huntingbol
Comdg 14th A.S. Bn

Army Form C. 2118.

WAR DIARY
or
INTELLIGENCE SUMMARY.
(Erase heading not required.)

Place	Date	Hour	Summary of Events and Information	Remarks and references to Appendices
BULLECOURT St Ledger Sector	1.2.18		Weather cold and foggy. Situation Quiet. Capt. H Shillow attended Court Martial at ERVILLERS. Capt. F&N Crophas returned from leave. Lt. Col. Thorne to G.H.Q Staff. Read a wire from Lieut R.H.Q. R.S.M. new award the Belgian Croix del guerre dated 31 Jan 1918 W.L.	
do.	2.2.18		Weather fine. Situation very quiet. 2nd Lt. Surly and 2nd Lt. Ratho to NOREUIL 2nd Lt. Duffeld returned from leave. Lt A.O. Abraham admitted to no.3 Can. hospital. W.L.	
do.	3.2.18		Weather fine. Situation Quiet. 14 WATS. I.H. relieves 14 KSLI in Ref.M Sector front. "D" Coy right front. "B" Coy left front. Dispositions "C" Coy right support. "A" Coy left support. Quiet relief. Capt. Killing proceeded on leave. W.L.	

FEBRUARY 1918
Volume - 21.
Army Form C. 2118.

WAR DIARY
INTELLIGENCE SUMMARY
(Erase heading not required.)

W¹ R. A. D. Bn

Instructions regarding War Diaries and Intelligence Summaries are contained in F. S. Regs., Part II. and the Staff Manual respectively. Title pages will be prepared in manuscript.

Place	Date	Hour	Summary of Events and Information	Remarks and references to Appendices
BULLECOURT RIENCOURT	4/2/18		Weather fine. Situation Quiet. No E. V. C. Valley shelled with a mixture of H.E. and gas shells. Hostile Artillery normal; a few shells round SYDNEY AVENUE. T.M.s fell around head of GABLE ALLEY. Aerial cards followed and R. & T. works in ALLEY. Hostile M.G.s active. Lt. W.E.G. killed proceeded on leave. 2 O.R. sent casualties situation.	W.K.
do	5/2/18		Weather fine. Hostile artillery very active around the night and early morning. Lines sent ady. ordered Heavy Minnies fired in that direction from it own - None. No casualties. Our front line shelled with 2.5 m.m. about 11 a.m. Remainder of day Quiet. 2 Lt. Walker returned from course. G.S.O. III visited our lines during the night 4/5/6.	W.K.
do	6/2/18		Weather fine. Situation Quiet; a few shells fell on RAILWAY RES. and a few 150 m.m. our front line between GABLE ALLEY and TOTTENHAM Alley round head of it.	W.K.

FEBRUARY 1918
Volume 2.1
Army Form C. 2118.

4th Bn. APO S40

WAR DIARY
or
INTELLIGENCE SUMMARY.
(Erase heading not required.)

France

Instructions regarding War Diaries and Intelligence Summaries are contained in F. S. Regs., Part II. and the Staff Manual respectively. Title pages will be prepared in manuscript.

Place	Date	Hour	Summary of Events and Information	Remarks and references to Appendices
BULLECOURT RIGHT SUBSECT.	7/2/18		Weather fair but dull and snowy. About 30 gas mines released at Ahens between 10.45 a.m - 11.15 a.m 114th M.G.Bn were relieved by 4th M.L.I. in front line trenches and were went into support. Dispositions: - R.H.Q. and "C" Coy at IGAREE CORNER. "A" & "D" Coys in MALEVIL-SCOUT Lane. "B" Coy in DEWSBURY TRENCH. WK	
BULLECOURT RIGHT SUPPORT BAC DU NORD.	8/2/18		Quiet relief. Weather dull with slight drizzle. Heavy bombardment & shelling from our front by the Bn. Since at 6 am. Several H.E. and Shrapnel shells burst nr HQ. EVIL during the afternoon. 2 Lt Kinnear proceeded on leave. WK	
do.	9/2/18		Weather fair. Aim to relieve front on Enemy preparations on evening shown from 5 am - 10 am. Otherwise situation quiet. General BYNG visited Bn H.Qrs. WK	

February 1918.
VOLUME 21.
Army Form C. 2118.

WAR DIARY or INTELLIGENCE SUMMARY.

(Erase heading not required.)

14th Bn. A.I.F. — 4th A Bde

Place	Date	Hour	Summary of Events and Information	Remarks and references to Appendices
BULLECOURT Bed Subs.	10/2/18		Weather fine. A shell destroyed our shelter at Tigress Corner & crushed Stokes artillery rather serious in N.U.R.E. via Vallee and between front system and support system. 14th A.I.F.H. were relieved by 16th N. and 5/6 S. Staffs and proceeded to back billets camp ERVILLERS. W.K. fired rebel.	
ERVILLERS	11/2/18		Weather fine. Battalion moved IR in the following order: H.Q. "A" Coy, "B" Coy, "C" Coy, "D" Coy. and marched to HENDECOURT. Capt. Sheaver proceeded on leave. Lieut. Wallison proceeded to U.K. for 6 months' tour of duty.	W.K.
HENDECOURT	12/2/18		Weather fine. Coys at disposal of Coy. commanders.	W.K.
do.	13/2/18		Weather rainy and warm. Coys at disposal of Coy. commanders. Lt. M. Hill proceeded to class.	W.K.

FEBRUARY 1918.
VOLUME - 21
Army Form C. 2118.

WAR DIARY
or
INTELLIGENCE SUMMARY.   4th Bn. A.I.F. ☉ H.Q.
(Erase heading not required.)

Place	Date	Hour	Summary of Events and Information	Remarks and references to Appendices
HENDECOURT	14/2/18		Weather wet and dull. Coys at Baths. And training according to programme. 2 Lt. R.H. Smith rejoined Batt. from hospital. Draft Pte. & N.C.O.R. arrived	
Do.	15/2/18		Weather wet and dull. Coys training in accordance with programme.	
Do.	16.2.18		Weather fine. Transport inspected by Brigadier General. Coys carried out training in accordance with programme. Capt Rutherford R.A.M.C. proceeded on leave, being relieved by Capt Hargrave R.A.M.C.	
Do.	17.2.18		Weather fine. Battalion attended Church parade. Capt Anderson Lt. returned from leave.	

February 1918
VOLUME 21
Army Form C. 2118.

WAR DIARY
or
INTELLIGENCE SUMMARY. 4th Bn A.I.F.
(Erase heading not required.)

Instructions regarding War Diaries and Intelligence
Summaries are contained in F. S. Regs., Part II.
and the Staff Manual respectively. Title pages
will be prepared in manuscript.

Place	Date	Hour	Summary of Events and Information	Remarks and references to Appendices
HENDECOURT.	18/2/18		Weather fine. Coys carried out training in accordance with programme. Brigadier-General inspected the Battalion. Battalion attended concert given by Arts concert party in the evening.	WK
do.	19/2/18		Weather fine. Coys carried out training in accordance with programme.	WK
do.	20/2/18		Weather dull; rain in the evening. Coys carried out training in accordance with programme. Capt B Claudius left for leave/13 tour March in U.K. Battalion concert in the evening.	WK
do.	21/2/18		Weather fair. Coys carried out training in accordance with programme. 2 Lt McKay joined the 20th Brigade T.M.B. 2 Lt Walker finished Henry on proceeded to VI Corps School. 2 Lt Melville proceeded on leave.	WK

FEBRUARY 1918.
VOLUME 21.

Army Form C. 2118.

WAR DIARY
or
INTELLIGENCE SUMMARY.

(Erase heading not required.)

Instructions regarding War Diaries and Intelligence Summaries are contained in F. S. Regs., Part II. and the Staff Manual respectively. Title pages will be prepared in manuscript.

Place	Date	Hour	Summary of Events and Information	Remarks and references to Appendices
HENDECOURT	26/2/18		Weather cold, wet in the morning. Batt. marched to NORTHUMBERLAND CAMP, MERCATEL starting at 9.30 a.m. in the following order:- H.Q., "A" Coy, "B" Coy, "C" Coy, "D" Coy. Lt. Col Benzie took over command of Batt. Lt. Col Johnstone relinquished command & Command of Batt.	
MERCATEL	27/2/18		Weather dull and cold. Coys carried out training in accordance with programme. Col W. E. G. Miller returned from leave 2nd Lt. J.D. McKay proceeded on leave	WK.
do	28/2/18		Weather fair. Ratcheson attended Army parade. 2 Lt. Kinnear returned from leave	WK.
do	29/2/18		Weather cold & wet. Coys carried out training in accordance with scheme. Lt. Regan proceeded on leave	WK.

FEBRUARY 1918
Volume 2t
Army Form C. 2118.

WAR DIARY
or
INTELLIGENCE SUMMARY
(Erase heading not required.)

4th B Arcts

Place	Date	Hour	Summary of Events and Information	Remarks and references to Appendices
MERCATEL	26/2/18		Weather dry but cold and windy. Coys carried out training in the morning. Major Miller took over command of "A" Coy. Capt Lenterman rejoined. Back from detachment with 46 R.I. 2nd Lieut Sharp returned from hospital. Two new draft for 50 O.R. at Hq H working in orderlies. Casualties: 2nd Lt Sg. Pilfers killed. Capt McClellan wounded and 15 O.R. wounded. 2nd Lt Davis proceeded to Third Army Musketry School W.K.	
do.	27/2/18		Weather fair; rain fell during the night. Coys carried out training in the morning. Lieut Kerr R.A.M.C. took over from Capt. Halpin U.S. M.C. W.K.	

FEBRUARY - 14
VOLUME 21
Army Form C. 2118.

WAR DIARY
or
INTELLIGENCE SUMMARY. 4th/5th Bn AIF
(Erase heading not required.)

Place	Date	Hour	Summary of Events and Information	Remarks and references to Appendices
MERCATEL	21/2/18		Weather fair. The Battalion marched from MERCATEL to BERLES-AU-BOIS. Started at 10.15 am and proceeded by the following route:- Road running S, M.2.8.d., M.2.6.c., M.3.c.a., M.3.d.c. - BOISLEUX-AU-MONT - BOIRY-STE-RICTRUDE - SUCRERIE - ADINFER - MONCHY-AU-BOIS - BIENVILLERS-AU-BOIS - BERLES-AU-BOIS arrived at 5.30 pm.	

R Runyu Lieut. Col.
Comdg. 4th Bn. A.I.F.

2nd March 1918

40th Division.
120th Infantry Brigade

WAR
DIARY

14th BATTALION

ARGYLE & SUTHERLAND HIGHLANDERS

MARCH 1 9 1 8

WAR DIARY or INTELLIGENCE SUMMARY

Army Form C. 2118.

MARCH 1918.
VOLUME XXII
14th Aug. & Futher Highrs

Place	Date	Hour	Summary of Events and Information	Remarks and references to Appendices
BERLES-au-BOIS	1/3/18		Weather dull and cold. Coy. training carried out in the morning. Coy. and specialist training in the afternoon.	JB 2 L
do.	2/3/18		Weather very cold with strong wind and snow. Coy training in the morning. Lt. M. Hill returned from leave.	wx.
do.	3/3/18		Weather cold and damp. Battalion attended divine service at 11.30 a.m. 2 Lt. Harton proceeded on leave.	wx.
do.	4/3/18		Weather cold & raining. Battalion carried out a practice attack on MONCHY-aux-BOIS. Formations - "A" Coy. and "C" Coy. in attacking waves. "B" Coy. moppers up. "D" Coy. as enemy.	wx.
do.	5/3/18		Weather fair. Coys. carried out training in the morning. Specialist training in the afternoon. 2 Lts W. Rose, and J.B. Cumming proceeded to G.H.Q. Lewis Guns School & withdrew demonstration.	D.

WAR DIARY
or
INTELLIGENCE SUMMARY.

Army Form C. 2118.

MARCH 1918.
VOLUME XXII
14th Aug. & Sutchis Heights.

Place	Date 1918 MARCH	Hour	Summary of Events and Information	Remarks and references to Appendices
BEAULES-au-BOIS.	6/3/18		Weather fine. Battalion carried out a tactical attack on MONCHY-au-BOIS formation:- "A" Coy and "C" Coy attacking. "B" Coy mopping up. "D" Coy in reserve.	left.
do.	7/3/18		Our 4th Brig. practised an attack. Weather fine. Corps carried out Gas drill. Battalion bathing parade. Battalion attended concert given by the GAMECOCKS in the evening. left.	
do.	8/3/18		Weather fine. Bde Commander inspected the battalion in the afternoon. 2nd Lieut. Cummings returned from C.I.A. Lewis Gun School. W.E.	
do.	9/3/18		Weather fine. 10th B attalion took part in Brigade scheme. Attack on QUESNOY-FM. Advised as reserves till first objective was taken and then leap frogged through them final objective.	W.E.

WAR DIARY
INTELLIGENCE SUMMARY.

MARCH 1918. VOLUME XXII

1st Arg. & Sutho. Highrs

Army Form C. 2118.

Place	Date 1918 MARCH	Hour	Summary of Events and Information	Remarks and references to Appendices
BERLES-AU-BOIS.	10/3/18		Weather fine. Battalion attended Divine Service at 11.30 am. 2/Lt Melville returned from leave.	
do	11/3/18		Weather fine. Corps concert and band in the morning. 2/Lt Munro gave a lecture to the Battalion in the afternoon on Education.	
do	12/3/18		Weather fine. 2/Lt Forester proceeded to U.K. for 6 months' tour of duty. 2/Lt Panton proceeded on leave. 2/Lt Still proceeded to G.H.Q. Lewis Gun School. 2/Lt Mackay returned from leave. The Battalion marched from BERLES-AU-BOIS to HAMELINCOURT, started at 6.45 a.m. Route:- BIENVILLERS, MONCHY-AU-BOIS, ADINFER, DOUCHY, AYETTE, MOYENNEVILLE. The B. Battalion took over accommodation at CLONMEL CAMP.	

R.J. Sanford Col
11/4

WAR DIARY
or
INTELLIGENCE SUMMARY.

(Erase heading not required.)

MARCH 1918.

VOLUME XX-II

1st Aug. & Sutton Highrs

Army Form C. 2118.

Place	Date	Hour	Summary of Events and Information	Remarks and references to Appendices
HAMELINE DUCT.	13/3/18		Weather fine. Battalion engaged in cleaning up. Recreational training in the afternoon. 2 Lt A Brown returned from leave.	WK
do.	14/3/18		Weather fine. Circuit training in the morning. Recreational training in the afternoon.	WK
do.	15/3/18		Weather fine. Coys carried out trench training in the morning, and trench training in the afternoon. 2 Lt Becker proceeded on leave.	WK
do.	16/3/18		Weather fine. Coys and specialist training as in the morning. Third B Company bathing parade.	WK
do.	17/3/18		Weather fine. H and B Coys attended Divine Service at 11.30 am. Capt D Coy on baths humer. Capt Learn returned from leave. Lt Whitelaw returned from Army G.S.	

Army Form C. 2118.

WAR DIARY
or
INTELLIGENCE SUMMARY.
(Erase heading not required.)

MARCH 1918.

VOLUME XX-11

14th Arg. & Sutld. Highrs.

Place	Date	Hour	Summary of Events and Information	Remarks and references to Appendices
HAMELINCOURT	18/3/18		Weather fair. Coys carried out training. Six Officers and twelve other ranks attended demonstration of Tank Tactics. Battalion concert in the evening. 25th with Gymnor proceded on leave.	W.R.
do	19/3/18		Weather dull & wet. Lectures were given by Coy Officers, and training was carried out in huts. Battalion provided a working party of 15 Officers and 500 O.R. for work in the Battle zone.	W.R.
do	20/3/18		Weather dull. 15 Officers and 50 O.R. attended demonstration of Tank Tactics at WAILLY.	W.R.
do	21/3/18		Weather fine. Battalion stood to at 5.30 a.m. and moved from 2.15 p.m. towards VAULX-VRAUCOURT. B.H.Q. were established in an Bde HQrs in the VAULX-MORY Rd. and the Battalion took up position in support to R.S.F. and [signatures]	

WAR DIARY or INTELLIGENCE SUMMARY

Army Form C. 2118.

MARCH 1918. VOLUME XVII.

1/4 Argyll & Suth'd Highrs

Place	Date 1918 MARCH	Hour	Summary of Events and Information	Remarks and references to Appendices
VAUX – VRAUCOURT	21/3/18	9 p.m.	Lunchers went out & left rested it Cemetery on VAUX – ECOUST Rd.	
		10.30 p.m.	A stray patrol worked down trench from C.13.b.5.0. & yelled, and drove the enemy out of the trench.	
do	22/3/18	3.25 a.m.	"A" Coy established themselves in this trench and C&D Coys moved forward and took up position on left of "A" Coy, and "B" Coy moved forward to support at Cemetery. The line was held from C.20.b.4 & K.C.13.a.b.9. The A/S.H. on right & 2nd R.S.F. and part of 2nd Bn to H/S Lancs who touched at Cemetery. Patrols found enemy blockhouses on either flank at VAUX-CORP.	
		6.40 a.m.	The enemy attacked heavily, but made no progress against the entire Bn, while they made an advance the line was held till well on the afternoon when we withdrew to positions in front of VRAUCOURT. Both withdrew and established itself in Army Line. Col. Walker was first wounded & killed.	W.K.
ARMY LINE	23/3/18		Weather fine. Situation quiet in our front all day and enemy he will look on our left was heavily attacked.	W.K.

WAR DIARY or INTELLIGENCE SUMMARY

Army Form C. 2118.

MARCH 1918 VOLUME XXII

14th Argyll & Suth'd Highrs

Place	Date	Hour	Summary of Events and Information	Remarks and references to Appendices
ARMY LINE	24/3/18	5/am	Weather fine. Situation fairly quiet. The night was spent consolidating position. At 5 am information received that enemy had broken our C.O's & Runners & would have broken thro' this line in front of FAVREUIL, approx through #3 Central, H.4.b. 9.0, H.7.10 Central, H.4.16.c, H.16.C. 9.0 and about two	
		7/15 pm	[continued] Two runners were sent here.	W.R.
BEHAGNIES	25/3/18	4/am	Weather fine. The Batt. held a line in front of BEHAGNIES in the morning. Enemy launched attacks against our right, continued thro'out the day. The line was maintained till it had when we withdrew	
		A/pm	took high ground in front of GOMIECOURT, orders for the relief of the Batt. were issued in the evening and the 14 ARGYLL withdrew in accordance thereto to DOUCHY.	W.R.
DOUCHY	26/3/18		Weather fine. In the afternoon the Batt. took up position in front of ADINFER WOOD. This was vacated at 12.30 am on 27/3/18. Total casualties 10 Officers 300 O.R.	

Army Form C. 2118.

WAR DIARY
or
INTELLIGENCE SUMMARY.
(Erase heading not required.)

MARCH 1918

VOLUME XXII

14th Aug'. Sutho' Highrs.

Place	Date 1918 MARCH	Hour	Summary of Events and Information	Remarks and references to Appendices
DOUCHY.	27/3/18.		Weather crisp rather dull. After church, the Batt. marched to WARLUZEL. Route:- AINFER, RANSART, RIVIERE, BEAUMETZ, GOUY-en-ARTOIS, FOSSEUX, BARLY, SOMBRIN.	
WARLUZEL	28/3/18		Weather dull & cold. Tool inspection by Doctor. Talent & Efficiencies. Allowance officers debate reported Battalion.	
WARLUZEL	29/3/18		Weather cold and rainy. Batt paraded at 10 am in the following order and marched to MONCHY BRETON. Four Officers and 190 OR who had taken part in the fighting proceeded to MONCHY BRETON in buses.	
MONCHY BRETON	30/3/18		Weather fair in the morning, dull in the afternoon. Battalion paraded at 9.45 am, marched to ST POL - BRUAY ST JEAN where they entrained and proceeded to Nom MONDE	

Army Form C. 2118.

WAR DIARY
or
INTELLIGENCE SUMMARY.
(Erase heading not required.)

MARCH 1918.

VOLUME XXII

4th Aug. Sutch's Afghs.

Place	Date	Hour	Summary of Events and Information	Remarks and references to Appendices
LE NOUVEAU MONDE	3/4/18		Weather fine. Battalion church parade at 3 pm. Battalion paraded at 6.30 p.m. in the following order: HQ, MGCO and marched to Rum huts easter in FLEURBAIX distr. where they relieved 9 KRR (quiet day)	

Signatures

D. D. & L., London, E.C.
(A8000) Wt. W1771/M231 750,000 5/17 Sch. 53 Forms/C2118/14

To all Ranks of the 40th Division.

I wish to thank the Division, one and all, for their splendid courage and behaviour. You know what the Commander-in-Chief and your Corps Commander think of you and I can only say you have done your duty like British Soldiers always do.

We shall, no doubt, be called upon again to fight for all we are worth.

We in the 40th Division, I know, will be ready again and I feel very proud to be the Divisional Commander of such a splendid body of men as you have proved to be. I thank you all from the bottom of my heart, and whatever may happen I feel complete confidence in the ultimate result with soldiers of your spirit and bravery under my command.

John Ponsonby

Major General,
Commanding 40th Division.

28/3/18.

Copy passed round Coys.
29/3/18

To be attached to war diary.

The following extract from a letter written by the Corps Commander to the Divisional Commander is forwarded for your information.

It should be communicated to all ranks.

" As regards your fighting troops, Infantry, Artillery and R.E., I cannot speak too highly. They have made a magnificent defence and, tired as they must be with so prolonged a struggle, they have stood like a stone wall between my right and the Germans.
All I can say is that I am deeply grateful and feel that they have nobly upheld the great fighting traditions of the British Army".

28/3/18.

(...................) Lt. Col.
General Staff, 40th Division.
****

Issued to all units.

2/Lt. S. McAdie. W.†M.

Officer Commanding
    14th Bn. A.& S.Highrs.

With reference to Casualties 21/27-3-18, attached is copy of official Casualty List. The following have since been reported from Hospital Lists:-
                                        159
    S/40859 Pte.Stoddart R.   172.
    301447   "   Kelly   G.   Km A.   23.
    S/17219   "   Johnston   W.   195
    301723   "   Brown   J.
    S/21596   "   Mullen   W.   Missing   81
    S/40846   "   Mathieson D.   6   276
                                    165

The following have Died of Wounds:-
    S/7221 Pte.Miller   H.
    S/40863 " Macdonald D.
    S/40847 " Miller   J.
    S/4279 L/C.Johnston   R.
    S/40821 Pte.Shaw   D.
    S/9155 Sgt.McLachlan D.
    S/9959 Pte.Falconer   A.   7
                                172

    The name of S/18107 A/Sgt.Riddick W. appears on a Burial Report, but con-firmation is awaited before this Casualty is officially reported.
    Included in your List of Wounded is S/40817 Pte.McInnes A. As this man was transferred to the Labour Corps on 23-1-18, his inclusion is not understood. The Casualty has been reported to the Labour Corps.
    Your telegrams duly received deleting the following from the List of "Missing":- S/11814 Pte.Dunsmore W.
                                S/9048   "   Richardson R.
    With regard to "Missing" believed killed, wounded, and prison-ers of war, kindly forward as soon as possible all available evidence in support of your belief.
    No Hospital report has yet been received regarding the follow-ing, reported by you "Wounded". Kindly verify.
    S/6693 Sgt.McFarlane   J.
    S/40781 Pte.Thomson   J.
    S/43200 " Jackson   C.   275824 Stewart g.
    300366   " Campbell   A.
    301947   " Smellie   J.

    The following Hospital reports have been received regarding two O.R. "Wounded", which also please verify:-
    325566 Pte.Campbell   J. Adm."Diarrhoea"
    S/13037 " McSherry   F. " "Rupture"

    S/21821 Pte.Anderson J. is reported by you "Wounded". Should this not be S/21812 Pte.Anderson J.? The latter has been admitted to Hospital "Wounded", but no Hospital report has been received regarding the former.
    In your List of "Missing"(C Coy) kindly verify following, whose Reg.Nos. are not fully given:- Ptes W.Stoddart & J.Watt.

                                    Major
                            Officer i/c Infantry Section No.1
17-4-18   G.H.Qrs. 3rd Echelon.

"Missing" corrected to July 1918.
        3 Off. 88 O.R's.

14th (Ser.) Bn-Argyll & Sutherland Highlanders

No.1 District   Daily Casualty List No.156

Reg.No.	Rank & Name	Casualties	P.R.
S/6693	Sgt. McFarlane J.	— Wm. R167.	
10318	" Logan C.		
325735	" Morrison R.		
S/12107	Cpl.(A/Sgt.) Riddick W.		
276951	Pte.(A/L/Sgt.) Aitken W.		
S/9025	" " Langlands W.		
S/3898	Pte.(A/Cpl.) Cook A.		
S/6283	" " Brown T.		
S/9066	L/C.(A/Cpl.) Turnbull W.		
S/9648	" " Wingate T.		
S/13412	" " Nairn A.		
S/40541	Pte.(A/Cpl.) McLean J.		
325240	" " Guthrie J.		
714	L/C. Fletcher A.		
S/6121	" McDade J.		
S/9859	" Ramsay A.		
S/9878	" Wilson A.		
S/12562	" Hutton J.		
S/13360	" Dryden A.		
S/14896	" Wilson J.		
S/13484	" Hamilton R.		
S/15878	" McArthur W.		
S/40164	" Fleming G.		
S/40588	" Jarvie D.		
300307	" Holborow F.		
300807	" Langlands W.		
577	Pte. McPherson H.		
1253	" Fleeting J.	W. 21/27-3-18	N
S/2568	" Clark J.		
S/4809	" Ballantyne J.	Reported by O.C. Bn.	
6421	" Gallacher C.	2-4-18	
S/6744	" Spankie G.		
S/7460	" Coventry J.		
S/7610	" Graham D.		
4/7833	" Coyle F.		
4/8928	" Brannigan P.		
4/8929	" McPhail J.		
S/8904	" Paterson J.		
S/9154	" Neill J.		
9241	" Miller G.		
S/9361	" McCoubrey J.		
S/9548	" Graham G.		
S/9649	" McFarlane J.		
S/9930	" McGillivray J.		
11261	" Cameron J.		
S/11389	" Etherson R.		
S/11710	" Bryans S.		
S/12024	" Fraser G.		
S/12026	" Johnston G.		
S/12351	" Scotland C.		
S/12429	" Hayes A.		
S/12560	" Adam J.		
S/12801	" Latimer J.		
S/12807	" Burley G.		
S/12837	" McIntyre W.		
S/12843	" Henderson J.		
S/13188	" Young W.		
S/13264	" Dickie D.		
S/13494	" Fyffe A.		
S/13867	" Blackie W.		
S/13880	" Stewart W.		
S/14715	" Crawford I.		
S/15995	" Anderson G.		
S/16037	" McSherry F.	— Cancel. R167	
S/16041	" Ross A.		

Second Sheet

14th (Ser.) Bn. Argyll & Sutherland Highlanders

No.1 District   Daily Casualty List No.156

Reg.No.	Rank.& Name	Casualties	P.R.
S/16338	Pte. Frisken W.		
S/16351	" Hart H.		
S/17000	" Porteous G.		
S/17073	" Hannah J.		
S/17411	" Graham W.		
S/17701	" Crighton W.		
S/18205	" Scott R.		
S/18250	" Young A.		
S/19461	" Grant D.		
S/19752	" Garrick J.		
S/20413	" Leitch J.		
S/21445	" McDonald W.		
S/21725	" Chambers D.		
S/21809	" Miller W.		
S/21812	" Anderson J.		
S/22047	" McLay W.		
S/22145	" McIlvar H.		
S/22234	" Enticknap H.		
S/22269	" Cameron J.		
S/22318	" Copeland H.		
S/22657	" Lindsay S.		
S/23829	" Cook H.		
S/23871	" Madelin W.		
S/40547	" Bradley P.		
S/40548	" Brown G.		
S/40552	" Campbell J.		
S/40589	" Jarvie J.		
S/40595	" Kirkhope J.	W. 21/27-3-18	N
S/40598	" Liddell J.		
S/40740	" Drysdale W.	Reported by O.C.Bn. 2-4-18	
S/40773	" McLeod A.		
S/40775	" Cochrane C.		
S/40798	" McDonald H.		
S/40781	" Thomson J.	W+M. R.167	
S/40800	" Curley F.		
S/40807	" Hamilton J.		
S/40818	" Nicolson A.		
S/40823	" Stewart A.		
S/40824	" Turner G.		
S/40826	" Goldie H.		
S/40830	" Clark G.		
S/40831	" Caldwell R.		
S/40836	" Leckie G.		
S/40839	" Paxton T.		
S/40855	" Laidlaw A.		
S/40882	" Sykes J.		
S/43035	" Kennedy J.		
S/43200	" Jackson C.	W+M. R.167	
S/43208	" Davidson W.		
202282	" McMillan W.		
202415	" McDonald L.		
275824	" Stewart J.	W+M. R.167	
276901	" Smith A.		
277005	" Blair R.		
277030	" Drysdale J.		
277040	" Wilson R.		
277099	" Millar A.		
277574	" Angely J.		
277594	" Paul J.		
277985	" Fowler J.		
278001	" Urquhart C.		
278243	" Martin J.		
278268	" Corrick F.		
278843	" Law G.		
300086	" McInnes A.		
300366	" Campbell A.	W+M. R.167	

Third Sheet

14th (Ser.) Bn. Argyll & Sutherland Highlanders

No.1 District   Daily Casualty List No.156

Reg.No.	Rank & Name	Casualties	P.R.
300819	Pte. Gillies W.		
301340	" Leitch A.		
301622	" McKimmie T.		
301947	" Smellie J.	W.&.M. R 167	
302017	" Downie T.		
302221	" Barrie P.		
302812	" Woods E.		
325043	" Riddell J.		
325303	" Wood A.		
325522	" Wilson D.		
325566	" Campbell J.	cancel: R 167	
325632	" O'Donell J.		
325819	" Wright J.	W. 21/27-3-18	N
350865	" Herd A.		
351147	" Bowdery W.	Reported by O.C.Bn.	
771	L/C. Anderson T.	2-4-18	
S/3569	" Jarrett E.		
S/5604	Pte. Durning W.		
S/17285	" McRobbie J.		
S/18288	" McAllister N.		
S/20895	" Wilson D.	In Bn. list of Missing	
S/22179	" McArthur A.	Hosp. entries show him W.	
S/23850	" Ferrier A.		
S/23855	" Myles D.		
S/40868	" Beattie R.		
S/40871	" Cunningham W.		
326605	" Kelso J.		
S/13335	Pte. Fawley M.	Adm.W. 23-3-18	N
		Reported by O.C.136 F.A. 23-3-18	

Total 159

10-4-18

Major
Officer i/c Infantry Section No.1
G.H.Qrs. 3rd Echelon.

S/40859 Pte Stoddart R.   To UK fr. 24 Gen. Hos.
                           GSW from R' 29.3.18
Bn. to verify.

14th (S) Bn Argyll & Sutherland Highrs.   No.155.

Casualties reported 9.4.18.   No.1.District.

Regtl No.	Rank & Name.	Casualties.	By whom reported.	P.R.
4382.L/Cpl (A/Sergt) Harris A.				
S/16070.L/Cpl (Act L/Sergt) Miller J.				
S/12365.L/Cpl (Act L/Sergt) Lannagan J.				
S/13591.Corpl Robson W.				
S/9899.L/Cpl (Act Corpl) Anderson P.H.				
S/9045.L/Cpl (Act Corpl) Milne T.		K in A.		
S/40424.L/Cpl Congdon S.		21-27/3/18.	O.C.Bn.	
S/40263.L/Cpl Garfirth L.			2.4.18.	N.
4/9443.Pte Irvine J.				
S/13645.Pte Roberts B.B.				
S/14353.Pte Fairley A McR.				
S/14371.Pte Wilson R.R.H.				
S/14391.Pte Morrison J.				
S/15986.Pte Wilson J.				
S/22185.Pte McCafferty J.				
S/23839.Pte Crombie J.				
S/40562.Pte Craig A.				
S/40785.Pte Whitelaw W.				
S/40878.Pte Mathew P.T.				
200727.Pte McKenna J.				
277677.Pte Mathieson J.				
325808.Pte Quigley A.				
350180.Pte McGregor A.				

23

Major.

Officer i/c Infantry Section No.1.
G H Qrs, 3rd Echelon.

O.19.

14th (Ser.) Bn. Argyll & Sutherland Highlanders

No.1 District
Daily Casualty List No.180

Reg.No.	Rank & Name	Casualty	P.R.
S/6562	Sgt.Murrie T.		
S/12008	Cpl.(A/Sgt) Harris D.		
S/13407	Cpl.Carmichael W.		
S/15550	Pte.(A/Sgt) Lorimer R.		
T-276851	Pte.(A/L/Sgt) Gillies W.		
S/8849	Cpl.Kidd J.		
S/12591	L/C.(A/Cpl) Loy W.		
8445	Pte.(A/Cpl) Carrigan J.		
S/40708	" " Walker J.		
S/2082	Pte.Leyden T.		
S/5905	" McKenzie J.		
S/5345	" Owens W.		
S/6812	" McPherson M.		
S/9140	" Cranston R.		
S/9848	" Wise W.		
S/10499	" Baird J.		
S/11281	" Lamb J.		
S/11467	" Murray A.		
S/12058	" Simpson J.		
S/12371	" Brien W.		
S/12592	" Hogarth G.		
S/12849	" Mathieson R.		
S/12858	" Bannatyne G.		
S/13363	" McCracken J.	Missing 21/27-3-18	N.
S/13364	" Auld W.	Reported by O.C.Bn.	
S/13457	" Stuart G.	2-4-18	
S/13681	" Millar T.		
S/14267	L/C.Davidson E.		
S/14337	Pte.Malcolmson J.		
S/14810	" Donegan P.		
S/15989	" Baxter W.		
S/16201	" Bewar R.		
S/16295	" Grant D.		
S/16344	" Whytock A.		
S/16578	L/C.Ewing J.N.		
S/17007	Pte.Johnstone A.		
S/18458	" Cook W.		
S/19644	" McLay R.		
S/21731	" Morrison J.		
S/21732	" Stewart R.		
S/21821	" Anderson J.		
S/22120	" Mitchell J.		
S/22169	" Findlay J.		
S/22264	" Howie O.		
S/22514	" Cockburn J.		
S/22518	" Curran R.		
S/22669	" Muego G.		
S/22671	" McLay W.		
S/23342	Pte.(A/Cpl) Oldham W.		
S/40231	Pte.Ivol C.		
S/40622	" Provan J.		
S/40753	" Wilkie J.		
S/40771	" Fraser D.		
S/40801	" McCance J.		
S/40805	" Balmer J.		
S/40811	" Lewis R.W.		
S/40842	" McPherson D.		
S/40861	" Telford A.		
S/40875	" Kinnaird A.		
S/40877	" McGee G.		
S/40879	" Monaghan W.		
S/40883	" Thomson A.		
270001	" Shearer J.		
276927	" Brimer A.		

Second Sheet

14th (Ser.) Bn. Argyll & Sutherland Highlanders

No.1 District   Daily Casualty List No.160

Reg.No.	Rank & Name	Casualty	N.
278278	Pte. Hampton W.		
277058	" Campbell J.		
277544	" Campbell J.		
277818	" Maitland N.		
278036	" Penny D.		
278088	" Murray C.		
278202	" Horsburgh W.		
278293	" McKenna W.	Missing 21/27-3-18	N.
300226	" Campbell D.	Reported by O.C.Bn.	
303066	" Gordon H.	2-4-18	
301021	" Smethurst W.		
301797	" Mulhearn J.	Cancel R.165	
325484	" McAllan J.		
350103	" Blyth W.		
350212	" McClure R.		
350497	" Downie T.	3 a 1/7" Bn 7-4-18	
S/40854	Pte. Haughie C.	Missing 24-3-18 Reported by O.C.40th Bn. M.G.Corps. 30-3-18	N.

17-4-18

Major
Officer i/c Infantry Section No.1
G.H.Qrs. 3rd Echelon.

14th (Ser.) Bn. Argyll & Sutherland Highlanders

No.1 District   Daily Casualty List No.160

Reg.No.	Rank & Name	Casualty	P.R.
S/6562	Sgt.Murrie T.		
S/12008	Cpl.(A/Sgt) Harris D.		
S/13407	Cpl.Carmichael W.		
S/15550	Pte.(A/Sgt) Lorimer R.		
276851	Pte.(A/L/Sgt) Gillies W.		
S/8849	Cpl.Kidd J.		
S/12591	L/C.(A/Cpl) Loy W.		
8445	Pte.(A/Cpl) Carrigan J.		
S/40708	" " Walker J.		
S/2082	Pte.Leyden T.		
3/5905	" McKenzie J.		
S/5345	" Owens W.		
S/6812	" McPherson M.		
S/9140	" Cranston R.		
S/9848	" Wise W.		
S/10499	" Baird J.		
S/11281	" Lamb J.		
S/11467	" Murray A.		
S/12058	" Simpson J.		
S/12371	" Brien W.		
S/12592	" Hogarth G.		
S/12849	" Mathieson R.		
S/12858	" Bannatyne G.	Missing 21/27-3-18	N.
S/13363	" McCracken J.	Reported by O.C.Bn.	
S/13364	" Auld W.	2-4-18	
S/13457	" Stuart G.		
S/13681	" Millar T.		
S/14267	L/Cpl Davidson E.		
S/14337	Pte. Malcolmson J.		
S/14810	" Donegan P.		
S/15989	" Baxter W.		
S/16201	" Lewar R.		
S/16295	" Grant D.		
S/16344	" Whytock A.		
S/16578	L/C.Ewing J.W.		
S/17067	Pte.Johnstone A.		
S/18458	" Cook W.		
S/19644	" McLay R.		
S/21731	" Morrison J.		
S/21732	" Stewart R.		
S/21821	" Anderson J.		
S/22120	" Mitchell J.		
S/22169	" Findlay J.		
S/22264	" Howie O.		
S/22514	" Cockburn J.		
S/22518	" Curran R.		
S/22669	" Muego G.		
S/22671	" McLay W.		
S/23842	Pte.(A/Cpl) Oldham W.		
S/40231	Pte.Ivol C.		
S/40622	" Provan J.		
S/40733	" Wilkie J.		
S/40771	" Fraser D.		
S/40801	" McCance J.		
S/40805	" Balmer J.		
S/40811	" Lewis R.W.		
S/40842	" McPherson D.		
S/40861	" Telford A.		
S/40875	" Kinnaird A.		
S/40877	" McGee G.		
S/40879	" Monaghan W.		
S/40883	" Thomson A.		
270001	" Shearer J.		
276927	" Brimer A.		

Second Sheet

14th (Ser.) Bn. Argyll & Sutherland Highlanders

No.1 District   Daily Casualty List No.160

Reg.No.	Rank & Name	Casualty	N.
278978	Pte. Hampton W.		
277058	" Campbell J.		
277544	" Campbell J.		
277818	" Maitland N.		
278036	" Penny D.		
278088	" Murray C.		
278202	" Horsburgh W.		
278293	" McKenna W.	Missing 21/27-3-18	N.
300226	" Campbell D.	Reported by O.C.Bn.	
303066	" Gordon H.	2-4-18	
301021	" Smethurst W.		
301797	" Mulhearn J.		
325484	" McAllan J.		
350103	" Blyth W.		
350212	" McClure R.		
350497	" Downie T.		
S/40854	Pte. Haughie C.	Missing 24-3-18 Reported by O.C.40th Bn. M.G.Corps. 30-3-18	N.

17-4-18

Major
Officer i/c Infantry Section No.1
G.H.Qrs. 3rd Echelon.

For Record

14th Bn. ARGYLL & SUTHERLAND HIGHLANDERS.

Nominal roll of Other Rank casualties during the recent operations 21st to 27th March, 1918.

Killed.

Regtl.
No.   Rank and Name.

"A" Company.

9899   Cpl. P. H. Anderson.
40562 Pte. A. Craig.
22185   "   J. McCafferty.
277577 "   J. Mathieson.   277677.
325806 "   A. Quigley.

"B" Company.

9045   Cpl. J. Milne.
15936 Pte. J. Wilson.

"C" Company.

4388   Sgt. A. Harris.
16070 Cpl. J. Miller.
12365   "   J. Lannigan.
40424 Cpl. S. Congdon.
40263 L/C. L. Garfirth.
23839 Pte. J. Crombie.
9445   Pte. J. Irvine.
350130 "   A. McGregor.
200727 "   J. McKenna.
14391   "   J. Morrison.
40785   "   W. Whitelaw.

"D" Company.

13591 Cpl. W. Robson.
14571 Pte. R.R.H. Wilson.
40878   "   P. Matthews.
13645   "   G. B. Roberts.
14353   "   A. M. Fairlie.

Killed -
Wounded -
Missing - (all kinds).

Casualties contd.

Wounded.

"A" Company.

10318 ✓	Sgt.	✓ C. Logan. ✓	
6283 ✓	Cpl.	✓ T.W.F. Brown.	
14996 ✓	L/C.	✓ J. J. Wilson.	
40588 ✓	"	✓ D. Jarvie.	
40547 ✓	pte.	✓ P. Bradley.	
40548 ✓	"	✓ G. Brown.	
11710 ✓	"	✓ S. Bryans.	
17701 ✓	"	✓ W. Crighton.	
40807 ✓	"	✓ J. Hamilton.	
9649 9469 ✓	"	✓ J. C. McFarlane. S/9649	
40821 ✗	"	D. Shaw.	D of W.
12562 ✓	L/C.	✓ J. Hutton.	
13484 ✓	"	✓ R. M. Hamilton.	
4309 ✓	pte.	✓ J. Ballantine.	
21725 ✓	"	✓ D. Chambers.	
40552 ✓	"	✓ J. Campbell.	
40826 ✓	"	✓ H. Goldie.	Hosp. N.Y.D. U.K
40773 ✓	"	✓ A. McLeod.	
277099 ✓	"	✓ A. Miller.	
40823 ✓	"	✓ A. Stewart.	
12560 ✓	"	✓ J. M. Adam.	
2568 ✓	"	✓ J. Clark.	
577	"	✓ H. McPherson. ✓	
17000 ✓	"	✓ G. Porteous.	
40824 ✓	"	✓ G. Turner.	
12807 ✓	"	✓ G. Burley.	
17073 ✓	"	✓ J. Hannah.	
40589 ✓	"	✓ J. Jarvie.	
22657 ✓	"	✓ S. Lindsay.	
12637 ✓	"	✓ W. McIntyre.	
✗ 40817	"	A. McInnes.	Trnsf. to L.C.(24 Sch. Bn)23-1-18. Reported to W.C. Hsp. phone. 10.4.18. 511754.
202415 ✓	"	✓ L. McDonald.	
40918 ✓	"	✓ A. Nicholson.	
13264 ✓	"	✓ D. C. Dickie.	

"B" Company.

323045 ✓	Sgt.	✓ Sheddell.	
15360 ✓	L/C.	✓ A. Dryden.	
13860 ✓	Pte.	✓ W. Stewart.	
351147 ✓	"	✓ W. Bowdry.	
43208 ✓	"	✓ W. Davidson.	
40836 ✓	"	✓ G. Lackie.	
9866 9986 ✓	Cpl.	✓ W. F. Turnbull. — S/9866	
40598 ✓	Pte.	✓ J. Liddell.	
14715 ✓	"	✓ I. Crawford.	
277005 ✓	"	✓ R. H. Blair. — 301340	
301346 ✓	"	✓ A. Leitch.	
40867 40807 ✗	"	J. Miller. — D of W 26-3-18 Cmo Etaples D of W
300307 ✓	L/C.	✓ F. R. Holborow.	
276951 ✓	L/Sgt.	✓ E. Aitken.	
6693 ✓	Sgt.	✓ J. McFarlane.	
40541 20021 ✓	A/Cpl.	✓ J. McLean. — S/40541 W. U.K.	
9859 ✓	L/Cpl.	✓ A. Ramsay.	
21445 ✓	Pte.	✓ W. McDonald.	
40839 ✓	"	✓ T. Paxton.	
202262 ✓	"	✓ W. McMillan.	
40595 ✓	"	✓ J. Kirkhope.	
277040 ✓	"	✓ R. Wilson.	
7221 ✗	"	H. Miller. — D of W.	
40740 ✓	"	✓ W. Drysdale.	
16351 ✓	"	✓ H. Hart.	
43035 ✓	"	✓ XX J. Kennedy.	
18261 ✓	"	✓ J. Cameron.	
278001 ✓	"	✓ Urquhart.	

771 L/C. Anderson G.
S/3569 " Orritt E

"B" Company, Wounded, contd.

```
     7833  ✓ pte. ✓F. Coyle.
   278843  ✓  "   ✓G. Law.
    43200  ✓ L/C ✓C. Jackson.
    22269  ✓ pte ✓J. Cameron.
2/ 325532  ✓  "  ✓D. Wilson. —— 325522
   277574  ✓  "  ✓J. Angeley.
   277594  ✓  "  ✓J. paul.
     8904  ✓  "  ✓J. B. paterson
    40830  ✓  "  ✓C. Clark.
    40831  ✓  "  ✓R. Caldwell.
S/11389  4389 ✓  "  ✓R. Etherston. S/11389
    13863  ✓  "  ✓W. Blackie. ——
   278243  ✓  "  ✓J. Martin.
 4/8929   ✓  "  ✓J. S. McPhail.
     6744 ✓    ✓ G Spankie.
```

"C" Company.

```
    12107 ✓ Sgt ✓W. Riddick.
     3898 ✓ Cpl.✓A. Cook.
     9648 ✓  "  ✓T. Wingate.
     6121 ✓ L/Cpl ✓J. McDade.
   300807 ✓  "  ✓W. Langlands.
     9959 ✗  "   A. Falconer. ✗ — D.ofW.
    1599 5 pte. ✓G. Anderson.
   302221 ✓  "  ✓P. Barrie.
    23829 ✓  "  ✓H. Cook.
    22318 ✓  "  ✓H. Copeland.
    22834 ✓  "  ✓H. Enticknap.
   277985 ✓  "  ✓J. Fowler.
    17411 ✓  "  ✓W. Graham.
    19782 ✓  "  ✓C. Garrick.
     6421 ✓  "  ✓C. Gallacher.
7610 7710 ✓  "  ✓D. Graham. —— S/7610.
    12429 ✓  "  ✓A. Hayes.
    40855 ✓  "  ✓A. Laidlaw.
    20413 ✓  "  ✓J. Leitch.
    40863 ✗  "   D. McDonald. D/W 25/2/18
     9361 ✓  "  ✓J. McCubbray.
    22145 ✓  "  ✓H. McIlvar.
   275624 ✓  "  ✓J. Stewart
   301947 ✓  "  ✓J. Smellie.
    40781 ✓  "  ✓J.N. Thomson.
   325303 ✓  "  ✓A. Wood.
   325019 ✓  "  ✓J.S. Wright. 325819
     6744       G Spankie
```

"D" Company.

```
      714 ✓ L/C.✓A. Fletcher.
    40164 ✓  "  ✓G. Fleming.
   325240 ✓ Cpl.✓J. Guthrie. From 1/8 Bn. 20.1.18 no pte
2— 350865 ✓ L/C.✓A. Herd. ——  D.ofW 28/2/18 18 C.H.
     4279 ✗  "   R. Johnston. ✗ D.ofW
     9025 ✓ L/Sgt ✓W.T. Langlands.
     9155 ✗ a/Sgt D. McLachlan ✗ D.ofW.
    23871 ✓ L/C ✓W. Madelin.
15878 15875 ✓ Sgt ✓W. McArthur. —— S/15878.
   325735 ✓ Sgt ✓R. Morrison. —— 325735
13412 15412 ✓ a/C/W ✓A. Nairn. —— S/13412
     9878 ✓ L/C ✓A.D. Wilson.
    21821½✓ pte.✓J. Anderson. —— S/21812. Two J. Wilsons S/21812 Wd.W. 21821 No two entry
  4/8928 ✓  "  ✓P. Brannigan.
   278268 ✓  "  ✓W. Corrick.
    40775 ✓  "  ✓C. Cochrane.
   300366 ✓ pte.✓A. Campbell.
     7460   pte. ✓J. Coventry.
   277030 ✓  "  ✓J. Drysdale.
    40800 ✓  "  ✓F. Curley.
   302017 ✓  "  ✓T. Downie.
```

"D" Company, Wounded, Contd.

```
 1253  ✓ Pte, ✓ J. Fleeting.
13494  ✓  "  ✓ A. Fyfe.
12024  ✓  "  ✓ G. Fraser.
19461  ✓  "  ✓ D. Grant.
306339 ✓  "  ✓ W. Gillies.
12843  ✓  "  ✓ J. Henderson.
12026  ✓  "  ✓ G. Johnstone.
16037  ✓  "  ✓ F. McSherry.
40798  ✓  "  ✓ N. McDonald.
22047  ✓  "  ✓ W. McLay.
301622 ✓  "  ✓ T. McKimmie.
300086 ✓  "  ✓ A. McInnes.
 0241  ✓  "  ✓ G. Millar.
~~21~~        ~~W. Miller~~
 9154  ✓  "  ✓ J. Y. Neill.
~~~~          ~~J. Primrose~~
18205/19025 ✓ " ✓ R. M. Scott. — S/18205
276901 ✓  "  ✓ A. Smith.
40882  ✓  "  ✓ J. Sykes.
302312 ✓  "  ✓ E. Woods.
13188  ✓  "  ✓ W. M. Young.
13250  ✓  "  ✓ A. Young.
 9548  ✓  "  ✓ G. Graham.
12801  ✓  "  ✓ J. C. Latimer.
325566 ✓  "  ✓ J. Campbell.
16041  ✓  "  ✓ A. D. Ross.
21809  ✓    ✓ Walker
12331  ✓    ✓ Scotland
~~225682~~ ✓ ✓ ~~Munn~~ J. O. Dougall. 325632.
```

"A" Company, Wounded.

```
 9950 ✓ Pte, ✓ J. A. McGillivray
16338 ✓  "  ✓ W. Frisken.
```

W.K.

```
  771    L/C  Anderson  J.    — Hos.
S/3569    "   Jarrett   E.    — Hos.
S/15878   "   McArthur  W.
S/40541  A/Cpl McLean   J.
S/12026   Pte  Johnston G.
S/18228   "   McGrotton  N
S/23853   "   Myles     D
S/40775       Cochrane  C
S/40831   "   Caldwell  R
S/40859   "   Stoddart  R
S/40868   "   Binnie    R
325733    Sgt  Morrison R
325043    Pte  Riddell  J.
326605    "   Kelso     J
```

Casualties, contd.

Missing

"A" Company.

10499	Pte.	J. Baird.	
301723	"	J. W. Brown.	JWK
303066	"	H. Gordon.	Hos W UK
3569	Cpl.	E. Jarrett.	Hos W UK
771	L/C.	T. Anderson.	Hos W UK
5604	Pte.	W. Durning.	" W
276135	"	S. Cummings.	" W
17219	"	W. Johnston.	
22179	"	A. McArthur.	
9848	"	W. Wise.	W Hos

"B" Company.

22150	Pte.	J. McKay.	W Hos NYDN
21731	"	J. Morrison.	
350043	"	J. Riddell.	Wounded
350497	"	T. Downie.	
279001	"	C. Urquhart.	Wounded
277001	"	J. Martyn.	Delete
18228	"	N. McAlister.	Hos W UK
301447	"	S. Kelly	Hos W — R.158
16201	"	R. Dewar.	
301797	"	J. Mulhearn.	
40346	"	D. Mathieson.	Joined (Sc) B.D. ex bCC 2.4.18 — 43 US W since 15.4.18
11467	"	A. Murray.	
326605	"	J. Kelson.	W UK
9046	"	R. Richardson.	Reported at Reinf. Camp. Tel from OC 13.4.18 A.40
14010/8	"	P. Donegan.	
21554	"	W. Mullin.	W Hos
40739	"	D. Cramb.	
14303	"	W. J. Fenwick.	} Delete
9140	L/C	R. Cranston.	

"C" Company.

15510	Sgt.	R. Lorimer.	
13407	Cpl.	W. Carmichael.	
40708	"	J. Walker.	
40231	L/C	C. Ivol.	
30120/301021	"	W. Smethurst.	
21858	Pte.	G. Bannatyne.	
313871	"	W. Brien.	
276927	"	A. Brimer.	
40622	"	J. Provan.	
40869/8	"	R. Beattie	W To UK
40871	"	W. Cunningham.	W Hos
18458	"	W. D. Cook.	
22516	"	R. Curran.	
22514	"	J. Cockburn.	
11814	"	D. Dinsmore.	since rejd BN. Tel OC 11.3.18
16295	"	D. Grant.	
17067	"	A. Johnston.	
6207	"	H. Johnston.	Hos NYDN
40875	"	A. Kinnaird.	W Hos
17235	"	J. McRobbie.	
22671	"	M. McLay.	
5905	"	J. McKenzie.	
22669	"	TM Muego.	
12053	"	J. Simpson.	
5147/40197	"	W. Stoddart.	Vimy
40861	"	A. Telford.	
50 203153	"	J. Watt.	(203153)

"C" Company Missing, contd

277495 Pte, J. Park.

"D" Company

	40771	Pte, D. J. Fraser.	
	300226	L/C. D. Campbell.	
3/	13364	Cpl. W. J. Auld.	
	3445	" J. Carrigan.	
	16578	L/C. J. Ewing.	
	276851	L/Sgt. W. H. Gillies.	
	12008	Sgt. D. Harrie.	
	3649	L/Sgt. J. Kidd.	
	218121	Pte, J. Anderson.	
	277544	" J. Campbell.	
	277058	" J. Campbell.	
	276948	" W. Hampton.	
	22264	" O. Howie.	
	273202	" W. Horsburgh.	
	2082	" T. Leyden.	
	40801	" J. McCance.	
	325484	" J. McAllan.	
	19644	" R. McLay.	
	40877	" G. McGee.	
	350212	" R. McClure.	
	40879	" W. Monaghan.	
	13681	" T. Miller.	
	23355	" D. Myles. — Hos W	
	325662	" J. O'Donnell	
	5345	" W. Owens.	
	278036	" D. Penny.	
	12561	" G. Scotland	
	270001	" J. Shearer.	
	40883	" A. Thomson.	
	16344	" A. Whytock.	
	273088	" G. Murray.	

Missing, believed killed

6812	Pte. M. McPherson.	"B" Coy.
12591	Cpl. W. Loy.	"D" "
23842	" W. H. Oldham	" "
12592	Pte, B. Hogarth.	" "
11281	" J. Lamb.	
13363	" J. McCracken.	
278293	" W. H. McKenna.	
12549	" R. S. Mathieson.	
22120	" J. Mitchell.	

Missing, believed wounded

| 21732 | Pte, R. Stewart | "B" Coy. |

Missing believed prisoner of War

| 6562 | Sgt, T. Murrie | "C" Coy. |

Missing 24.3.18   Reported by 40th. Bn. MGC.
S/40854   Houghie C.

Wounded and Missing

"A" Company

15989	Pte.	W. Baxter	
40605	"	J. Balmer	
40811	"	R. Lewis	
40733	"	J. Wilkie	
20895	"	D. Wilson	20895 W.How

"B" Company

277848	Pte.	N. Maitland	
408024	"	D. McPherson	
~~240~~	~~L/C~~	~~R. Gronson~~	
350103	Pte.	W. Blyth	

"C" Company

12783	Sgt.	G. Summers	15752
14337	"	J. M°Colmson	
14267	L/C.	E. Davidson	
13457	"	G. Stuart	
~~23850~~	Pte.	~~A. Ferrier~~	W.How
22169	"	J. Findlay	

Not on any list

S/40859 Stoddart R
13335   Fawley M

Comdg. 14th Argyll & Sutherland Highlanders.

2nd April, 1918

S/40854 √ Haughie C. Reported by MGC.

www.ingramcontent.com/pod-product-compliance
Lightning Source LLC
Chambersburg PA
CBHW080925230426
43668CB00014B/2200